this is the
samoyed

by joan mcdonald brearley

Cover:
Harold McLaughlin captures all the snow-white beauty of the Samoyed breed in this magnificent puppy picture photographed at his Silveracres Kennels in Morrison, Colorado.

Frontispiece:
Kubla Khan Teddy Bear, first in Puppy Dog Class at six months at a San Diego Specialty Show. Sired by Ch. Sam O'Khan's Kubla Khan *ex* Ch. Orions Capella of Tsar-Khan. Bred and owned by Patricia Morehouse, Los Angeles.

ISBN 0-87666-379-X

Distributed in the U.S.A. by T.F.H. Publications, Inc., 211 West Sylvania Avenue, P.O. Box 27, Neptune City, N.J. 07753; in England by T.F.H. (Gt. Britain) Ltd., 13 Nutley Lane, Reigate, Surrey; in Canada to the book store and library trade by Clarke, Irwin & Company, Clarwin House, 791 St. Clair Avenue West, Toronto 10, Ontario; in Canada to the pet trade by Rolf C. Hagen Ltd., 3225 Sartelon Street, Montreal 382, Quebec; in Southeast Asia by Y.W. Ong, 9 Lorong 36 Geylang, Singapore 14; in Australia and the south Pacific by Pet Imports Pty. Ltd., P.O. Box 149, Brookvale 2100, N.S.W., Australia. Published by T.F.H. Publications, Inc. Ltd., The British Crown Colony of Hong Kong.

CONTENTS

ACKNOWLEDGMENTS
ABOUT THE AUTHOR
1. ANCIENT HISTORY 13
Treatment of the Dogs. . . Feeding in Ancient Times. . . Natural
Instinct. . . Whelping in the Wilds. . . Bitches in Season. . . The
Sacrificial Dog. . . Myths and Legends. . . Early Explorers and
Expeditions. . . Stonehenge on the Esquimaux Dog. . . The Social
Hierarchy
2. THE SAMOYED IN ITS HOMELAND 23
Gaining World Attention. . . Ancestry Established
3. THE SAMOYED IN ENGLAND 28
4. THE SAMOYED IN AMERICA 36
First Samoyed Champion. . . The Samoyed Club of America. . .
Some Specialty Show Highlights. . . America's Top-Winning
Samoyed. . . American Kennel Club Registrations
5. AKC STANDARD FOR THE BREED 59
The Story of the Standard
6. SAMOYED TEMPERAMENT AND PERSONALITY 65
Adjustment to Family Life. . . Excellent House Dogs. . . The Age
of Maturity. . . The Teen-Agers. . . Home Exercise. . . Indoor or
Outdoor Dog?. . . Chewing a Strong Habit
7. THE SAMOYED AS A SLED AND RACING DOG 78
Early Sleds. . . Sled Dog Training—Harnessing the Puppies. . .
Sled Dog's Career a Short One. . . Harnessing Methods. . . Early
Team Dogs. . . Geldings. . . Early Team Training. . . Darwin's
Theory on Sled Dogs. . . The Great Serum Run. . . Early Samoyed
Racing. . . The All-Alaska Sweepstakes. . . Racing Today. . .
Team Racing. . . Starting the Puppy. . . Early Training for the
Racing Dog. . . The Training Ground. . . Disposition and Attitude
. . . Forming Your Teams. . . Securing Racing Information. . . The
Day of the Race. . . Racing Manners. . . Professional Racing
Teams. . . Professional Racing Dogs. . . Sled Dog Racing Events
. . . World Championship Sled Dog Derby. . . Racing in Alaska. . .
Racing in Canada. . . The Huslia Heritage and the Huslia Hustlers
. . . Women Mushers. . . The Women's World Championship. . .
A Glossary of Racing Terms

8. BUYING YOUR SAMOYED PUPPY........................111
The Puppy You Buy... Male or Female?... The Planned Parenthood Behind Your Puppy... Puppies and Worms... Veterinary Inspection... The Conditions of Sale... Buying a Show Puppy... The Purchase Price... The Cost of Buying Adult Stock

9. GROOMING YOUR SAMOYED 131
Samoyed Bathing Area... The Actual Bath... The Drying Process... Grooming the Puppy... The Problem of Shedding... Foot Care... Eye Care... Ear Care... Teeth

10. GENETICS 141

11. BREEDING YOUR SAMOYED.............................145
The Health of the Breeding Stock... The Day of the Mating... How Much Does the Stud Fee Cost?... The Actual Mating... Artificial Insemination... The Gestation Period... Probing for Puppies... Alerting Your Veterinarian... Do You Need a Veterinarian in Attendance?... Labor... The Arrival of the Puppies... Feeding the Bitch Between Births... Breech Births... Dry Births ... The Twenty-Four-Hour Checkup... False Pregnancy... Caesarean Section... Episiotomy... Socializing Your Puppy... Rearing the Family... Evaluating the Litter... Spaying and Castrating... Sterilizing for Health... The Power of Pedigrees

12. TRAINING AND OBEDIENCE FOR YOUR SAMOYED 179
When to Start Training... The Reward Method... How Long Should the Lessons Be?... What You Need to Start Training... What to Teach First... The "Down" Command... The Stand for Examination... Formal School Training... Advanced Training and Obedience Trials... The Companion Dog Excellent Degree ... The Utility Dog Degree... The Tracking Dog Degree... The Samoyed in Obedience

13. SHOWING YOUR SAMOYED 201
Match Shows... The Point Shows... The Prize Ribbons and What They Stand For... Qualifying for Championship... Obedience Trials... Junior Showmanship Competition... Dog Show Photographers... Two Types of Dog Shows... Benched or Unbenched Dog Shows... Professional Handlers... Do You Really Need a Handler... The Cost of Campaigning a Dog With a Handler

14. FEEDING AND NUTRITION 223
Feeding Puppies... Weaning the Puppies... Feeding the Adult Dog... The All Meat Diet Controversy... Obesity... Orphaned Puppies... How to Feed the Newborn Puppies... Gastric Torsion ... Feeding the Racing Dog... Drinking Water

15. GENERAL CARE AND MANAGEMENT OF YOUR SAMOYED 239
Tattooing... Outdoor Housebreaking... Other Important Outdoor Manners... Geriatrics... Dog Insurance... The High Cost of Burial... In the Event of Your Death... Keeping Records

16. YOUR DOG, YOUR VETERINARIAN, AND YOU! 247
Aspirin: A Danger. . . What the Thermometer Can Tell You. . .
Coprophagy. . . Masturbation. . . Rabies. . . Vaccinations. . .
Snakebite. . . Emergencies. . . The First Aid Kit. . . How Not to
Poison Your Dog. . . Symptoms of Poisoning. . . The Curse of
Allergy. . . Do All Dogs Chew?. . . Bones. . . Hip Dysplasia. . .
Elbow Dysplasia. . . Patellar Dysplasia. . . HD Program in Great
Britain. . . The United States Registry
17. THE BLIGHT OF PARASITES 279
Internal Parasites
18. DICTIONARY OF DOG DISEASES 287
19. PURSUING A CAREER IN DOGS 331
Part Time Kennel Work. . . Professional Handlers. . . Dog Train-
ing. . . Grooming Parlors. . . The Pet Shop. . . Dog Judging. . .
Miscellaneous
20. SAMOYED STORIES 347
Laika in Space. . . Samoyeds in Education. . . The Name's the
Same. . . Samoyeds in Public Relations. . . Food for Thought. . .
Lucky Winner. . . Samoyed Loyalty
21. GLOSSARY OF DOG TERMS. 359
INDEX

The magnificent import Ch. Kiskas Karaholme Cherokee, photographed in Bryce Canyon, Utah. Painter is owned by Mr. and Mrs. Robert H.
Ward of Calabasas, California. The Wards, owners of the famous
Starctic Samoyeds Kennel, are charter members of SCLA, honorary
members of the Samoyed Club of San Diego, and past presidents and
30-year members of the Samoyed Club of America. They are also active in the organization for Working Samoyeds.

ACKNOWLEDGMENTS

The author is particularly grateful to all those who have contributed information and photographs for this book on this most beautiful breed, with special thanks to Ruth Bates Young for her extra effort and contributions, to Robert R. Shomer, DVM, for the usual expert counsel, to Stephen McDonald for additional research, and to the Samoyed—a breed that has given so much pleasure to us down through the years.

Ch. Boreas Blue Velvet Paint finished for championship at 2 years and 3 months of age. Bred, owned and handled by Frank and Clair Schlegel of Ogden, Utah. Blue was sired by Ch. Kiskas Karaholme Cherokee *ex* White Velvet of Sawinjaq.

White Velvet of Sawinjaq, whelped in December 1970, with her first litter, whelped in October 1972, and sired by Ch. Kiskas Karaholme Cherokee. The litter, pictured at two weeks of age, was bred by Velvet's owners, Frank and Clair Schlegel of Ogden, Utah.

DEDICATION

to

EDITH MAY BREESE

who always smiles, I dedicate this book about the breed that is said to smile. . .

Pictured left is Ch. Miss Hollie, C.D. and her son Holihouse Dancing Paw Prince. Prince's sire was Ch. Kondako's Dancing Bear. Hollie and Dannie are owned by Patricia A. Eik of Trenton, New Jersey. Photography by Thomas W. Schupan.

The name

SAMOYED

is pronounced

sam-a-YED

(accent on last syllable)

In Germany the Samoyed is called *SAMOJEDENSPITS*. . .

In Russia it is *SAMOYEDSKAJA LAIKA*

(and all dogs in the Spitz group

bear the label of *Laika*)

ABOUT THE AUTHOR. . .

JOAN McDONALD BREARLEY

Joan Brearley has loved animals ever since she was old enough to know what they were. Over the years there has been a constant succession of dogs, cats, birds, fish, rabbits, snakes, turtles, alligators, squirrels, lizards, etc., for her own personal menagerie. Through these same years she has owned over thirty different breeds of purebred dogs, as well as countless mixtures, since the door was never closed to a needy or homeless animal.

A graduate of the American Academy of Dramatic Arts, Joan started her career as a writer for movie magazines, actress and dancer. She also studied journalism at Columbia University and has been a radio, television and magazine writer, writing for some of the major New York City agencies. She was also a television producer-director for a major network on such shows as *Nick Carter, Master Detective*, and has written, cast, directed, produced and, on occasion, starred in television film commercials. She has written material for such personalities as Dick Van Dyke, Bill Stern, Herman Hickman, Dione Lucas, Amy Vanderbilt and many others prominent in the entertainment world.

Her accomplishments in the dog fancy include being an American Kennel Club approved judge, breeder-exhibitor of top show dogs, writer for various dog magazines, author or co-author of many breed

Hutchinson's Encyclopedia offers the theory that while the wolf coloration of the Husky may bear out the general impression that Huskies at least were frequently wolf-crossed, if that were the case most Huskies would be all white, because the Arctic wolf is white. Also, the Arctic wolf is a much larger animal than the Husky, often weighing 150 pounds. They also carry their tails down while the Husky dogs carry them up and over their backs. And strangely enough, the Arctic wolf is the only animal a Husky is afraid to attack.

Additionally, pure-bred wolves have been trained and used to a limited extent as sled animals. They proved most unsatisfactory, since they did not have the endurance so necessary for a good sled dog! The only conclusion can be that while the Husky may have originally descended from wolves, there has since been only what could be considered as occasional cross-breedings.

According to Dr. Edward Moffat Weyer, Jr., one of the foremost students of the Eskimo, "It seems altogether likely that the dogs have crossed to some extent with wolves. The skeletal similarity points to a relationship."

Perhaps the most obvious difference seems to be in behavioral pattern of the wolf and of the jackal. While both the wolf and the jackal packs recognize a leader, the wolf packs support a graduated order of superiority from the leader down, in a one, two, three "pecking order." The jackals, on the other hand, are said to recognize a leader, but the rest of the pack share equally in rank, with no dog taking second place to any other dog in importance.

With this comparison in mind, and going beyond the wolf-like physical appearance of today's Samoyeds, and knowing that they have been interbred with wolves over the centuries, we must also note that their social behavior resembles that of the jackal. In spite of the virtually complete domestication of the Samoyed today, they observe the "leader of the pack" social pattern, which is one of the reasons they fit in so nicely with our family living. The dog joins the family "pack" and recognizes the dominant member of the family as his "leader." This is the person to whom obedience is paid and to whom his allegiance belongs. But it also upholds the jackal social behavior pattern in that he gets along equally well with all other members of the family "pack," a trait attributed to animals descending morphologically from the jackal.

2. THE SAMOYED
IN ITS HOMELAND

The vast frozen and bleak wilderness of northern Russia known as Siberia and its tribesmen, the Samoyed people, are responsible for the propagation of the lovely white working dog which we know now by the same name.

Generally believed to have migrated to this seemingly endless wasteland along the Arctic Ocean, stretching from the White Sea to the Yenisei River, the Samoyeds, or Nentsi, and their dogs date back to over a thousand years before Christ, making the Samoyed one of the oldest breeds of dogs existing today.

Legend has it that originally the Samoyed people sprang from ancient tribes which roamed the then-fertile Gobi Desert and were eventually forced northward by the Tartars all the way to the Gulf of Ob at the northern valley of the Yenisei River and all the way to the Taimyr Peninsula in Siberia. Here, with the aid of their dogs, they managed to thrive on frozen wastelands for many hundreds of years.

Their dogs served them well as reindeer herders and for fighting off marauding wolf packs. They towed their boats, helped with hunting and fishing and kept the family warm under deerskin covers in the tent-like huts called chooms or yurts made of reindeer skins and wooden poles. They called their white dogs *Bjelkier*, which means white dog that breeds white. The Bjelkiers were usually cherished by their owners, not only for their working abilities and endurance but also as defenders of the home. A close familial interdependency therefore has become inherent in the Samoyed, which is what makes it such an ideal family dog. Today the Samoyed gives the same loyalty to his owners that it once gave to the leader of the pack or the head of the family group.

The Samoyeds are a strongly Mongolian people in type. They are of short, stocky stature, dark-skinned, with slanting eyes and straight black hair.

The Nentsi, who inhabited the northwest Siberian tundra, were the Urgo-Samoyeds; they lived during the Bronze Age in the Minusink Basin of the upper Yenesei River. They worked the land and were especially skilled in copperware.

The Yurak or Tawgy Samoyeds were reindeer nomads for the most part, and the Ostyak Samoyeds were hunters and fishers and lived mostly in tents rather than the more permanent chooms built by the herding tribes. The famous Finnish ethnographer M. Castren researched the Samoyeds in the latter part of the nineteenth century and found herds of reindeer estimated at 40,000 head in the lower Pechora Basin alone. Almost a century earlier, in 1792, an explorer named Richard Kerr gave the Samoyed dog the name of *Canis sibiricus*.

The area along the White Sea coast inhabited by the Nentsi was referred to at one time as the Nentsi National Area, and it is through this region that it is believed some of the ancient men of the north must have found their way across the Bering Strait to North America. The American Indian does resemble the Asiatic Mongol, and even today "Eskimos" live on both sides of the Bering Strait and all through the Aleutian Islands.

What remains of the Samoyed people today are located along the wooded plains along the banks of the river Ob, from the Mongolian frontier along to the Gulfs of Ob and Taz. While this is a considerable stretch of land, the tribes are scattered, some being found as far as the Khatanga basin and as far northwest as the island of Novaya Zemlya. Several decades ago it was reported that the best examples of the Samoyed could be found in the Tobolsk, Pechora and Yeniseisk districts. But more recently, unless one would travel in the area in person, it would not be possible to say what the current native Samoyeds look like, since so little information comes out of Russia.

GAINING WORLD ATTENTION

It was the exciting polar expeditions at the turn of the twentieth century that brought world attention to the remarkable Northern dogs and their feats of endurance and spirit against great hardships. We recognize the extensive use of the Samoyed dogs for transport by most of the important European expeditions to the Arctic and Antarctic. Samoyed teams are part of recorded history with the accounts of Borchgrevink (alternatively spelled Borchgrevnik and Borchgrevinks), Amundsen, and with Shackleton in the Antarctic and with Dr. Fridtjof Nansen and with Abruzzi in the Arctic. The American explorers Fiala and Baldwin also used Samoyed dog teams. Nansen's account of his farthest northern trip with Samoyeds on the first *Fram* expedition is a classic tale of shared endurance between man and dog.

In this 1894-1895 adventure, Nansen was the first explorer to use the Samoyed as a draft animal for his trip to the North Pole. Not all the dogs could meet the rigors of both ocean voyage and the long pull, however. Of the original 33 taken on the voyage, few survived. Of 16 used on a sled team trying to reach the Pole, not one returned. As provisions ran low, the weaker dogs were destroyed to feed the others. Oddly enough, they refused to eat the meat, and it was then used to sustain the human members of the expedition.

24

Rear Admiral Richard E. Byrd, famous polar explorer who used Northern breeds in various expeditions.

Those dogs which had been left aboard the ship miraculously survived and even reproduced. Most of their young could not subsist on their diets of bear meat and evaporated milk, so few returned to Norway aboard the *Fram*. There is no reference to them in any of the pedigrees around that time.

It was during these same years in the late 1800's that world horizons began to broaden. Both explorers and trappers began to venture up into Siberia and came back with tales about the beautiful white dogs in the north. Some they obtained through nefarious schemes, and others they brought back through legitimate purchase. The first of these reached England by 1889. The Prince of Wales (later to become King Edward VII) had a Samoyed dog that was all white except for its black head. In 1899 a Mr. Edgar Farman, a Bulldog fancier, exhibited a Samoyed named Real Arctic at the Colchester, England dog show. Also a Mr. Frank Sewell is reported to have owned an all-sable brown Samoyed named Tinsey.

ANCESTRY ESTABLISHED

Major F. Jackson had somewhat better luck in acquiring some of these dogs for his expedition. He returned to England with several Samoyeds. Among them were two bitches which were to become famous—Kvik and Flo. These two females were bred to the G. Kilburn-Scott dogs and produced some champions later on. The famous Jacko, which Major Jackson presented to Queen Alexandra, was another one of them. The ancestry of present-day Samoyeds can in many instances be traced back to some of these dogs. Another beauty was named Russ, a member of the Duke of Abruzzi's expedition. He was acquired through purchase from Trondjhem, a dog dealer of the time.

Ninety dogs sailed on the *Southern Cross* on the Borchgrevinks Expedition. Written entries were made aboard ship regarding the behavior of the dogs. Notations made by Borchgrevinks read: "It was surprising to see how certain dogs took to certain men, and in leisure hours you would see some of the members of the expedition selecting a quiet corner and petting their dogs."

It is also interesting to note that on this same voyage body weights on 31 dogs were kept. The average weight was in the fifties, but ranged from 28 to 64 pounds, a fact which might account for some of the dispute on size which raged in England during the time when the breed was becoming established. And quite a contrast with today's sturdy specimens!

It was this Borchgrevinks Expedition which included the famous dog Antarctic Buck, rescued by Mrs. Clara Kilburn-Scott, whose touching story is related in our Samoyed Stories chapter further on in the book.

There were 52 dogs and four sledges on the Amundsen expedition to the South Pole. Round-trip they covered 1,860 miles in just under

A magnificent portrait of Agnes Mason's Samoyed dog team, this one showing the team next to a giant waterfall in Idaho. Rex is the lead dog; the team is accompanied by driver-trainer Lloyd Van Sickle and his wife Alta.

one hundred days. Etah, a solid white Samoyed, was Amundsen's lead dog when on December 14, 1911 they reached the South Pole, and Etah earned the title of being the first known dog to get there. She later became the cherished pet of the Princess de Montyglyon and was one of the few expedition dogs to live out a long and full life, fully appreciated for her worthy achievement.

3. THE SAMOYED IN ENGLAND

The Breed Becomes Officially Known As "The Samoyed"

In 1889 Mrs. Kilburn-Scott's husband "officially" introduced the Samoyed to England. Mr. Scott, a member of the Royal Zoological Society, brought one of them back from an expedition. He had purchased the dog from a tribe of Samoyeds at an encampment in the Archangel province in northwestern Russia. He immediately named the breed Samoyed, after the people who had developed it. The name was originally written as Samoyede, but the "e" was dropped by the British in 1923 and by the American Kennel Club in 1947. The impressive dog he acquired as his first specimen he named Sabarka, and Sabarka did much to create and establish interest in the breed from the moment it arrived on English soil. In 1896 Whirtay Petchora was imported by the Kilburn-Scotts to be his mate. Lady Stilway, a friend of the Kilburn-Scotts, then imported Musti from Russia as a mate for her dog, which came from the first litter bred in England.

After several other importations by the Kilburn-Scotts, their kennels were established, and many of the progeny from this kennel were used on future expeditions to the North. One of Mr. Kilburn-Scott's most notable dogs was one he purchased after the Borchgrevinks expedition. The dog was born aboard ship on the way to the Antarctic. Written comment about the dog went as follows:

"He stands 21½ or 22 inches tall and is measured 35 inches long from the tip of his nose to the tip of his tail. He has the fine open forehead, great ruff on neck, spreading tail and hair around the toes which are so characteristic of the breed. His fur is snowy white all over with a gloss on the hair which is peculiar to the breed. He is a most lovable dog and, before being brought to England, he was shown to Jack London (who wrote so charmingly about Arctic dogs and their characteristics,) who declared that Buck was one of the finest Arctic dogs he had seen. So typical a Samoyed is a great accession to the breed."

Other Samoyeds which made history in the breed and were owned by the Kilburn-Scotts were their Ch. Antarctic Bru, bred by a Miss

Perdita, by Gainsborough, features a "Mrs. Robinson" with what is obviously one of the early Samoyeds. It is interesting to note that the background and the Samoyed-type dog is exactly the same as the background for Gainsborough's *The Morning Walk*, painted in 1785, almost a century before the Samoyed was supposedly introduced officially to England. Both *Perdita* and *The Morning Walk* are on display at the National Gallery in London. Mrs. Robinson also bears a striking resemblance to the woman portrayed by Thomas Gainsborough in *The Morning Walk*.

Marker in 1915; Polar Light, bred by a Mrs. Simon in 1923 and winner of the championship at Crufts for five consecutive years; and Siberian Keeno, to name a few.

Another early import was a dog named Sam, presented to a Miss Puxley by an explorer after an expedition; Sam's name appears on some of the important early pedigrees. Sam was followed by two Russian imports, one named Moustan, direct from the kennels of Grand Duke Nicholas, and about whom we shall learn more later. After Moustan came Hasova, who was traded for a gun!

Shortly after Antarctic Buck had come and gone, Ayesha was imported to England from the island of Novaya Zemlya in 1910. She was entirely white with the very blackest points, which her daughters passed on to their progeny also. She and Buck left a strong influence in the breed. Ayesha was imported and owned by Mr. F. Gordon Colman and was secured for him largely through the efforts of Mr. E. Gray-Landsberg.

In appreciation for his trouble Mr. Colman presented Mrs. Landsberg with Peter, a dog sired by his stud Black Nordbrin, who was sired by the black and white dog Ch. Alacbra, one of the colored descendants of the Kilburn-Scotts' original importation from Russia. So enthralled was Mrs. Landsberg with the breed at this point that she implored her husband to wire his business agents all over northern Europe to secure another Samoyed for her. A puppy bitch was obtained in Finland but died of distemper after three months in quarantine.

In 1925, when trade relations were resumed with Russia, Mrs. Landsberg obtained some dogs direct from the few remaining Samoyed tribes east of the Yenisei River in northern Siberia. Yugor of Halfway was one; he survived shipment direct to England after crossing many miles of frozen tundra to his new home. Bred to Polka of Halfway, a granddaughter of the imported Ayesha, they produced magnificent puppies, one of which became the mainstay of a French kennel; another produced a future Canadian champion. A daughter of Yugor, named Yugarello, was the dam of Mrs. Stuart Thynne's famous stud Balto.

Soon after the importation of Samoyeds by Mr. and Mrs. Kilburn-Scott, the Hon. Mrs. McLaren Morrison and Mrs. F. Ringer imported several other specimens. We must recall, however, that at this point in time they were not necessarily the spectacular all-white variety we know today. They included black and tan and black and white Samoyeds. It was only later on, when the British began to express a definite interest in the pure whites, that they adopted and adhered to the Samoyed tribe's revelation that where Samoyed dogs were concerned "white breeds white." Miss Marion Keyte-Perry and Mrs. Gray-Landsberg both did much to establish the pure whites as the favorite with the British dog fancy.

English Champion Demetrio of Kobe pictured at seven years of age. He was later owned by a Canadian and accidentally killed by a train.

Mrs. Stuart Thynne was active in the breed during these first decades of the twentieth century and was equally as well-known as her Ch. Kieff and Ch. Viking. The mating of her Nastja to Miss J.V. Thomson-Glover's beautiful sire Snow Cloud had a noticeable influence on the breed at that time. Many champions both in England and later in America go back to this careful blending of bloodlines. Mrs. Thynne's Viking was a potent stud force at her kennel until his death in 1920, and he was a popular favorite in the show ring from 1911 until he died. He attained his championship in 1915.

Both Viking and Kieff were used extensively at stud even during World War I, when breeding was of necessity greatly curtailed, and was followed by a muzzling order in 1919. Kieff's get was eventually crossed with another famous stud dog, Mustan of Farningham, and produced successful results for their breed, helping him to make his mark in the breed. Kieff was immortalized in the designs of Nymphenberg pottery, and it is said that his stuffed and preserved body resides in the British Museum.

The "original" English Taz.

A classic pose captured on film by the famous dog photographer William Brown shows Ch. Sport of the Arctic, imported from England by Natalie Rogers of Sun Valley, Idaho and New York City. While Sport lived at the Waldorf Astoria Hotel in New York the elevator boys used to try to test him on which floor he should get off for home. . . and Sport always knew which stop was *really* where he lived!

The English-bred Ch. Destiny of Top Acres, owned by Ruth B. Young of Medway, Ohio.

Mrs. F.A. Cammack was important to the breed. She purchased her first three Samoyeds in 1906 from Mrs. McLaren Morrison and eventually became the owner of Ayesha. Her champions Kosko and Zahra did much to establish the breed, but by her own admission Mrs. Cammack admits it was Ayesha who made the most important contribution to Samoyeds. Mrs. Cammack has said that Ayesha never whelped a second-rate puppy and was almost faultless in conformation. The war also hampered her breeding program, or there is no telling what contribution she might have attained! Mrs. Cammack's Ch. Winter was a most important bitch, bred in 1924, and was a daughter of Ch. Kieff out of Nanook.

Other top breeders of the period were Mrs. L.D. Ingle, who bred Toula of Tazov in 1928; Mrs. D. Edwards, who bred the fine Ch. Surf of the Arctic in 1928, among other fine dogs; a Miss Lurcock, owner of the Arctic Kennels; and a Miss Timmins, who was among the first to become prominent as a breeder.

Snowland Fyodor, an English Samoyed of several years ago.

There was also Mrs. D.L. Perry, and her Kobe Kennels, who in the 1930's became well-known in the show rings. She first exhibited dogs she had purchased from their breeder, Mrs. Edwards, and then went on to win with her home-breds Magnus of Kobe and White Fang of Kobe, born in 1935. Lady May Boothby owned Pearla of Kobe, bred in 1931 by Mr. F. Paddy, and also owned Boris of the Glacier, another outstanding example of the Samoyed.

Miss I. Creveld and her Ch. Siberian Shaman came into prominence around this time. Shaman was from the Taimir Kennels and went back to the early Farningham lines. Mrs. C.M. Stuckey showed Ch. Edelweiss, whelped in 1928 and still winning in 1934. The Iceland Kennel Samoyeds owned by a Miss Quinlan also captured Challenge Certificates as Mrs. McLaren Morrison diligently pursued her efforts to increase entries in the breed at the dog shows. And it was in 1935 that Ivan of Taz, owned by a Mr. Andrews, caused a sensation by winning five first prizes, Best of Sex and Best Dog at the Abergavenny Championship show in England at 22 months of age. A Mrs. Michael was another breed enthusiast who showed Samoyeds and claims the honor of having bred the first Welsh champion.

As Samoyeds' popularity grew and entries at the shows increased markedly during the next decade, breed clubs began to be formed. The two most substantial bodies guiding the breed around the 1950's were the British Samoyed Club and the Samoyed Association.

While official recognition came almost simultaneously for Samoyeds in England and America, the first accepted Standard for the breed was adopted in England in 1909, based on points set down by Miss Keyte-Perry. Practically the same Standard was established for the breed in the United States and only later was rewritten on points set down by Mrs. Kilburn-Scott. The Standard in the U.S.A. was once again rewritten in 1956, though practically all of Mrs. Kilburn-Scott's points still apply. Fortunately, the conformation of the Samoyed was set so true that little has been done to change it. . . and hurrah for that!

The Samoyed people have lost almost all their identity because of the Soviet persecution of small ethnic groups, and most of the original Samoyed stock disappeared with the Samoyed people. The obligation to carry on this breed became a personal responsibility of every new owner as the original stock faded away in its native land. Since their fabulous coat protects them from the bitter cold and somewhat insulates them against the heat, Samoyeds have become popular in all climates, and today we can find the Samoyed thriving and admired all over the world. Those who have owned the breed have found it the ideal dog, little changed from its original natural beauty and conformation. . . The stuffed and mounted body of Ch. Siberian Keeno resides at the Natural History Museum at South Kensington, England, as a constant reminder of what the true Samoyed conformation should be.

4. THE SAMOYED IN AMERICA

The first Samoyed was registered with the American Kennel Club in 1906. A dog, Moustan of Argenteau, already a champion in Russia, was brought to the United States in 1904 by Princess de Montyglyon. The Princess, an ardent dog show enthusiast, arrived with two Collies, two Chow Chows and four Samoyeds, one of which was the illustrious Moustan.

Moustan was one of the favorite Samoyeds belonging to the Grand Duke Nicholas, brother of the Czar of Russia. Moustan was a gift to the Princess from the Grand Duke after she had found the dog following her down the aisle at a dog show, dragging his bench chain behind him. . . She had wanted to buy the dog, but the Grand Duke advised her that there was no money that could buy him. The dog in the end was presented to her as a gift along with a basket of orchids!

Subsequently Moustan appeared in the show ring in the United States in the Miscellaneous class, since his ancestry was unknown, though he was rumored to be both a son of the famous Antarctic Buck and a survivor of the Nansen expedition. Pedigrees indicate that few of the early registrations represented dogs which were the background for our show dogs of today, which stemmed from dogs imported from established English kennels just before and right after World War I. Russian importations were negligible during the 1920's, and with the deterioration of Russian-American relations and the closed door policy, none since have appeared on the scene, to the best of our knowledge.

FIRST SAMOYED CHAMPION

Moustan's son, Ch. de Witte of Argenteau, became the first American champion Samoyed in 1907, though his dam, Sora, was also of unknown parentage. Another of the Princess' Samoyeds, Martyska of Argenteau, also became a champion, in 1908. So dedicated was the Princess to this beautiful breed that when she wrote her memoirs she dedicated the book to her Samoyed Etah, one of the lead dogs from the Amundsen expedition which she had acquired.

While her dogs were usually the only Samoyed entries at the dog shows during the first decade of the twentieth century, it wasn't long before their striking white beauty caught the eye of the dog fanciers and new exhibitors and breeders began to appear. Next on the scene was Mrs. Ada Van Heusen, a Chow Chow enthusiast and owner of the Greenacre Kennels. In 1912 Mrs. Van Heusen imported four Samoyeds, and her Tamera became the first bitch to win a championship in this country.

Miss Elizabeth Hudson came into the breed in 1908, and others such as Mrs. King Wainwright, Mrs. Sidney Borg, Miss Ruth Nichols, Mrs. Frank Romer, owner of the Yurak Kennels, Thomas Girvan, Mr. and Mrs. F.L. Vinton, owners of the Obi Kennels, the Harry Reids and their Norka Kennels, Top of the World Kennels, and Miss Mildred Sheridan, whose Parke-Cliffe Kennels is still in operation and the oldest of them all, also were prominent at this time.

By the end of World War I, the American Kennel Club had recorded 40 Samoyed registrations; the registrations included 15 English imports, three from the kennels of the Czar, one from France and two from China. While not exactly astronomical figures by any stretch of the imagination, the breed was nonetheless established in the hearts of a few dedicated breeders with important kennels and was on its way to a steady place in American dogdom.

In the early 1920's the well-known dog authority Percy Roberts, then a handler and today a judge, imported Tobolsk for Mrs. Romer's Yurak Kennels. Ch. Tobolsk was soon being touted as the greatest Samoyed ever to be seen in America. There were those who criticized him, of course, but he more than made his mark in the breed as a stud force and show dog; bred to many bitches of merit, he produced quality puppies which did more than their share of winning and producing quality also. Actually at this period in time all Samoyeds were being criticized and denied ribbons in the show ring, as uniformity of size in the breed was a distinct problem.

In the 1920's Ch. Donerna's Barin also rose to fame in the breed. Imported by the Alfred Seeleys for their Donerna Kennels in New York, Barin was a great sled dog, produced over one hundred purebred offspring and traced his ancestry to Antarctic Buck within two generations.

THE SAMOYED CLUB OF AMERICA

1923 was the year of the founding of the Samoyed Club of America. A group of Samoyed fanciers gathered for the annual Westminster show in New York City on February 14. While only 40 Samoyeds had been registered during the first two decades of the century, the American Kennel Club had to admit that the 1923 entry did represent considerable interest in the breed, and the club was formed and recognized by the AKC in May of the same year.

One of the old-time greats—Gorka, bred and owned by Mrs. Horace Mann of Trenton, New Jersey. In his initial appearance at the Trenton Kennel Club Show on December 7 and 8, 1928, he won first from Novice Class and went on to Best in the Working Group. Gorka was born July 15, 1927 and was sired by Ch. Yukon Mit; his dam was Nona of Donevna, a daughter of the well-known Ch. Donevna's Barin.

After the English judge J. Willoughby Mitchell from London had caused a sensation by withholding Reserve Winners ribbons, based on questionable ancestry of the dogs at this 1923 show, the fanciers gathered to start their club and draw up a constitution to assure the pure breeding of the Samoyed. It was to be exhibited in the Non-Sporting group.

The English Standard for the breed was adopted with certain exceptions. They designated in no uncertain terms that black coloring or black spots would automatically disqualify a dog from the ring, and they called particular attention to the incredibly good disposition of the breed. It was everyone's wish that the ideal disposition and temperament of the   Samoyed be known as one which could fit into anyone's family, though previously the Samoyed had largely been regarded as being strictly a working dog and one which required a cold climate.

Fewer than 300 Samoyeds had been registered at the time of the formation of this parent club, and a handful of prominent kennels accounted for most of the registrations, working and exhibiting diligently to bring their breed into the public eye.

SOME SPECIALTY SHOW HIGHLIGHTS

The first Samoyed Club of America specialty show was held in conjunction with the Tuxedo Kennel Club Show in Tuxedo, New York, on September 14, 1929. Judge Louis Smirnow had an entry of forty, and his choice for Best of Breed was Mr. and Mrs. H. Reid's Ch. Tiger Boy of Norka, a scant three weeks after his arrival in this country. This import from England, purchased by the Reids as a show dog and stud force for their Norka Kennels, was already a champion in his native land and caused a sensation in the breed here. He had also sired in England before his departure but produced impressive get in the States bearing the Norka kennel prefix. One of his sons was the 1939 Best of Breed winner at the 1939 Westminster Kennel Club show. His name was Norka's Viking.

By the mid-1940's Samoyeds had spread across the nation, necessitating additional club branches if the breed were going to be properly "monitored" to protect it against indiscriminate breeding. Pacific, Midwestern and Eastern clubs sprang into existence, and with the cessation of World War II the breed mushroomed and established new interest everywhere.

In 1946 the parent club was hosted by the new Midwest Division, and a Specialty was held in conjunction with the Chicago International event. The late judge Alva Rosenberg officiated and from an entry of 46 chose J.J. Marshall's Ch. Frolnick of Sammar as Best of Breed and watched it move on to win the Working Group. This show represented a gathering of Samoyeds from all over the United States; the arrangements for this successful event were handled by Colonel Ed-

Colonel and Mrs. Edward Wentworth with their Samoyed Ditko.

The late Mr. Ruick of Indianapolis, Indiana, with his Ch. Prince Kofski; Mr. Ruick was a well-known Samoyed fancier several years ago.

ward Wentworth, devotee of the breed and Chief Steward for the Chicago club. Colonel Wentworth was a vice-president for the Armour Packing Company and did not exhibit at this show, held at the Chicago stockyards.

While 1948 was the silver anniversary of the Samoyed Club of America, with Agnes Mason serving as its president, it was in 1949, at Mrs. Geraldine Dodge's world-famous Morris and Essex Kennel Club show, that the breed was to draw its largest entry to that date: 81 Samoyeds appeared in the ring for judge M. Rosenbaum. One of the Specials entered, Ch. Noel of Snowland, though not the supreme Best of Breed winner, made an impressive appearance on a television program about this famous dog show.

1949 was also the year in which the first Samoyed to win a Best in Show emerged. The colorful judge Marie Meyer made history for the breed on April 10 by placing a Samoyed puppy bitch named Sweet Missy of Sammar all the way to Best in Show. The show was the Toledo Kennel Club event and the proud owners Mr. and Mrs. J.J. Marshall, Jr. Best of Breed and first in the Group were awarded by breeder-judge Anastasia McBain. Missy's sire, Dr. Ivens' import Ch. Mar-

The first occasion on which a Samoyed won Best In Show in the United States came on April 10, 1949, when the renowned judge Marie Meyer presented the coveted award to Sweet Missy of Sammar, owned by Mrs. Joe Marshall. E.F. Chittenden, President of the sponsoring club, is pictured on extreme left as Michael Di Salle (then mayor of Toledo) presents the trophy. Missy's sire was Ch. Martingate Snowland Taz, and her dam was Ch. Frolene of Sammar. A Frasie Studio photo.

Champion Martingale Snowland Taz, owned by Dr. William Ivens of Philadelphia and given to Elena Miller of New York.

A 1957 photograph of "Rocky," the great Ch. Yurok of Whitecliff, a Working Group winner with many placements, including two firsts.

Champion Yorza II, owned by Mrs. John May of Trenton, New Jersey, looks over wins earned at the Philadelphia Kennel Club in November, 1949.

tingale Snowland Taz, won Best of Opposite Sex that same year at Morris and Essex.

This first Best in Show win for a Samoyed brought great attention to the breed and opened the door to many more top wins for them during the 1950's. Top contender during the second half of the 1950's was Ch. Yurok of Whitecliff with five Best in Show all-breed wins, 25 Group Firsts and 98 Group Placings. He won over a hundred Bests of Breed as well. These awards had won Yurok a place among the nation's Top Ten dogs in all the breeds, according to the Phillips System rating for show dogs. Created by Irene Phillips Khatoonian, the Phillips System allowed a point for each other dog defeated in the show ring, which could, and frequently did, total in the thousands for the top contenders. Yurok was handled by Mrs. Jean Blank, who co-owned him with Lena and Percy Matheron, all of them from California.

During the 1950's geographical factors made it possible for another Samoyed to soar to the top with five Best in Show wins. Ch. Silver Spray of Wychwood was his name, and there wasn't another five-show winner until the second half of the 1960's, when James and

Joan Sheet's Ch. Sam O'Khan's Chingis Khan climbed to the top. Jingo also made it to the Top Ten list in the Phillips System as top-winning Samoyed for 1967 and 1969. I know, because I was recording the Phillips System ratings while editor of *Popular Dogs* magazine, the magazine that featured the Phillips System winners each year during my tenure as its editor from 1967 to 1972. It was exciting to watch Jingo climbing to the top of the charts. He was also the winner of the A.E. Mason Trophy for top-winning Samoyed during the last three years (1966; 67; 68) the trophy was presented, and he won the Juliet Goodrich Trust Fund Trophy in 1969 and 1970, the first two years it was presented.

The J.M. Doyles also set a record in the second half of the 1950's when their Ch. Nordly's Sammy won the parent club Specialty four years in a row, from 1956 through 1959, under judges Marie Meyer, Charles Swartz, Wh. H. Reeves and Major B. Godsol.

Ch. Verla's Prince Comet pictured winning under judge Christian Knudsen at Harbor Cities Kennel Club in California in June, 1950. Comet was owner-handled by Shirley Ann Hill. Photo by Joan Ludwig.

Agnes Mason's famous Samoyed dog team. The lead dog's name is Rex, and Lloyd Van Sickle is the driver, shown here with Alta Van Sickle in this magnificent California snow scene.

But the time was "ripe" for top Sammys. Following the lean, restricting World War II years, there was new interest in the breed, good imports were beginning to come to this country once again, and the Samoyed was coming into its own with registrations now over a thousand per year. The parent club Specialty on August 3, 1952 saw Shirley Hill's remarkable Ch. Verla's Prince Comet win Best of Breed under judge J.W. Cross, which was a repeat win from the 1950 Specialty show held with Harbor Cities and an entry of 110. That year judge Chris Knudsen gave Prince the Specialty Best of Breed and saw him go on to a Group Fourth.

But the club's thirteenth event, which Prince won so handily, provided the breed with an opportunity to demonstrate to the public the great working ability of the Samoyed. The show was held at a race track in California, and after the judging there were sled races which created tremendous interest. Five teams of five dogs each competed, and a special exhibition of a 25-dog team pulling an automobile was evidence of their great strength. The famous Rex of White Way was lead dog and also led a team of 15 other Samoyeds, including eight bench champions, for the benefit of a television audience.

The 1953 Specialty Show winners of the Samoyed Club of America, held in conjunction with the Westchester Kennel Club annual show: Best of Breed was Champion Zor of Altai, owned by Alta V. and H. Lee Roy Ruth. Best of Opposite Sex (pictured on the right) was White Barks Petrovna, owned by White Bark Kennels. Ruth Stillman was the judge.

A 1957 photograph of the beautiful Ch. Pratikas Pilot.

A winning show dog of yesteryear: Ch. Drujok with his owner, Mrs. J.T. Roth of Cincinnati, Ohio, pictured at a dog show in March, 1944. Photo by Percy T. Jones.

Ch. Silvertips Scion of Wychwood wins Best In Show at a Rhode Island Kennel Club Show in the mid-1950's.

In 1953 the Samoyed Club of America voted to hold its annual meetings in the locale of the club president's home town, and for the first time since its inception the annual meeting was held outside New York City, though not too far afield at that. The fourteenth annual Specialty was held in conjunction with the Westchester Kennel Club event and drew an entry of 40 for judge Ruth Stillman. Her choice for Best of Breed was Alta and Roy Ruth's Ch. Zor of Altai.

The parent club show in 1962 (in Purchase, New York) was also held with the Westchester Kennel Club show and was a special memorial show for Ardath Chamberlain. The club invited her husband Clifford to judge as an added tribute to the woman who had served the

The lovely Snowpack Loucka of Kobe winning Best Dog in the Working Group at the Genessee Valley Kennel Club Show in Rochester, New York, on October 14, 1956. The judge was William L. Kendrick. Loucka was owned by Bernice B. Ashdown of Manhassett, New York.

Ch. Snowshone III winning Best In Show at the Portland Oregon Kennel Club Show in March, 1957, handled by Bob Hastings for owner Mr. William Dawson. James Trullinger judged; Mrs. Porter Washington presents the trophy.

Ch. Dey's Kim of Breezewood goes Winners Dog at the Chicago International Show in 1955. Owned by Betty Marie Kimp-flin of Chicago.

Ch. Lucky Labon Vanum, owned by Mrs. B.P. Dawes of Cupertino, California. This photograph was taken December 19, 1949.

Best In Show dog at the 40th annual dog show of the Eastern Dog Club in Boston, Massachusetts, in February, 1953 was the Beautiful Ch. Silver Spray of Wychwood, owned by Bernice B. Ashdown of Manhasset, New York and handled by Charles Rollins, Eastern Dog Club president. Paul T. Haskell presents the trophies. The judge at this show was Theodore Hollander. Photo by Evelyn Shafer.

Snow Crystal, photographed in June, 1946. Bred and owned by Ruth Bates Young and sold to the Powers of Detroit, Michigan. The sire was American and Canadian Ch. Kola Snow Cloud.

A handsome trio of Sammys. On the right is the great Ch. Martingate Snowland Taz, imported by Dr. William Ivens of Pennsylvania several years ago.

Ch. Sport of the Arctic photographed with some friends in St. Moritz, Switzerland in 1939. Natalie Rogers is on the left and her secretary Ilse Liebman on the right. The gentleman is not identified. Soon after this photograph was taken Sport was sent to the Brumbys' kennel in Long Island to be conditioned for East Coast dog shows. He also sired a litter for the Top Acres kennel.

A great Samoyed from the 1940's: Ch. Tazson, photographed on March 17, 1949 on the occasion of his third birthday. He was a son of Ch. Martingate Snowland Taz and was owned by Mrs. Borghild Ulfeng of New Jersey.

Samoyed Club of America as a Publicity Director and had "championed" the breed for over 30 years. From the 32 entries Mr. Chamberlain chose Mrs. E.L. Miller's Ch. Elkanglo's Dash O'Silver as Best of Breed.

An independent Specialty show was held in 1964 for the first time, thanks largely to the efforts of Richard Brechenridge, Lloyd Bristol, Robert Ward and Robert Bowles. The Southern Group of the Pacific Coast Division hosted the event at the Miramar Hotel in Santa Barbara, California.

Albert E. Van Court, one of the first judges to place a Samoyed Best in Show, was chosen to officiate. It was a good choice. . . he drew an entry of 92, including 21 champions. A class bitch, Shondra of Drayalene, owned by Joe Dyer of Idaho, was the Best of Breed winner. Subsequent independent Specialty shows have been held by the parent club since this first successful event.

Betty Kimpflin, old-time Samoyed fancier from Hot Springs, Arkansas, photographed with two of her Sammys, Tchory and Leja in May, 1950.

AMERICA'S TOP-WINNING SAMOYED

Records are made to be broken, and as the years rolled by it was inevitable that a top show dog would come along to head the list of winners in the Samoyed breed.

This remarkably beautiful dog was American, Canadian and Bermudian Champion Lulhaven's Snowmist Ensign. Tiki, as he was called by his co-owners Ott Hyatt and Sonny White of Bellevue, Washington, was the pure-white showman that captured the title of top-

American and Canadian Ch. Saroma's Polar Prince pictured winning Best In Show. "Peppy" is owned by Martha and Richard Beal of Mercer Island, Washington, and his chief claim to fame in addition to his Best In Show career is the fact that he is the sire of the top-winning Sammy in the history of the breed, Ch. Lulhaven's Snowmist Ensign. However, he can also claim fame in his own right because of being the Samoyed Club of America's National Stud Dog Trophy winner in 1968, the top-winning Samoyed in the USA for 1964 (in both the Phillips System and the Samoyed Club Annual Award System) and the sire of Best In Show winners. "Stormy" was whelped March 20, 1961 and was bred by Valerie Robbins of Renton, Washington. Sire: American and Canadian Ch. Tod-Acres Fang; dam: Ch. Leordan Taku Glacier.

The greatest winning Samoyed in the history of the breed: Ch. Lulhaven's Snowmist Ensign owned by Ott R. Hyat and Sonny White of Bellevue, Washington. "Tiki" is captured in this remarkable likeness painted in 1972 by Cougleton. His record at retirement was 24 Bests In Show, 47 Group Firsts and 100 Bests of Breed in two years of being campaigned by handler Pat Tripp.

winning Samoyed in the history of the breed. As of this writing (1975) he still holds the record with a grand total of 24 Bests in Show, 47 Group Firsts and 100 Bests of Breed. His exceptionally competent handler during his illustrious career in the show ring was Mrs. Pat Tripp of Canada, who obviously adored the dog and always presented him in immaculate condition, thereby doing much to show the dog-loving public how truly beautiful the Samoyed could be.

The author remembers seeing Tiki in Bermuda while he was competing for his Bermudian title. Pat Tripp and he made a stunning sight against the lush Bermuda foliage and flowers with Tiki's pristine white and Pat's pastel-colored outfits that set him off so well.

There were always *oh's* and *ah's* from the crowd when they made their entrance into the ring and cheers from owners of all breeds when he won. . . a real tribute in the dog fancy. But Tiki had that kind of charm; he was a magnificent specimen of the breed, a grand showman with outgoing personality, and Pat Tripp knew exactly how to make the most of it! They were quite a pair! And they made the early 1970's an exciting time in the show ring for Samoyeds.

AMERICAN KENNEL CLUB REGISTRATIONS

While the first Samoyed was registered in 1906 (the only one that year), and with no noticeable increase until the mid-1920's, by the mid-1950's registrations numbered over a thousand. By 1973 they numbered just under ten thousand! The 9,912 registrations for that year put Samoyeds in twenty-ninth position.

Though not anywhere near the almost 200,000 Poodles which rank #1, the count of almost 10,000 does indicate a steady, safe increase in interest in the fancy where the Samoyed's great beauty and pleasing conformation is obviously more and more appreciated.

Fortunately, obedience title winners are on the increase as well, since we want to be sure the Samoyed is always able to do what he was bred to do. . . work! Also there are those who are still devoted to sled work and racing, a source of great satisfaction to both the participating owners and the dogs themselves.

5. AKC STANDARD FOR THE BREED

GENERAL CONFORMATION— (a) *General Appearance—*The Samoyed, being essentially a working dog, should present a picture of beauty, alertness and strength, with agility, dignity and grace. As his work lies in cold climates, his coat should be heavy and weather resistant, well groomed, and of good quality rather than quantity. The male carries more of a "ruff" than the female. He should not be long in the back as a weak back would make him practically useless for his legitimate work, but at the same time, a close-coupled body would also place him at a great disadvantage as a draft dog. Breeders should aim for the happy medium, a body not long but muscular, allowing liberty, with a deep chest and well-sprung ribs, strong neck, straight front and especially strong loins. Males should be masculine in appearance and deportment without unwarranted aggressiveness; bitches feminine without weakness of structure or apparent softness of temperament. Bitches may be slightly longer in back than males. They should both give the appearance of being capable of great endurance but be free from coarseness. Because of the depth of chest required, the legs should be moderately long. A very short-legged dog is to be deprecated. Hindquarters should be particularly well developed, stifles well bent and any suggestion of unsound stifles or cowhocks severely penalized. General appearance should include movement and general conformation, indicating balance and good substance.

(b) *Substance—*Substance is that sufficiency of bone and muscle which rounds out a balance with the frame. The bone is heavier than would be expected in a dog of this size but not so massive as to prevent the speed and agility most desirable in a Samoyed. In all builds, bone should be in proportion to body size. The Samoyed should never be so heavy as to appear clumsy nor so light as to appear racy. The weight should be in proportion to the height.

(c) *Height—*Males—21 to 23½ inches; females—19 to 21 inches at the withers. An oversized or undersized Samoyed is to be penalized according to the extent of the deviation.

(d) *Coat* (Texture & Condition)—The Samoyed is a double-coated dog. The body should be well-covered with an undercoat of soft, short,

An impressive pen and ink headstudy of one of Ruth Bates Young's Samoyeds by artist Ernest Hart.

thick, close wool with longer and harsh hair growing through it to form the outer coat, which stands straight out from the body and should be free from curl. The coat should form a ruff around the neck and shoulders, framing the head (more on males than on females). Quality of coat should be weather resistant and considered more than quantity. A droopy coat is undesirable. The coat should glisten with a silver sheen. The female does not usually carry as long a coat as most males and it is softer in texture.

(e) *Color*—Samoyeds should be pure white, white and biscuit, cream, or all biscuit. Any other colors disqualify.

MOVEMENT—(a) *Gait*—The Samoyed should trot, not pace. He should move with a quick agile stride that is well timed. The gait should be free, balanced and vigorous, with good reach in the forequarters and good driving power in the hindquarters. When trotting, there should be a strong rear action drive. Moving at a slow walk or trot, they will not single track, but as speed increases the legs gradually angle inward until the pads are finally falling on a line directly under the longitudinal center of the body. As the pad marks converge the forelegs and hind legs are carried straight forward in traveling, the stifles not turned in nor out. The back should remain strong, firm and level. A choppy or stilted gait should be penalized.

(b) *Rear End*—Upper thighs should be well developed. Stifles well bent—approximately 45 degrees to the ground. Hocks should be well developed, sharply defined and set at approximately 30 per cent of hip height. The hind legs should be parallel when viewed from the rear in a natural stance, strong, well developed, turning neither in nor out. Straight stifles are objectionable. Double jointedness or cowhocks are a fault. Cowhocks should only be determined if the dog has had an opportunity to move properly.

(c) *Front End*—Legs should be parallel and straight to the pasterns. The pasterns should be strong, sturdy and straight, but flexible with some spring for proper let-down of feet. Because of depth of chest, legs should be moderately long. Length of leg from the ground to the elbow should be approximately 55 per cent of the total height at the withers—a very short-legged dog is to be deprecated. Shoulders should be long and sloping, with a lay-back of 45 degrees and be firmly set. Out at the shoulders or out at the elbow should be penalized. The withers separation should be approximately 1-1½ inches.

(d) *Feet*—Large, long, flattish—a hare-foot, slightly spread but not splayed; toes arched; pads thick and tough, with protective growth of hair between the toes. Feet should turn neither in nor out in a natural stance but may turn in slightly in the act of pulling. Turning out, pigeon-toed, round or cat-footed or splayed are faults. Feathers on feet are not too essential but are more profuse on females than on males.

HEAD—(a) *Conformation*—Skull is wedge-shaped, broad, slightly crowned, not round or apple-headed, and should form an equilateral triangle on lines between the inner base of the ears and the center point of the stop. *Muzzle*—Muzzle of medium length and medium width, neither coarse nor snipy; should taper toward the nose and be in proportion to the size of the dog and the width of skull. The muzzle must have depth. *Stop*—Not too abrupt, nevertheless well defined. *Lips*—Should be black for preference and slightly curved up at the corners of the mouth, giving the "Samoyed smile." Lip lines should not have the appearance of being coarse nor should the flews drop predominately at corners of the mouth.

EARS—Strong and thick, erect, triangular and slightly rounded at the tips; should not be large or pointed, nor should they be small and "bear-eared." Ears should conform to head size and the size of the dog; they should be set well apart but be within the border of the outer edge of the head; they should be mobile and well covered inside with hair; hair full and stand-off before the ears. Length of ear should be the same measurement as the distance from inner base of ear to outer corner of eye.

EYES—Should be dark for preference; should be placed well apart and deep-set; almond shaped with lower lid slanting toward an imaginary point approximating the base of ears. Dark eye rims for preference. Round or protruding eyes penalized. Blue eyes disqualifying.

NOSE—Black for preference but brown, liver, or Dudley nose not penalized. Color of nose sometimes changes with age and weather.

JAWS AND TEETH—Strong, well set teeth, snugly overlapping with scissors bite. Undershot or overshot should be penalized. (b) *Expression*—The expression, referred to as "Samoyed expression," is very important and is indicated by sparkle of the eyes, animation and lighting up of the face when alert or intent on anything. Expression is made up of a combination of eyes, ears and mouth. The ears should be erect when alert; the mouth should be slightly curved up at the corners to form the "Samoyed smile."

TORSO—(a) *Neck*—Strong, well muscled, carried proudly erect, set on sloping shoulders to carry head with dignity when at attention. Neck should blend into shoulders with a graceful arch.
(b) *Chest*—Should be deep, with ribs well sprung out from the spine and flattened at the sides to allow proper movement of the shoulders and freedom for the front legs. Should not be barrel-chested. Perfect depth of chest approximates the point of elbows, and the deepest part of the chest should be back of the forelegs—near the ninth rib. Heart and lung room are secured more by body depth than width.
(c) *Loin and Back*—The withers form the highest part of the back. Loins strong and slightly arched. The back should be straight to the

A perfect example of why the Samoyed is referred to as the dog that smiles. . . this happy puppy is owned by Ruth Young of Medway, Ohio.

loin, medium in length, very muscular and neither long nor short-coupled. The dog should be "just off square"—the length being approximately 5 per cent more than the height. Females allowed to be slightly longer than males. The belly should be well shaped and tightly muscled and, with the rear of the thorax, should swing up in a pleasing curve (tuck-up). Croup must be full, slightly sloping, and must continue imperceptibly to the tail root.

TAIL—The tail should be moderately long with the tail bone terminating approximately at the hock when down. It should be profusely covered with long hair and carried forward over the back or side when alert, but sometimes dropped when at rest. It should not be high or low set and should be mobile and loose—not tight over the hock. A double hook is a fault. A judge should see the tail over the back once when judging.

DISPOSITION—Intelligent, gentle, loyal, adaptable, alert, full of action, eager to serve, friendly but conservative, not distrustful or shy, not overly aggressive. Unprovoked aggressiveness to be severely penalized.

Disqualifications

Any color other than pure white, cream, biscuit, or white and biscuit. Blue eyes.

Approved April, 9, 1963

THE STORY OF THE STANDARD

In the early 1900's Ernest Kilburn-Scott laid down the framework for the first Standard for the breed in England. When the Kennel Club made it "official" in 1909 it was virtually unchanged and remained so even after the original Samoyed association came into being in 1911. The present day English Standard for the Samoyed is still very close to Mr. Scott's initial version.

Americans, Canadians, and eventually the Australians, though making minor changes, all took on the English Standard which has served the breed well.

After World War II, however, with registration increasing considerably, the parent club felt that the Standard should be revised. President S.K. Ruick created a Standard Committee and appointed Agnes Mason as Chairman. In 1952 other breeder-judges were added to the committee; Gertrude Adams became Chairman, since Mrs. Mason was now President. Members of the committee now consisted of Helen Harris, Berta Ruick, Lucile Miller, Martha Humphriss, Louis Smirnow, Robert Ward, Vera Lawrence, Joe E. Scott, C.H. Chamberlain, Miles Vernon, B.P. Dawes, Mrs. Robert Seekins, Warren Shelley, Georgia Gleason and Charles Burr.

An illustrated Standard was considered; the issue of height of bitches, weight, correct description of the head and stress on good disposition were all matters of great concern and importance to the committee.

After almost twelve years of deliberation the new Standard for the breed was approved by the American Kennel Club in 1957. On April 9, 1963, another change was made: the scale of points for judging the dog was eliminated, thereby placing emphasis on the overall conformation of the dog.

6. SAMOYED TEMPERAMENT AND PERSONALITY

To coin a phrase, "Just ask the man who owns one!"

Samoyed owners will delight in telling you all the wonderful attributes of the breed, in addition, of course, to the obvious beauty of the snow-white coat and the flashing black eyes. This marvelous dog has a most outgoing personality which makes it an ideal dog for children.

Little Karissa Anderson with Sacha, her favorite pillow! Photographed in 1971 with Kirsten's Sacha of Pinehill, Karissa is the daughter of Major and Mrs. Anderson of Fairborn, Ohio.

This is a factor which is greatly responsible for the breed's being classed and praised as a working dog and also having the distinction of being cherished as a family dog as well.

ADJUSTMENT TO FAMILY LIFE

While some Sammys will choose their favorite member of the household, they are completely trustworthy with all the family! Another reason the Samoyed can be termed a family dog is its remarkable ability to fit in with almost any kind of domestic life.

All through their history in the Arctic, they served as sled dogs used for hauling or herding reindeer. The dogs were brought into the home in the evening and actually slept with members of the family, helping to keep them warm during the long frigid nights. The bitches had their litters by the fire, and the young puppies were raised as members of the family also. Being an integral part of the domestic scene is a trait which has remained with the Samoyed down through the years and has endeared the breed to dog owners who are inclined to make their dogs regular members of their family.

It can be truly stated that the Samoyed is a happy dog that adjusts well, no matter what kind of life his owner chooses for him. He is

Little Michael Ward and two Sammy puppy pals express their joy in each other's company! The two puppies, Sugar Bear and Jenny, are owned by Jackie Simpson of Dover, Delaware; Michael is owned by Mrs. Jenny Ward of Montoursville, Pennsylvania.

Six-week-old Sammy puppies owned by Jennette Gifford of Carmel, Indiana.

content to live indoors or outdoors; to enter the show ring and display his gay spirit and beautiful coat and conformation; or to work hard and loyally at hauling or herding. The Samoyed aims to please. Therefore, success is also reported in the field of obedience training for Samoyeds because of their great desire to please their masters.

EXCELLENT HOUSE DOGS

The medium size of Samoyeds is also a point in their favor. They are small enough not to overwhelm a child at play, and yet sturdy and solid enough not to be injured easily by rough handling at the hands of the children they watch over. This same medium size qualifies them as house—or even apartment size—dogs. They are not at all clumsy indoors, and they are not jumpers. The only problem will be their persistent desire to be next to you on the couch or to share your favorite chair, whether you are in it or not!

They make excellent guard dogs since they are strongly inclined to alert their owners to the approach of strangers. Yet they do not bark unnecessarily. So, when they bark, you would do well to investigate the cause. . .

White on white:
Joyce Cain's
Samoyed and
his friend the
white cat.

Samoyed breeders will tell you that the bitches make good mothers and are generally easy whelpers of good-sized litters. Being basically adjusted to family living, Sammys are not overly protective of their young and seem to delight in the attentions bestowed on their puppies. This is a good thing, since the puppies are such adorable black-button-eyed little snowballs it is next to impossible for anyone to resist them! Most Samoyed puppies are spoiled by their owners who feel compelled to enjoy every available moment with the puppies before they are sold and leave for their new homes with their new owners.

The only point to make on the negative side of the Samoyed temperament is that the male studs are inclined to fight among themselves. But this is a fact found to apply to most breeds and can also be said to be a problem which lies mostly with large breeding kennels

A charming family of Samoyeds with their proud and handsome young master.

where the studs are in keen competition with one another. Even a small breeding kennel will usually keep only one stud to service the bitches no matter how many females are included in the breeding program.

As for the all-around concept of the perfect family dog, there is no question that the Samoyed fits the picture with beauty, brains, and bright disposition. . . in the show ring they are incomparable!

THE AGE OF MATURITY

The American Kennel Club claims a dog is no longer a puppy when it reaches one year of age. Full maturity comes to the Samoyed around two to three years of age. Maturity depends, of course, on the particular bloodline and also on the size of the dog. The slow developer usually holds its prime for a longer span than the dog which matures earlier or, as some do, at one year of age.

While many Sammys are worthy of their appearance in the show rings at seven and eight years of age, the early-maturing dog can be well past his prime at two. There are few dogs more beautiful than the Samoyed in full bloom. If your dog is past his prime he should not be shown in the ring no matter how much he loves dog shows! You do a disservice to your dog and to the breed by putting a dog that is no longer at his peak against younger dogs.

THE TEEN-AGERS

You will find that at about six months of age, here again depending on how slowly or quickly your dog is maturing, your Sammy will go through a very awkward stage, just as most teenagers do. At this point you must have faith in the pedigree, the sire, the dam, and your devotion to diet and exercise. Chances are the dog will turn out well if you have done everything else right!

HOME EXERCISE

If you own just one Samoyed, you will find it will establish its own exercise schedule, especially if it is exercised on a leash. If your dog is lucky enough (and we hope all dogs are!) to have a backyard to run around in, you will find that he sets his own exercise pattern. You will notice that almost all dogs form set patterns of pacing a fence or chasing after children at play or, in the case of the Samoyed, indulging in one of their favorite pastimes. . . digging holes!

Digging is second nature for the Samoyed, since for all of its history it has been burrowing in the snow to insure its very survival in the polar blizzards. Samoyeds in the Arctic would dig a hole in the snow and then curl their plumy tails around their feet and faces to keep warm or to protect themselves or their young against the driving storms. So whether your dog resides in the wilds of Canada, remote Siberia or a Florida mangrove, a place to dig would be most appreciated!

Adorable red-haired Tracy Outerbridge of Bailey's Bay, Bermuda, cuddles up to the prize-winning Samoyed Lulhaven's Snowmist Ensign in Bermuda to compete in the week of dog shows which is a major event in Bermuda each year. Handled by Pat Tripp for owners Ott Hyatt and Sonny White of Bellevue, Washington. Ensign distinguished himself at the shows by capturing a Best In Show award at the 1971 events. Photo, Bermuda News Bureau.

If providing digging space just isn't possible, the best method of correction is watching the dog during regular exercise periods and offering rawhide or nylon bones or some other type of distraction as the desire to dig strikes. A platform of wooden two-by-fours over stones, or a concrete run, also eliminates the problem.

INDOOR OR OUTDOOR DOG?

Samoyeds are a breed which can feel at home living either indoors or outdoors. If your dog indicates he prefers the outdoor life, with only occasional visits inside with the family, it would be wise to respect his wishes and provide the necessary protection and shelter outdoors. By protection, I mean safety from dognappers, teasing children, or cruel neighbors. . . and the elements. You must provide shelter in the form of a dog house or lean-to; you should also provide shade from the sun. Shade is especially important; not only does the sun burn the beautiful white coat, but the heavy coat means the dog feels the heat more readily than some of the other breeds, and you must never forget this.

Clean, cool water must be provided at all times, and feeding at night is preferable for dogs that live out, since it eliminates the danger of the sun's souring the food if it is not eaten up right away.

At Cape Breton with the ocean for a background these three beautiful Samoyeds make a breath-taking picture. International Champion Kola is on the right, International Champion Bomber is in the middle.

Margaret Ochi's Ch. Winterway's Yukiko, photographed by Josephine Seelig at Rockville, Maryland. Yukiko's sire was Ch. Kondako's Dancing Bear *ex* Ch. Kim's Lady Bug.

Ch. Narguess of Top Acres, owned by General Allen of Ft. Knox, Kentucky.

Mrs. Fred Mills and three of her Sams in Chattanooga, Tennessee.

The glorious Kobe's Michelle of Encino, pictured in April, 1971 at seven months of age. Margaret R. Tucker of Encino, California is the breeder; Robert A. Faulkner of Dayton, Ohio is the owner.

If your dog is to live indoors with you with several excursions into the backyard for exercise or a couple of nice long walks during the course of the day, there are several responsibilities you must assume to insure his good behavior. The dog should have a place to call his own in the house where he has water and his feeding dish and can gather his toys and bones for enjoying at his leisure. This spot should be established in close proximity to where the greatest family activity is centered, for a house dog will want to be as much a member of the family as possible. I might also mention that he should have a bed of his own, but if he is like most other dogs I have known, he will prefer to choose for himself where he sleeps, and it will very likely be *your* bed or as close to it as he can get!

CHEWING A STRONG HABIT

Another thing to watch out for with the house dog is chewing! Next to digging, Sammys love to chew—sometimes even on themselves! Doorknobs, chair legs and chair arms, shoes, etc., are all possibilities, if not probabilities. Until you are absolutely certain that your dog has not developed this habit and can be trusted you would do well to keep a close eye on him.

Wanda and Bob Krauss have titled this beautiful picture "In my element. . .". It shows one of their beautiful K-Way Samoyeds in Madison, Wisconsin.

A sled for Christmas. . . what every child wants, and apparently every Samoyed too! These adorable puppies photographed by their owner, photographer Harold McLaughlin of Morrison, Colorado.

Charles Van Ornum, who is with the Cincinnati Symphony Orchestra, practices at home with Ch. Major Bee, C.D.X. close at hand. Major couldn't get much closer to the music if he wanted to. Major is co-owned by Charles and Marjorie Van Ornum of Cincinnati, Ohio; this photograph was taken in March of 1965.

Leaving any animal alone in the house while you are gone, even for a short period of time, can produce boredom to the point where he will seek solace in one of the above mentioned "pacifiers," making him chew or dig for "spite" because you have left him behind. A pair of Samoyeds can be sufficient company for each other and prevent such destructive behavior also. Better still, take the dog with you and make him a full-time member of the family. You'll both be happier!

7. THE SAMOYED AS A SLED AND RACING DOG

EARLY SLEDS

The first sleds or komiatics were made from whale bone or driftwood gathered from ice floes or the tundra during the thaws. The runners were usually wooden, preferably hickory, and extended as far as 5 to 30 feet in length, with 12 feet being the average. Reindeer antlers tied to the sled with strips of walrus hide were sometimes used as handle bars. The baskets were made of seal or walrus hide; on some sleds runners were made from parts of the jawbones of whales. In an emergency sleds could be made from cuttings of ice, frozen together and carved to their individual needs.

SLED DOG TRAINING— HARNESSING THE PUPPIES

Harnessing began when the puppies were a few months old, sometimes as early as two months of age. It was not uncommon to see entire litters of puppies tied up behind their mother learning to pull in unison. Such teams often made the best and most efficient workers.

SLED DOG'S CAREER A SHORT ONE

Seven years was about the limit for a sled dog, though some of the stronger dogs were used for a dozen or more years. But it was strictly downhill from about seven years on. Others were lost to frostbite, hunger, accidents on the trail, dog fights, disease or ending up second best in a bout with a bear or other animal.

HARNESSING METHODS

There were basically three kinds of harnessing in ancient times, as there are today. One method of harnessing was attaching the dogs in pairs on both sides of a main line that was attached to the middle of the front of the sled. This was, of course, the ideal method of hauling large, heavy loads.

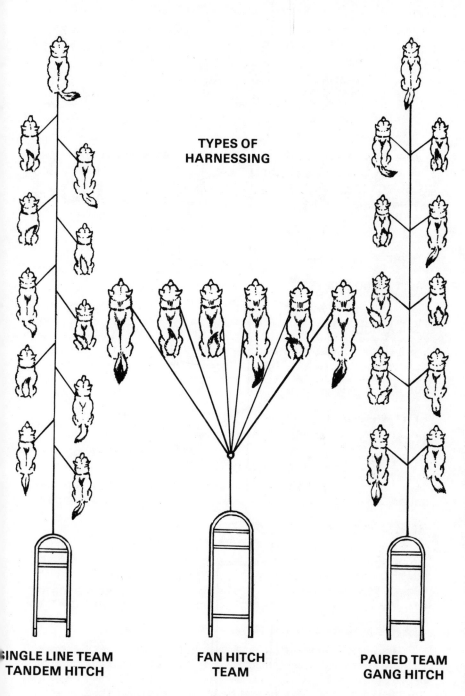

TYPES OF
HARNESSING

SINGLE LINE TEAM
TANDEM HITCH

FAN HITCH
TEAM

PAIRED TEAM
GANG HITCH

Types of harnessing. Drawings by Ernest H. Hart.

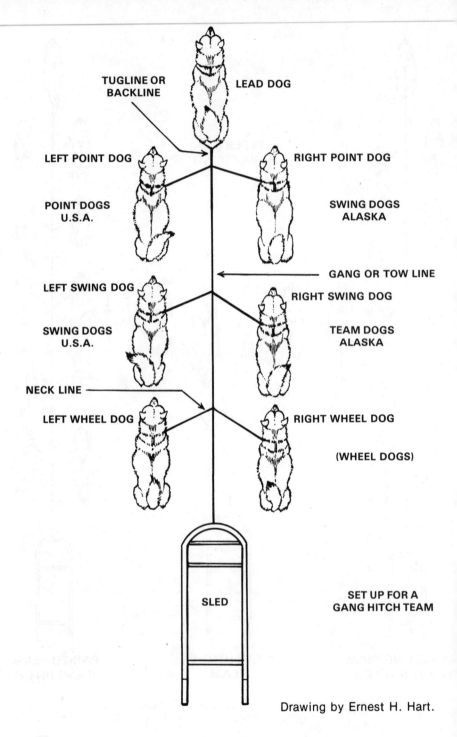

TUGLINE OR BACKLINE

LEAD DOG

LEFT POINT DOG

RIGHT POINT DOG

POINT DOGS U.S.A.

SWING DOGS ALASKA

GANG OR TOW LINE

LEFT SWING DOG

RIGHT SWING DOG

SWING DOGS U.S.A.

TEAM DOGS ALASKA

NECK LINE

LEFT WHEEL DOG

RIGHT WHEEL DOG

(WHEEL DOGS)

SLED

SET UP FOR A GANG HITCH TEAM

Drawing by Ernest H. Hart.

Mrs. Alyce Seekins, Jr. of Troy, New York, is a beautiful sight to see as she races her Samoyed team across the snow. This photograph was featured in the December, 1956, issue of *Popular Dogs* magazine.

The second method of harnessing the dogs was with them attached singly, alternately placed on a single tow line to the sled. They used about six or seven dogs on this single team haul. The logic behind the single line was to avoid excessive loss in crevasse accidents and to prevent dogs from going over precipices during snowstorms.

The third harnessing method was the fan attachment, where several dogs ran side by side, being attached at a single point and with a single tow line to the sled. This method was satisfactory only on clear wide-open terrain.

EARLY TEAM DOGS

In the wilds of the North the Samoyed team dogs were completely different from those we see in more modern times. They were scrappy and vicious, and brutal fights among the dogs were commonplace. All life was a challenge, a defense against the elements, the winning of a female, a fight for food or territory or status among the rest of the dogs.

If there was a fight for leadership between two dogs, it would be a fight to the death. The entire pack would swarm around, waiting eagerly to demolish and devour whichever dog turned out to be the loser. No amount of beating on the part of the owner can hold off the pack when the loser in a dog fight goes down. The same applies when for some reason the pack ostracizes one of its members. It may lag behind the rest at first, but sooner or later the pack will gang up on it, close in and finish it off. And what's more—the dog will know it is a goner and will do little to defend itself.

The lead dog realizes this as well. The moment it shows the first sign of weakness or illness or oncoming age it must immediately be replaced or it will meet the same fate as the outcast dog. A demonstration of the survival of the fittest in its most extreme context.

GELDINGS

The above represent a few reasons why more and more frequently geldings were used on the teams. They ate much less food, did not fight as much among themselves and could be quartered together in small places. The dogs were gelded with an iron knife, and at times only the lead dog on a team was a whole male, making his job of maintaining law and order much easier.

EARLY TEAM TRAINING

On occasion there were dogs which never could "make the team." These dogs were either killed, and probably eaten, or kept strictly for herding. Quarrelsome dogs had their teeth pulled out or the points broken off. By the time they reached 18 months of age the new young dogs were ready to join the teams in prominent positions, and the older dogs were weeded out.

With this regular complete turnover of the team, you can readily understand the importance of the lead dog. He leads and the rest follow *him*, not the driver. Your team is only as good as your lead dog. And it is perfectly possible for a lead dog to bring the team home when the driver is lost on the trail, and against the most unbelievable odds. They may turn up snowblind during a blizzard, but they've kept to the trail and have gotten the team home safely.

When Samoyed dogs are well treated and well fed they take great pleasure in this work, and the closer the relationship between the driver and the lead dog the better the team will function. The winning drivers in the racing events today never forget this either!

DARWIN'S THEORY ON SLED DOGS

In his *The Descent of Man* Charles Darwin presents an enlightening theory on animals and their reasoning powers with specific reference to the Northern breeds. ". . . Only a few persons now dispute that animals possess some power of reasoning. Animals may constantly

Wanda Krauss works out her team on wheels on the grass when there is no snow.

be seen to pause, deliberate, and resolve. It is a significant fact that the more the habits of any particular animal are studied by a naturalist, the more he attributes to reason and the less to unlearnt instincts. . . . For instance, Dr. Hayes, in his work on *The Open Polar Sea*, repeatedly remarks that his dogs, instead of continuing to draw the sledges in a compact body, diverged and separated when they came to thin ice, so that their weight might be more evenly distributed. This was often the first warning which the travelers received that the ice was becoming thin and dangerous. Now, did the dogs act thus from the experience of each individual dog, or from the example of the older and wiser dogs, or from an inherited habit, that is from instinct? This instinct may possibly have arisen since the time, long ago, when dogs were first employed by the natives in drawing their sledges; or the Arctic wolves, the parent-stock of the Esquimaux dog, may have acquired an instinct impelling them not to attack their prey in a close pack, when on thin ice."

THE GREAT SERUM RUN

Another incidence to bear out Darwin's theory of the "on thin ice" instinct in the Northern breeds was evidenced in 1925 during the Great Serum Run in Alaska when a series of relay teams fought a diphtheria epidemic. One of the greatest tales of heroism ever to come out of the frozen North occurred when these brave drivers and their stalwart sled dogs fought their way through fifty below zero weather and an 80-mile an hour blizzard to deliver the serum to the inhabitants of Nome to halt the epidemic of diphtheria. . .

In spite of the waist-high drifts and the mountainous crags of the pack ice, they covered the distance of 655 miles in five and a half days under the most excruciating circumstances, safely delivering the 20-pound package containing the precious 300,000 units of antitoxin serum. At 5:30 a.m. on the morning of February 2, 1925, Gunnar Kasson and his half-frozen team of dogs with bloody, torn feet pulled into Nome and handed over the serum to Curtis Welch of the United States Public Health Service.

Exhausted, Kasson still paid tribute to his lead dog. Newspapers all over the world carried his words of praise for Balto: "Damn fine dog! I've been mushing in Alaska since 1903. This was the toughest I've ever had on the trails. But Balto, he brought us through."

Kasson was referring to Balto's scenting the trail when Kasson got lost on the bare ice and had run into an overflow while crossing

Ch. Sayan of Woodland, pictured here winning Best of Breed under judge Nick Kay, is handled by William Holbrook for owners Bob and Evelyn Kite of Woodland Hills, California. Sired by Ch. Kazan of Kentwood *ex* Snow Heather Radandt, Sayan is one of only two Samoyeds to win three Parent Club Specialty shows. This Specialty was held in September, 1966. Agnes Mason, one of the most respected and revered pioneers in the breed, presents the trophy.

the Topkok River. Balto's "instinct" brought them back to land and onto the trail which eventually led them to Nome, their ultimate destination. It was just one of the occasions on which Balto came through and helped earn him the title of the best lead dog in Alaska. . .

EARLY SAMOYED RACING

The turn of the century marked the era of the great Alaskan Gold Rush. By 1906 a little village named Nome had burst into a boom town because of it! It was the leading gold mining town in the world, but once winter set in and froze the Bering Sea, it had little more than the telegraph and native dog teams with which to keep in contact with the rest of the world.

The dog teams suddenly became an essential means of transportation for the natives as well as members of the mining companies. In order to assure the stamina and performance of the vitally necessary dogs, the Nome Kennel Club was organized in 1907. The man responsible was a lawyer named Albert Fink, who was to serve as the first president of the club. The All-Alaska Sweepstakes races were the means devised to create interest in the dogs, and the Club set the first running for 1908.

THE ALL-ALASKA SWEEPSTAKES

A race course between Nome and Candle on the Seward Peninsula was drawn, which would represent a 408-mile round trip trail with a $10,000 first prize! It was to be run each April, the exact date depending on weather conditions. The course was to follow as closely as possible the Nome to Candle telephone line, and it was a course which presented every possible kind of terrain.

During the first years of the competition the winners consisted mostly of mixed-breed teams, which included almost all varieties of what were termed "northern breeds," with the team being called what they most resembled in appearances, i.e., mixed-Malamute team, mixed-Husky team, etc. These mixtures even included a Malamute-Foxhound team which placed third in the 1915 race, and Samoyeds were mentioned as well. Unfortunately, World War I hit even Alaska pretty hard in 1918, and some of the greatest dog team races ever run in Alaska came to an abrupt halt.

RACING TODAY

For the true dog lover there is a sense of great joy in seeing his favorite breed performing the tasks which God intended for them to do. So it is for the Samoyed owner. However, this isn't always possible for the Samoyed, since there are few reindeer to herd in the United States. Consequently, Samoyed admirers have turned to the sport of racing, or having their dogs actually work at hauling. The spirit and drive witnessed in observing a team of beautiful Samoyeds competing in a race or pulling a sled bring a special kind of pleasure, and the dogs themselves excel at "doing what comes naturally."

TEAM RACING

The one-dog Samoyed owner gets his measure of pleasure just by owning a Sammy, but the trend has been that more and more of the one-dog owners are getting the racing bug and have a litter of puppies which they find they have bred specifically to make up a team. Racing is not only fun but also a marvelous way of exercising their dogs as they compete against other Samoyed teams or against Huskies. Racing dog clubs are sprouting up all over the country, and where actual snow is scarce they race on sleds with wheels.

Relatively few Samoyeds become outstanding racing dogs. If they are good, it is usually because top quality racing dogs are in their background and show in their pedigree. Just as a good "nose" is almost always hereditary with a Beagle, so is the desire to run inherent in the Samoyed.

If they are good racers they are usually not too heavy, well angulated, with longer legs and lighter bones, with large and strong feet, a long and deep chest and an independence that sets them apart from others in the kennel.

If these qualifications are wrapped up in your dog, you are still only half way there! You must remember that the dog still has to be properly trained and be able to run with all the other dogs on the team, and *then*, if you don't have a top notch lead dog you probably won't win anyway, especially if the dog doesn't have the most essential ingredient of all—the innate desire to run! The most worrisome thing about the breed today is that so many of the Samoyeds being bred just do not have that desire to run above all else. Without it, you can never have better than a good team; you will never have a top-winning team!

STARTING THE PUPPY

There are probably few better breeds for racing or pulling than the Samoyed, because of his stamina and sustained power over long distances. Whether your dog will just race, or race and pull weight, training should start around two or three months of age. Start with a soft harness and let him drag a small log or board around. Judge the weight of the log by the weight of the dog. Don't let it be so heavy that the puppy could not possibly move it without a struggle; if you do that, he'll lose interest or get discouraged. By the same token, don't let it be so light that it will catch up with him on the down grade, or he'll never learn the meaning of what it is to "pull." Try what you think is just right, and then observe the puppy's behavior with it for a while; make any necessary adjustments at this time and, of course, as the puppy continues to grow.

Ch. Elrond Czar of Rivendale, winner of the 1971 Samoyed Club of America Specialty Show under judge H.M. Cresap. Owned by Mr. and Mrs. Edward Stowell Gaffney, "Ron" captured this win over 136 entries including 30 of the nation's top Sammy Specials. The same weekend he took Best of Breed over an entry of 71 at a Tuxedo Kennel Club show under judge Romona Van Court. Handled by Jim Manley; Joan Scovin is pictured presenting one of the trophies at this major event held at Far Hills, New Jersey.

At this time, while the puppy is learning to pull, he should be encouraged to pull along a given path, so that the idea of a trail can be established in his mind should you wish to enter competition in the future.

EARLY TRAINING FOR THE RACING DOG

I have just stressed how important it is that each dog destined to race have the innate desire to run and win. This eagerness to compete will enable the trainer to start his harness training at an earlier age and thereby give a head start to the dog on the training as well as conditioning him to his purpose of running and pulling.

If you are fortunate enough to live in snow country, your sled, harness and towline will be your initial equipment for training. If you live in a comparatively snowless area you will need a three-wheeled balanced substitute for training. Training should be a serious matter and in no way the same as or comparable to playtime. Start with each dog individually pulling some weight. This individual training will help you determine which of the puppies has the strongest desire to pull ahead in spite of the weight. You will find that invariably the dog with the strongest desire to pull will make the best lead dog by the time your training nears completion.

THE TRAINING GROUND

One of the most difficult aspects of training will be finding the proper place to train the puppies. If you do not live in the country it will be necessary to locate a park or wooded area, or better still, a local race track where the dogs can run a distance with minimum danger of interruption by uncertain terrain. Too many distractions in populated areas will throw puppies or young dogs off until they are used to what is expected of them. With too many spectators around there is always the danger of having the team bowl them over if they get in the way. Therefore, until the puppies get used to running and keeping on the trail, bridle paths, fields and or farm lands are best places to work out. Remember the safety of others when tearing down a path with a team of sled dogs! Under no circumstances train

Getting off to an early start for their sled team training, these seven-week-old puppies were photographed in 1963; they grew up to be the Suruka Orr sled dogs.

your dogs on the street or a concrete surface. The irritation to the pads of the feet somehow prevents the dogs from reaching out to their full stride, so they never become good distance runners in a race. Ideal conditions are snow or sand, but if such surfaces are not available, train on dirt surfaces to prevent the hackneyed gait of the dogs which are trying to preserve their own feet, or which will pull up with bloody pads if forced to run on pavement.

As the puppies grow and begin their working together, you will undoubtedly have joined a club in your area where members are equally interested in racing. You will learn a great deal from your association with other members, and it is advisable to take full advantage of their advice, knowledge and experience. But there still are going to be many hours of training on your own where a few essential rules will apply.

Important to remember in your training is this: do not teach too many commands. Young puppies can not retain too many words, and expecting too much of them too soon will only confuse them and perhaps make them lose interest entirely. Remember to praise them lavishly for their good work and efforts. Remember to keep your puppies and dogs in top racing condition so that they will be able to give what is expected of them without draining every last bit of energy. Remember common sense rules which apply to racing as well as obedience or show training; namely, do not feed or water immediately before training, and exercise the puppies before starting the training so there will be no interruption. And perhaps most important of all, do not go on to another command or lesson until the dog has already learned the last one!

You will find that your puppy can cover a mile comfortably by the time he is eight months old, which should increase to 15 or 16 miles at the peak of his training and performance at two years of age.

DISPOSITION AND ATTITUDE

One of the determining factors in selecting your team will be each dog's disposition. The training may have gone along very well, but if the dog is a "scrapper" and will be undependable when harnessed with other dogs in a team, you will eventually run into trouble. While it is allowable to remove a dog from a team during a race, it would make more sense to have all members of your team able to finish if you really want to win and need that full team to do it!

When we talk about Samoyeds being smart in their own special way, we must explain that at times there is an almost obvious "holding back" or lack of complete communication between you and the dog, which manifests itself noticeably in their training for racing competition. When a Samoyed is being trained to race he will usually pace himself to fit the distance he must cover on his own. Therefore, it is wise when training the dog for the race to steadily increase the distance each day, rather than varying the ground mileage to be covered from one day to the next. Increasing distance each day will increase his desire to always "go further," and to the end of the race.

FORMING YOUR TEAMS

A tenet in animal behavior studies acknowledges that there is a leader in every pack. So it is with a racing team. Your lead dog must be the most respected member of your kennel or the other dogs simply will not give their all and "follow the leader." Whatever the sex of the lead dog, put your next two fastest dogs behind the lead dog and your biggest, or strongest, two at the wheel positions.

While your lead dog will assert himself to keep order in the pack, to maintain a good team you must have harmony among all members of the team. Drivers will find that on occasion if they buy dogs from other teams to add to their own, the new dog is apt not to pull and will be dragged by the rest unless he feels he has been accepted by the other dogs as a member of the pack. Puppies from the same litter, trained together, often make the best teams for this reason. They "grow into the saddle."

Practice makes perfect, as the saying goes, and hours of practice and training are necessary to get all your dogs working together as a team. There is no easy way to accomplish this other than hard work. It is a magnificent challenge.

SECURING RACING INFORMATION

If you have decided that you wish to enter a team in a race, you must write to the race-giving club well in advance asking for all pertinent information along with an entry blank. Ask the race marshall for specific information regarding not only the race, but information on joining the club, which you will want to do eventually, if you haven't already. State the size of your team, and ascertain at this time whether it is necessary to be a member of the club in order to enter the race. With some clubs this is a requirement.

While waiting for this information to reach you, consider once again whether or not you are *really ready* to enter your first race. Ask yourself whether your dogs are sufficiently trained, run well together, fight in harness, stick to the trail, tangle with other teams, can be distracted by people or other animals on the sidelines? And perhaps most important of all, are all the dogs equal in strength and endurance, and do they all really want to run more than anything else?!?

THE DAY OF THE RACE

You've entered your first race and have received your notification and rules regarding the race, time, place and requirements. Needless to say, the beginner should arrive early to observe the pro-

California mountain snow scene in January, 1949, Mr. and Mrs. John Morgan of England are passengers on a sled dog team led by "Rex."

cedures others follow and have plenty of time to ask questions. Be sure you park in the correct area, stake your dogs out in the proper area, exercise them, and determine within plenty of time when the drivers' meeting will be held so that you can attend it.

While you are waiting for the meeting to begin, take the time to reread the rules of the race. As a beginner you may forget. . . and knowing what to do when and where can make a difference! Also check out your equipment.

Always include a complete substitute for your harness and tow lines, collars, leashes, etc., in your tack box. Accidents do happen, and it would be a shame to miss your first experience because a break left you without complete equipment. Don't be afraid to ask questions or to ask for help. Remember that everyone else was a beginner once also, and most of them remember how much it meant to them to have a helping hand or a genuine good word of advice.

Remember good manners during the race. Don't spoil someone else's chances because of your mistake or mistakes. They will be watching out for you if they know you are new at the game, but it is your responsibility not to spoil the race for others. You are expected to know the passing rules, re-passing rules, etc., and you will gain more respect for your sportsmanship and knowledge than you will for trying to stick it out when you should get out of the race. No one expects you to win your first race anyway! But whether you win or lose, once you've gotten into the competition you will become addicted to the sport and sooner or later you will win if your dogs are good and properly trained.

RACING MANNERS

Need we say that bad language, complaining and excuses, rough handling of your dogs (for any reason whatsoever!) drinking or pushing your dogs beyond their endurance are strictly taboo? How you conduct yourself under any and all conditions will determine how much help and respect you win from your fellow drivers, and if you want to continue in the racing field you had better stick to the rules or you will find yourself strictly an outsider. And that isn't the name of the game!

PROFESSIONAL RACING TEAMS

You must realize that racing for fun and pleasure or in local club meets or contests is entirely different from the professional racing meets where the stakes and purses are high and the owners and drivers are out to win. Professional racing teams are serious business, and it is a completely different world for the professional racing dog!

The trainers and drivers of the professional teams are usually those dedicated to doing nothing else but training and racing the dogs. It is their profession; the lives of the dogs are dedicated to racing and winning.

Cowboy movie stars Dale Evans and Roy Rogers stop to admire Agnes Mason's famous dog sled team at the Sportsmans Show in Los Angeles in April, 1969. The Masons' dogs have won at the Sienna Dog Derby races in California.

This intent and purpose begins with the picking of the dogs which show—above all else—the natural desire to run and to win. The training is more rigorous, the culling more ruthless, and the proper rearing and selection of the dogs even more essential. Professional team owners will spare no expense and will travel the globe to acquire just the right dog to enhance their team. The studying of pedigrees becomes almost a science, and the health, care and feeding of their teams is of major concern.

While the purses for the winners of the big races are large, so are the costs of maintaining a professional team. The costs far exceed the winnings, and before one considers getting into the professional aspect of this sport, financial considerations must be taken into account.

With the professional racing teams there is also a more strict, concentrated training schedule. The dogs must be kept in top racing condition all the time, not just before racing seasons, which means they must not become overweight. Bad dispositions are weeded out at the first moment of discovery, grooming and training are on a regular schedule and more frequent, and the serious racing training begins in earnest at six or seven months of age.

Most racing dogs are staked out at about three to four months old, and the confined conditions seem to heighten their desire to run.

PROFESSIONAL RACING DOGS

While there are more professional racing teams now than ever before, there are not as many as one would expect. There are reasons for this. . . the owners of the professional teams are interested to a great extent in the money prizes and will use any dog—purebred or otherwise—if the dog will run to win. Expenses are high to maintain and breed purebred Samoyeds exclusively while waiting for the top ones to come along. Mixed breeds offer more opportunities to buy up the fastest dogs in spite of their ancestry, giving the owners a "faster team faster!" So unless money is no object, more of the pros will not stick to one breed, but will shop around. Though price may be no object, there is a time limit involved. It is only the dedicated Samoyed lover who also races and can afford to support a team of purebreds who brings out a matched team that has a good chance of winning!

Night scene. Joyce Cain's Samoyed on night patrol in the snow at the Cain home in Ripon, Wisconsin.

SLED DOG RACING EVENTS
Sled Dog Racing in Idaho

1917 was the first year of the American Dog Derby in Ashtown, Idaho. This event is still held for racing enthusiasts. Today, however, the club holds several racing events in several different towns each year. They feature ten mile courses each day for two days. This is quite a different schedule from the 1917 event, when a half dozen teams of mixed breeds raced from West Yellowstone, Montana to Ashtown, Idaho—a distance of 75 miles!

Two of the Poviers' Samoyeds pose with their sled. The sled weighs 36 pounds and is made of hickory. Laura and Leo Povier and their Sammys live in Highland Park, Michigan.

Sled Dog Racing in Minnesota

The St. Paul, Minnesota, Winter Carnival in 1962 was the site of the first sled dog racing in the state, in conjunction with the special events at the State Fair.

In 1965 the North Star Sled Dog Club, Inc. was started as a racing club, and by 1969 the club decided to sponsor a major national racing event at the Winter Carnival; they called it "East Meets West." A total of 55 teams competed that year in St. Paul, representing 11 states and Canada. The event was a major breakthrough for racing enthusiasts and has been growing in popularity and competition ever since. The purses get larger each year and the spectators increase notably as well.

While a reasonably new group, the club membership keeps increasing and participating in other racing events, and plans for the future are bright.

Mutt Races

Each year the All American Championship Sled Dog Races are held in Ely, Minnesota, and feature mutt races as part of the special events program. These mutt races are usually held following a torchlight parade, and are run for boys and girls from six to eight years of age, eight to ten years of age, and children from ten to twelve years of age. Each child runs a single hitch, and the one dog may be of any type or breed. The only differential is that they separate the experienced and trained sled dogs from the amateur dogs and run them in separate categories.

There is no entry fee and, of course, trophies are provided for the winners. This is always a popular event with racing enthusiasts of all ages.

Beauty Queens

The Ely event also has been known to feature a beauty queen to appear in the torchlight parade. In 1971, and a repeat performance in 1972, it was Britt-Inger Johannsen, a former Miss Scandinavia and former Miss Sweden, invited by the Sled Dog Committee to head up the parade and to judge such events as a "beard contest" where she rubbed cheeks with those racing participants who sported "beavers."

Special Events

The sled dog gathering usually opens with a community center show which features the latest in sleds, equipment, accessories and demonstrations of anything and everything pertaining to racing, including items which can be purchased.

This is followed on Friday night by a torchlight parade, with the aforementioned beauty queen, sleds, snowmobiles, floats, and the like. The parade is followed by the special events program, which features weight pulling contests, celebrity races, ski-jorring, a scramble race, a beard contest and the kids' mutt races. Entertainment of the indoor variety follows the activities in these categories.

Saturday sees the first heats of the All American Championship Sled Dog Race. Usually over 100 teams compete. Saturday night there is a banquet and entertainment, and on Sunday the second heats are run; prizes are awarded at the completion of the day's events.

There is over $5000 in prize money awarded to the racers as well as hundreds of dollars worth of trophies to the winners who manage to triumph on one of the finest racing trails in the world. The best known racers from all over the United States (including Alaska, of course) and Canada manage to show up to compete.

Because of the great beauty of the dogs, and the excitement of the chase, there is always a great deal of spectator enthusiasm as well as newspaper, radio and television coverage and stories in major magazines all over the world. Over 20,000 fans show up to cheer on their favorite dog teams. The Chamber of Commerce of Ely, Minnesota, can be proud of their Expo-Mini Sports Show and Sled Dog Races which are the biggest winter sports events in northern Minnesota.

This Samoyed and the Santa and reindeer seem to be waiting for some Christmas snow to appear so they can be on their way!

WORLD CHAMPIONSHIP SLED DOG DERBY

On the eastern seaboard the sledding event takes over the main street of Laconia, New Hampshire when the racing enthusiasts participate in this major event. Snow making machines cover the main street with snow if none has fallen from the sky. Laconia also presents a Musher's Ball and crowns a Musher's Queen amid much fanfare.

RACING IN ALASKA

The first All-Alaska Sweepstakes race was run in 1908, with the Nome Kennel Club providing pennants and each team choosing its racing colors to gain instant recognition to win glory. Training began in the late fall for the spring races, and many hours were spent over the long winter months training the dogs for this big event.

The only communication with the outside world was by radio and with the dog teams which brought the mail. In those days the teams left at two-hour intervals, but this wide difference was later reduced to the point where the teams left within minutes—or even seconds—of each other.

In extremely cold weather the dogs were rubbed down with alcohol; they sometimes even wore blankets and flannel moccasins for their feet or eye covers for their eyes. So important was the winning of the races that the drivers fed and bedded down their dogs before they considered their own comforts, so that the dogs would be in good condition to run again the next day.

Even today Alaska considers sled dog racing as its very own sport and features two of the world's most famous races, the North American Championship Race, held in Fairbanks, and the Fur Rendezvous, or the Rondy, in Anchorage. The Fur Rendezvous began in 1936, and by the following year fur trappers in the area were selling their furs *and* racing their dogs. The rendezvous became a virtual festival for everyone, with a fur auction, parties, dances, and exhibitions all being held at the one gathering place. But even from the beginning the dog racing was the main event, and today the 75-mile race still is!

There was a brief halt in the festivities from 1924 to 1936 when only the races were held with the carnival atmosphere, and again during World War II (1942 through 1945) but the annual event was eagerly resumed in 1946 and is gaining in popularity with each year! The schools close on the Friday of the Rendezvous, and the city turns out *en masse* to watch the four-dog team demonstrations which became the regular feature in 1946.

The North American race is 70 miles in length and both events are run in three heats which divide the distance in three parts, over three days. After the third day the winner is announced and the celebrating begins anew!

There are also state championship races held in Kenai and Soldotna, and also one in Tok. In 1967 the Iditarod Trail Race was also held; it was referred to as an "endurance" event and used part of the trail used years ago to bring gold from Iditorod to Knik at the turn of the century. There are attempts being made to open up this rugged trail once again as an 800-mile endurance race. Plans are to restore the shelter cabins to house food for the dogs every fifty miles. Participants will use sleeping bags and carry survival equipment and the committee looks toward $2000 in gold as the reward for the winner!

Racing in Alaska, which had diminished during World War II, picked up again with new enthusiasm in the late 1940's, when the Alaska Dog Musher's Association was formed in Fairbanks. In 1949, in Anchorage, the Alaska Sled Dog and Racing Association was organized.

CHILDREN AND RACING IN ALASKA

At the end of December each year in Anchorage, Alaska, the Junior Alaskan Sled Dog and Racing Association opens its season. The club holds a meeting each Friday night to discuss weather and trail conditions and to draw for starting positions for the race at the Anchorage Tudor Track. Races are held each week throughout the month of January.

Champion Velko, bred by Ruth Young of the Top Acres Kennels in Medway, Ohio and owned by Joan Lueck of Oxford, Michigan. Sire was Ch. Beta Sigma's Mufti; dam was Sparkle's M'Liss of Top Acres.

These juniors must adhere to all the rules and regulations followed by the adults, which are held on the same trails as the adults run and are often eight to twelve miles long. To be a junior musher, the child must be from six to eighteen years of age. There are five classes of junior races consisting of one-, two-, three-, five- and seven-dog teams. The one-doggers race for a quarter of a mile on a straight track, while the two-dog class and most of the three-dog classes run three miles. The five- and seven-dog classes increase the mileage still farther, running a six-mile trail for the opening race with a vote determining the length of future races.

An armful of charm. . . four of Marjorie Van Ornum's litter of Sammy puppies.

RACING IN CANADA

In Canada the major race is the PAS held in Manitoba. This race is not widely known but is acknowledged to be the longest and the toughest in the world. The dogs travel a distance of anywhere from 100 to 150 miles during the three-day race.

The Quebec race, while not as long, covers a 100-mile distance. The purses for these races are large and the drivers take the winning of these two events very seriously.

THE HUSLIA HERITAGE AND THE HUSLIA HUSTLERS

The Athabascan Indian village named Huslia, which has given to the racing world in Alaska so many of its top dogs and top drivers, is situated 260 miles northwest of Fairbanks on a river about one mile from the Koyukuk. The village remains very remote, still steeped in its Indian culture, but with modern ways and communications now gradually creeping up on it.

Jimmy Hunington was a trapper originally but gained fame for Huslia when in 1939 he entered the dog derbies in Nome. Jimmy borrowed dogs, got a team together and by mushing and getting a ride on a mail plane (along with his 14 dogs!) arrived in Fairbanks to race in the North American Race intent on winning enough money to open his own trading post in Huslia. He placed fourth but went home broke because he was unable to collect his prize money.

The desire to race stayed with him, and in 1956 the villagers urged him to try again and loaned him their best dogs; he emerged the winner of the North American Race in Fairbanks and the Fur Rendezvous in Anchorage. He thereby became known as The Huslia Hustler, until 1958, when George Attla, Jr., also from Huslia, appeared on the scene; George now carries the title as well! Looking at the line-up of any big Alaskan race today, you'll probably find either a winning team of dogs and/or drivers from Huslia!

In 1958 George Attla, Jr. appeared in his first Rondy Race and won handily with a 12-dog team. He owned only one of them, his lead dog named Tennessee. The rest of the dogs belonged to members of his family. Today, after having won the Rondy again in 1962, 1968 and 1972, George is the Huslia Hustler—the greatest hustler of them all!

George Attla was born in 1933, one of eight children born to George and Eliza Attla. A form of tuberculosis caused the fusing of the bones in George's knee, but the defect in no way stopped him from sled racing; in addition to the four Rondy wins, he has captured the number one spot in just about every other major race in Alaska.

George is also known as a great dog trainer. In addition to training his own dogs, he sometimes trains dogs for his competition! He excels in training lead dogs which have made winning teams for many of his competitors in the major races. . . some of which have beaten his team!

George has recently authored a book titled *Everything I Know About Training and Racing Sled Dogs*, in collaboration with Bella Levorsen, a racing enthusiast in her own right, which reveals George's secrets of success as a World Champion Racer four times to date! His 1972 racing records at Bemidji, Minnesota, Ely, Minnesota, Kalkaska, Michigan, Anchorage, Nenana, Fairbanks, Tok and Tanana, Alaska, earned George Attla the Gold Medal from the International Sled Dog Racing Association's first annual competition for a Point Champion.

WOMEN MUSHERS

It seems women have always shared their husbands' interest in driving dog teams and racing. Dog racers are all familiar with the successes of Short Seeley, Lorna Demidoff and Louise Lombard, who in 1949 was the only woman entered in the 90-mile Ottawa, Canada, Dog Sled Derby, competing right along with her husband.

Mrs. E.P. Ricker, now Mrs. Nansen, was driving dog teams in 1928 and placed second at the Lake Placid fourth annual Sled Dog Derby in 1931. Bunty Dunlap, Mrs. Ricker's daughter, went on to follow in her mother's footsteps and became a top sled dog driver. And don't let us forget Jean Bryar, a winner of the North American Women's Championship in Alaska, the first woman from the States to do it. She also gave a good account of herself in many of the gruelling Canadian races, not to mention New Hampshire events. Millie Turner was active at the New England events in the 1930's and 1940's, and Natalie Norris and Joyce Wells have been active at the Rondy races.

Today's representatives are Kit Macinnes, Rosie Losonsky, Vera Wright, Barbara Parker, Shari Wright, Shirley Gavin, Anne Wing, Carol Lundgren and Carol Sheppard. In addition, let's stand by to see what Darlene Huckins will do!

No doubt about it, the women are active in the sport and play by the men's rules. A strong case for sled dog racing as a family sport!

THE WOMEN'S WORLD CHAMPIONSHIP

1953 was the first year of the Women's World Championship Sled Dog Races in Alaska, an event that has been run every year since except for 1956. The same rules apply to the women's races as apply to the regular races, and the women train their own dogs.

In the beginning the purses were small, but by 1972 the winner walked away with a $1000 prize. But then again, the race was not

Pixie, a puppy sold to Fred and Eva Wills of Chattanooga, Tennessee.

A magnificent headstudy of Ch. Snowlines Joi Shashan, photographed by the famed dog photographer Joan Ludwig. Joli is the proud pos-
session of Mary and Leon Mayfield of California.

Mrs. John May of Trenton, New Jersey and two of her Samoyeds in their favorite setting. . . snow!

always as long. The early days featured a two-day race of 20 miles, but by 1972 the winner is determined after three days of racing twelve miles eacy day for a total run of 36 miles. The total time is tallied to determine the winner.

The teams usually average 9 or 11 dogs, and there are on an average of ten to fifteen teams competing for the purse and the title of top female musher in Alaska—and the world!

The Women's World Championship Race Winners

1953 - Joyce Wells
1954 - Natalie Norris
1955 - Kit Macinnes
1957 - Rosie Losonsky
1958 - Vera Wright
1959 - Kit Macinnes
1960 - Kit Macinnes
1961 - Kit Macinnes
1962 - Barbara Parker
1963 - Barbara Parker
1964 - Barbara Parker
1965 - Sheri Wright
1966 - Shirley Gavin
1967 - Shari Wright
1968 - Anne Wing
1969 - Shirley Gavin
1970 - Shirley Gavin
1971 - Carol Lundgren
1972 - Carol Sheppard

A beautiful photograph of American and Canadian Ch. Oakwood Farm's Kari J'Go Diko, bred and owned by Joan Lueck of Oakwood Farm, Oxford, Michigan. Diko was sired by Ch. Sam O'Khan's Chingis Khan ex American and Canadian Ch. Oakwood Farm's Silver Kari.

A GLOSSARY OF RACING TERMS

ALASKAN HUSKY: A name appled to any Arctic-type cross-bred dog, usually a Husky, Malamute, Samoyed or Eskimo cross.

ALASKAN MALAMUTE: Used more for hauling than racing because of its great size and endurance.

ATTITUDE RUN: A short "fun" race.

BABICHE: Strips of rawhide used to join the parts of a sled.

BACKLINE: A line from the harness to the towline. Sometimes referred to as a tugline.

BASKET: The section of the sled which carries either passenger or cargo.

BRAKE: The metal fork stepped on by the driver to bring the sled to a halt. A fork on the underside of the sled which hits the ground and stops the sled.

BRIDLE: The collection of ropes gathered with a ring to which the towline is attached.

CART TRAINING: When there is no snow, training dogs with a three- or four-wheel cart is undertaken. Also carts are used in racing in warm climates.

CHAIN: Lengths of chain are used to stake a dog outdoors; usually about six feet in length and attached with snaps at the dog's collar and to the stake.

CHIEF STEWARD: Chief steward takes the other stewards out to their posts. He remains at start and finish lines.

CHUTE: The first several feet beyond the starting line is referred to as the chute.

DNF: Letters standing for Did Not Finish, which means a racer did not finish the race.

DOG BOX: The compartment mounted on a truck in which the dogs are transported to and from the racing site.

DRAGGING: When a dog is dragged along by his neckline, either after he falters, or if he is merely lagging behind.

GANGLINE: Center line fastened to the sled and to which the dogs are hitched. Also known as towline.

GEE: A term used with the dog to indicate a right turn.

GO: Same as start, begin, etc. Response to this word can mean the difference between getting off to a head start or merely starting along with the others.

HANDLE BAR: Topmost portion at the rear of the sled to which the driver holds on.

HARNESS: The webbing which covers the dog and is attached to the lines.

HAW: Term used to indicate a left turn.

HEAT: A heat is one race.

HOLDING AREA: A section near the racing site where dogs are staked until race time.

Ch. Star Acres Sian, Samoyed show winner with Patricia Morehouse, Kubla Khan Kennels, Los Angeles, California.

Ch. Gentle Giant of Snow Country, whelped in May, 1972 and co-owned by Clifton J. and Mary R. Fryer, Marcliff Samoyeds, Paradise, Pennsylvania.

HOOK, SNOW HOOK: A metal hook attached to the bridle of the sled by a line to hold the team in place. It can be driven into the ground or attached to a stationary object.

HOOK-UP AREA: Same as holding area—a place where the dogs are held until race time.

INDIAN DOG: A dog bred and owned by an Indian in an Indian village.

JINGLER: A collection of bells or noisy trinkets used to get the attention of the dogs and spur them on.

LEAD DOG: The dog at the head of the team, usually the fastest, most experienced and best trained.

LEADER: Same as a lead dog.

LOWER 48 or LOWER 49: Term used when referring to racing in any of the United States other than Alaska.

MARSHALL: A term used when referring to the racing official in charge at the race.

MUSH: Originally a French term meaning to walk or to march. While mush can be a term used for starting a team, more often "Let's Go!" or "Take Off!" work just as well. Usually only in the movies do the drivers yell Mush!

MUSHER: The term applied to the driver of a team.

NECKLINE: A light line that hooks the dog's collar to the towline.

NO: Word used to keep the dogs on the trail should they start to veer off, or to stop them from chewing on the line, to ward off a scrap, etc.

PEDALING: When the driver keeps one foot on the runner of the sled and pedals or pushes with the other.

PUMPING: A term used meaning the same as pedaling.

PUNCHING THROUGH: When the dog's feet break through the crust of ice on top of the snow they are said to punch through. The term punchy is the word used for the snow.

RACE MARSHALL: Man in charge of the races.

RIGGING: All the lines collectively to which dogs are hooked.

RUNNERS: Two bottom strips of wood on which the sled runs and are covered with steel or plastic strips called runner shoes.

SIBERIAN HUSKY: Purebred dog used extensively in sled racing.

SKI-JORRING: A short race with the driver on skis rather than with a sled. Line is attached around his waist with a slip knot.

SLED BAG: The canvas bag which holds items necessary to the race and usually carried in the basket.

SNOW BERM: The ridges of snow made along the side of the roads by the snow plows.

SNOW FENCE: Fencing made of wooden upright slats fastened together with wire used to mark off areas or to prevent heavy drifting of snow.

SNOW HOOK: A hook used to stake a team temporarily.

STANCHIONS: Vertical parts of a sled.

STARTER: The man who starts the race.

STAY: Same as Whoa, or stop or halt. Used to stop the dogs at end of race or any other reason. Choose one and stick with it.

STEWARD: One of the officials placed along the trail to avoid trouble at traffic spots, sharp curves, etc. They must stay on the trail until the last team has passed.

STOVE UP: When a dog pulls up lame, or stiff.

SWING DOGS: Dog that runs directly behind the leader either on the right side of the tow line (right swing dog) or on the left side (left swing dog).

Bred and owned by Joan Lueck, her American and Canadian Ch. Oakwood Farm's Kari J'Go Diko relaxes at home. The Luecks' Oakwood Farm is in Oxford, Michigan.

TEAM DOGS: Dogs hitched into the team between the swing dogs and the wheel dogs.

TO MUSH DOGS: To drive a team.

TOWLINE, OR GANGLINE: The center line fastened to the sled and to which the dogs are hitched.

TRAIL!: Term shouted by mushers to ask another driver for the right of way.

TUGLINE OR TUG: Line from harness to the towline, same as backline.

VET CHECK: Before each race a veterinarian checks over each dog to see that it has not been drugged, if it is in good health and running condition, etc.

WHEEL DOGS: The two dogs directly in front of the sled which determine the direction of the sled.

WHIP: Usually whips are not permitted, but if they are, they must be under three feet in length so that they cannot touch the dogs.

WHOA!: With dogs, as this horses, this means one thing—STOP!

8. BUYING YOUR SAMOYED PUPPY

There are several paths that will lead you to a litter of puppies where you can find the puppy of your choice. Write to the parent club and ask for the names and addresses of members who have puppies for sale. The addresses of Samoyed clubs can be obtained by writing the American Kennel Club, 51 Madison Avenue, New York, N.Y. 10010. They keep an accurate, up-to-date list of reputable breeders from whom you can seek information on obtaining a good healthy puppy. You might also check listings in the classified ads of major newspapers. The various dog magazines also carry listings and usually a column each month which features information and news on the breed.

It is to your advantage to attend a few dog shows in the area where purebred dogs of just about every breed are being exhibited in the show ring. Even if you do not wish to buy a show dog, you should be familiar with what the better specimens look like so that you may at least get a decent looking representative of the breed for your money. You will learn a lot by observing the dogs in action in the show ring, or in a public place where their personalities come to the fore. The dog show catalogue will list the dogs and their owners with local kennel names and breeders whom you can visit to see the types and colors they are breeding and winning with at the shows. Exhibitors at these shows are usually delighted to talk to people about their dogs and the specific characteristics of their particular breed.

Once you have chosen the Samoyed above all others because you admire its exceptional beauty, intelligence and personality, and because you feel the breed will fit in with your family's way of life, it is wise to do a little research on it. The American Kennel Club library, your local library, bookshops and the breed clubs can usually supply you with a list of reading matter or written material on the breed, past and present. Then, once you have drenched yourself in the breed's illustrious history and have definitely decided that this is the breed for you, it is time to start writing letters and making phone calls to set up appointments to see litters of puppies.

A word of caution here: don't let your choice of a kennel be determined by its nearness to your home, and then buy the first cute puppy

Equally inquisitive, Samoyed puppy and kitten explore each other. . . and become friends.

that races up to you or licks the end of your nose. All puppies are cute, and naturally you will have a preference among those you see. But don't let preferences sway you into buying the wrong puppy.

If you are buying your dog as a family pet, a preference might not be a serious offense. But if you have had, say, a color preference since you first considered this breed, you would be wise to stick to it. If you are buying a show dog, all physical features must meet with the Standard for the breed. In considering your purchase you must think clearly, choose carefully, and make the very best possible choice. You will, of course, learn to love whichever puppy you finally decide upon, but a case of "love at first sight" can be disappointing and expensive later on if a show career was your primary objective.

To get the broadest possible concept of what is for sale and the current market prices, it is recommended that you visit as many kennels and private breeders as you can. With today's reasonably safe, inexpensive and rapid non-stop flights on the major airlines, it is possible to secure dogs from far-off places at nominal additional charges, allowing you to buy the valuable bloodlines of your choice if you have a thought toward a breeding program in the future.

While it is always safest to actually *see* the dog you are buying, there are enough reputable breeders and kennels to be found for you to buy a dog with a minimum of risk once you have made up your mind what you want, and when you have decided whether you will buy in your own country or import to satisfy your concept of the breed Standard. If you are going to breed dogs, breeding Standard type can be a moral obligation, and your concern should be with buying the best bloodlines and individual animals obtainable, in spite of cost or distance.

It is customary for the purchaser to pay the shipping charges, and the airlines are most willing to supply flight information and prices upon request. Rental on the shipping crate, if the owner does not provide one for the dog, is nominal. While unfortunate incidents have occurred on the airlines in the transporting of animals by air, the major airlines are making improvements in safety measures and have reached the point of reasonable safety and cost. Barring unforeseen circumstances, the safe arrival of a dog you might buy can pretty much be assured if both seller and purchaser adhere to and follow up on even the most minute details from both ends.

Breeder Helga Gruber presents this adorable picture of two five-week-old Samoyed puppies sired by American and Canadian Ch. Oakwood Farm's Kari J'Go Diko *ex* Khingan's Queen of Sheba.

THE PUPPY YOU BUY

Let us assume you want to enjoy all the cute antics of a young puppy and decide to buy a six-to-eight-week-old puppy. This is about the age when a puppy is weaned, wormed and ready to go out into the world with a responsible new owner. It is better not to buy a puppy under six weeks of age; it simply is not yet ready to leave the mother or the security of the other puppies. At eight to twelve weeks of age you will be able to notice much about the appearance and the behavior. Puppies, as they are recalled in our fondest childhood memories, are gay and active and bouncy, as well they should be! The normal puppy should be interested, alert, and curious, especially about a stranger. If a puppy acts a little reserved or distant, however, such

A Samoyed puppy at play. If you can't fight it, *eat* it! A Harold McLaughlin photograph.

A typical adorable
Samoyed puppy.

act need not be misconstrued as shyness or fear. It merely indicates
he hasn't made up his mind whether he likes you as yet! By the same
token, he should not be fearful or terrified by a stranger—and especially should not show any fear of his owner!

In direct contrast, the puppy should not be ridiculously over-ac-
tive either. The puppy that frantically bounds around the room and is
never still is not especially desirable. And beware of the "spinners"!
Spinners are the puppies or dogs that have become neurotic from being kept in cramped quarters or in crates and behave in an emotional-
ly unstable manner when let loose in adequate space. When let out
they run in circles and seemingly "go wild." Puppies with this kind of
traumatic background seldom ever regain full composure or adjust
to the big outside world. The puppy which has had the proper exercise
and appropriate living quarters will have a normal, though spirited,
outlook on life and will do his utmost to win you over without having to
go into a tailspin.

Starctic Snowbasin Sioux, C.D., highest-scoring Samoyed in trial at the SCLA Specialty show in September, 1974. Sioux is pictured here winning the first leg at the first trial under judge Ray Muller with a score of 194½. Sioux finished for her Companion Dog title in three shows with her two other scores of 195. Owner-handler is Dolly Ward of Calabasas, California.

If the general behavior and appearance of the dog thus far appeal to you, it is time for you to observe him more closely for additional physical requirements. First of all, you cannot expect to find in the puppy all the coat he will bear upon maturity. That will come with time and good food, and will be additionally enhanced by the many wonderful grooming aids which can be found on the market today. Needless to say, the healthy puppy's coat should have a nice shine to it, and the more dense at this age, the better the coat will be when the dog reaches adulthood.

Look for clear, dark, sparkling eyes, free of discharge. Dark eye rims and lids are indications of good pigmentation, which is important in a breeding program, and even for generally pleasing good looks.

When the time comes to select your puppy, take an experienced breeder along with you if this is possible. If it is not possible, take the Standard for the breed with you. Try to interpret the Standard as best you can by making comparisons between the puppies you see.

Check the bite completely and carefully. While the first set of teeth can be misleading, even the placement of teeth at this young age can be a fairly accurate indication of what the bite will be in the grown dog. The gums should be a good healthy pink in color, and the teeth should be clear, clean and white. Any brown cast to them could mean a past case of distemper and would assuredly count against the dog in the show ring and against the dog's general appearance at maturity.

Puppies take anything and everything into their mouths to chew on while they are teething, and a lot of infectious diseases are transmitted this way. The aforementioned distemper is one, and the brown teeth as a result of this disease never clear. The puppy's breath should not be sour or even unpleasant or strong. Any acrid odor could indicate a poor mixture of food, or low quality of meat, especially if it is being fed raw. Many breeders have compared the breath of a healthy puppy to that of fresh toast, or as being vaguely like garlic. At any rate, a puppy should never be fed just table scraps, but should have a well-balanced diet containing a good dry puppy chow and a good grade of fresh meat. Poor meat and too much cereal or fillers tend to make the puppy too fat. We like puppies to be in good flesh, but not fat from the wrong kind of food.

It goes without saying that we want to find clean puppies. The breeder or owners who shows you a dirty puppy is one from whom to

Many breeders keep close watch on the weight of the puppies in each litter. This photo by Harold McLaughlin.

A litter of Samoyeds just seven days old, bred by Richard Peskin of Clinton, New Jersey. Sire was Oni-Agra's Chiefson *ex* Taymyra Eenya.

Three-week-old puppy owned by the Richard Peskins of Clinton, New Jersey.

A Samoyed litter photographed at seven weeks of age at the Driftwaye Kennels of Richard and Joan Peskin, Clinton, New Jersey.

Driftwayes Oni-Agra Radinka, photographed at eleven months of age. This bitch was Best Samoyed Puppy at a Delaware Water Gap Kennel Club all-breed match show and is owned and bred by Richard and Joan Peskin of the Driftwaye Kennels in Clinton, New Jersey.

steer away! Look closely at the skin. Rub the fur the wrong way or against the grain; make sure it is not spotted with insect bites or red, blotchy sores or dry scales. The vent area around the tail should not show evidences of diarrhea or inflammation. By the same token, the puppy's fur should not be matted with dry excrement or smell of urine.

True enough, you can wipe dirty eyes, clean dirty ears and give the puppy a bath when you get it home, but these things are all indications of how the puppy has been cared for during the important formative first months of its life, and can vitally influence its future health and development. There are many reputable breeders raising healthy puppies that have been reared in proper places and under the proper conditions in clean housing, so why take a chance on a series of veterinary bills and a questionable constitution?

MALE OR FEMALE?

The choice of sex in your puppy is also something that must be given serious thought before you buy. For the pet owner, the sex that would best suit the family life you enjoy would be the paramount

Pixie, owned by Ruth Bates Young, "all dressed up!"

A typical litter of quality puppies bred by the Kubla Khan Kennels in Los Angeles, California captured on film at six weeks of age by famed dog photographer Joan Ludwig.

choice to consider. For the breeder or exhibitor, there are other vital considerations. If you are looking for a stud to establish a kennel, it is essential that you select a dog with both testicles evident, even at a tender age, and verified by a veterinarian before the sale is finalized if there is any doubt.

The visibility of only one testicle, known as monorchidism, automatically disqualifies the dog from the show ring or from a breeding program, though monorchids are capable of siring. Additionally, it must be noted that monorchids frequently sire dogs with the same deficiency, and to introduce this into a bloodline knowingly is an unwritten sin in the fancy. Also, a monorchid can sire dogs that are completely sterile. Such dogs are referred to as cryptorchids and have no testicles.

If you want the dog to be a member of the family, the best selection would probably be a female. You can always go out for stud service if you should decide to breed. You can choose the bloodlines doing the most winning because they should be bred true to type, and you will not have to foot the bill for the financing of a show career. You can always keep a male from your first litter that will bear your own "kennel name" if you have decided to proceed in the kennel "business."

Dinner is served at the Harold McLaughlin household and this Sammy puppy has made up his mind what he would like.

An additional consideration in the male versus female decision for the private owners is that with males there might be the problem of leg-lifting and with females there is the inconvenience while they are in season. However, this need not be the problem it used to be— pet shops sell "pants" for both sexes, which help to control the situation.

THE PLANNED PARENTHOOD BEHIND YOUR PUPPY

Never be afraid to ask pertinent questions about the puppy, as well as questions about the sire and dam. Feel free to ask the breeder if you might see the dam, the purpose of your visit to determine her general health and her appearance as a representative of the breed. Ask also to see the sire if the breeder is the owner. Ask what the puppy has been fed and should be fed after weaning. Ask to see the pedigree, and inquire if the litter or the individual puppies have been registered with the American Kennel Club, how many of the temporary and/or permanent inoculations the puppy has had, when and if the puppy has been wormed and whether it has had any illness, disease or infection.

You need not ask if the puppy is housebroken. . . it won't mean much. He may have gotten the idea as to where "the place" is where he lives now, but he will need new training to learn where "the place" is in his new home! And you can't really expect too much from puppies at this age anyway. Housebreaking is entirely up to the new owner. We know puppies always eliminate when they first awaken and sometimes dribble when they get excited. If friends and relatives are coming over to see the new puppy, make sure he is walked just before he greets them at the front door. This will help.

The normal time period for puppies around three months of age to eliminate is about every two or three hours. As the time draws near, either take the puppy out or indicate the newspapers for the same purpose. Housebreaking is never easy, but anticipation is about 90 per cent of solving the problem. The schools that offer to housebreak your dog are virtually useless. Here again the puppy will learn the "place" at the schoolhouse, but coming home he will need special training for the new location.

A reputable breeder will welcome any and all questions you might ask and will voluntarily offer additional information, if only to

Four adorable puppies sired by Ch. Sport of the Arctic, bred by Ruth Bates Young, Top Acre Kennels, Medway, Ohio.

A litter of one-month-old puppies posing for their first formal family portrait. Sire was Ch. Destiny of Top Acres and the dam Barnella of Top Acres.

brag about the tedious and loving care he has given the litter. He will also sell a puppy on a 24-hour veterinary approval. This means you have a full day to get the puppy to a veterinarian of your choice to get his opinion on the general health of the puppy before you make a final decision. There should also be veterinary certificates and full particulars on the dates and types of inoculations the puppy has been given up to that time.

PUPPIES AND WORMS

Let us give further attention to the unhappy and very unpleasant subject of worms. Generally speaking, most all puppies—even those raised in clean quarters—come into contact with worms early in life. The worms can be passed down from the mother before birth or picked up during the puppies' first encounters with the earth or their kennel facilities. To say that you must not buy a puppy because of an infestation of worms is nonsensical. You might be passing up a fine animal that can be freed of worms in one short treatment, although a heavy infestation of worms of any kind in a young dog is dangerous and debilitating.

The extent of the infection can be readily determined by a veterinarian, and you might take his word as to whether the future health and conformation of the dog has been damaged. He can prescribe the dosage and supply the medication at the time and you will already have one of your problems solved. The kinds and varieties of worms and how to detect them is described in detail elsewhere in this book and we advise you to check the matter out further if there is any doubt in your mind as to the problems of worms in dogs.

VETERINARY INSPECTION

While your veterinarian is going over the puppy you have selected to purchase, you might just as well ask him for his opinion of it as a breed as well as the facts about its general health. While few veterinarins can claim to be breed conformation experts, they usually have a good eye for a worthy specimen and can advise you where to go for further information. Perhaps your veterinarian could also recommend other breeders if you should want another opinion. The veterinarian can point out structural faults or organic problems that affect all breeds and can usually judge whether an animal has been abused or mishandled and whether it is oversized or undersized.

I would like to emphasize here that it is only through this type of close cooperation between owners and veterinarians that we can expect to reap the harvest of modern research in the veterinary field.

Snowland Pyote, pictured here in show pose at three and one-half months of age. He is a great-grandson of the famous Fyodor and was sired by Christofjon of Snowland *ex* Snowland Dorvana.

Two of the Robert Levering children and their Sammy puppies sired by Ch. Barney Boy.

Most reliable veterinarians are more than eager to learn about various breeds of purebred dogs, and we in turn must acknowledge and apply what they have proved through experience and research in their field. We can buy and breed the best dog in the world, but when disease strikes we are only as safe as our veterinarian is capable—so let's keep them informed breed by breed, and dog by dog. The veterinarian represents the difference between life and death!

THE CONDITIONS OF SALE

While it is customary to pay for the puppy before you take it away with you, you should be able to give the breeder a deposit if there is any doubt about the puppy's health. You might also (depending on local laws) postdate a check to cover the 24-hour veterinary approval. If you decide to take the puppy, the breeder is required to supply you with a pedigree, along with the puppy's registration paper. He is also obliged to supply you with complete information about the inoculations and American Kennel Club instructions on how to transfer ownership of the puppy into your name.

A six-week-old puppy steps out. . . and is photographed by her owner, Ruth Bates Young of Medway, Ohio.

Patricia Morehouse's treasured Sammy puppy sired by the famous Champion Sam O'Khan's Kubla Khan. This photograph by Joan Ludwig captures the typical adorable puppy expression which endears the breed to so many dog fanciers.

Velko's Seya at eight weeks of age. A daughter of Ch. Velko of Chipaquiza, Seya was bred and is owned by Joan Lueck.

Some breeders will offer buyers time payment plans for convenience if the price on a show dog is very high or if deferred payments are the only way you can purchase the dog. However, any such terms must be worked out between buyer and breeder and should be put in writing to avoid later complications.

You will find most breeders cooperative if they believe you are sincere in your love for the puppy and that you will give it the proper home and the show ring career it deserves (if it is sold as a show quality specimen of the breed). Remember, when buying a show dog, it is impossible to guarantee nature. A breeder can only tell you what he *believes* will develop into a show dog. . . so be sure your breeder is an honest one.

Also, if you purchase a show prospect and promise to show the dog, you definitely should show it! It is a waste to have a beautiful dog that deserves recognition in the show ring sitting at home as a family pet, and it is unfair to the breeder. This is especially true if the breeder offered you a reduced price because of the advertising his kennel and bloodlines would receive by your showing the dog in the ring. If you want a pet, buy a pet. Be honest about it, and let the breeder decide on this basis which is the best dog for you. Your conscience will be clear and you'll both be doing a real service to the breed.

BUYING A SHOW PUPPY

If you are positive about breeding and showing your dog, make it clear that you intend to do so so that the breeder will sell you the best possible puppy. If you are dealing with an established kennel, you will have to rely partially if not entirely on their choice, since they know their bloodlines and what they can expect from the breeding. They know how their stock develops, and it would be foolish of them to sell you a puppy that could not stand up as a show specimen representing their stock in the ring.

However, you must also realize that the breeder may be keeping the best puppy in the litter to show and breed himself. If this is the case, you might be wise to select the best puppy of the opposite sex so that the dogs will not be competing against one another in the show rings for their championship title.

THE PURCHASE PRICE

Prices vary on all puppies, of course, but a good show prospect at six weeks to six months of age will sell for several hundred dollars. If the puppy is really outstanding, and the pedigree and parentage is

Two Driftwaye Samoyeds at play. They are owned by Richard and Joan Peskin of Clinton, New Jersey.

Joyce Cain's Sugay Daddi pictured as a puppy; photographed by Polly J. Knoll.

also outstanding, the price will be even higher. Honest breeders, however, will be around the same figure, so price should not be a deciding factor in your choice. If there is any question as to the current price range, a few telephone calls to different kennels will give you a good average. Breeders will usually stand behind their puppies; should something drastically wrong develop, such as hip dysplasia, etc., their obligation to make an adjustment is usually honored. Therefore, your cost is covered.

THE COST OF BUYING ADULT STOCK

Prices for adult dogs fluctuate greatly. Some grown dogs are offered free of charge to good homes; others are put out with owners on breeders' terms. But don't count on getting a "bargain" if it doesn't cost you anything! Good dogs are always in demand, and worthy studs or brood bitches are expensive. Prices for them can easily go up into the four-figure range. Take an expert with you if you intend to make this sort of investment. Just make sure the "expert" is free of professional jealousy and will offer an unprejudiced opinion. If you are reasonably familiar with the Standard, and get the expert's opinion, between the two you can usually come up with a proper decision.

Buying grown stock does remove some of the risk if you are planning a kennel. You will know exactly what you are getting for your foundation stock and will also save time on getting your kennel started.

9. GROOMING YOUR SAMOYED

It goes without saying that the white dog requires some extra care and grooming to look his best, whether it is a show dog or just a member of the family. No other coat shows the dirt as much as a white one and, if the Samoyed is to look its best, the whiter the white the better. If your dog is a working dog, he is going to look and smell like one, which means baths on a pretty regular basis if he is to be allowed in the house or the show ring! Even when they get wet from a walk in the rain, all the wet fur means you are going to notice the "wet dog smell," and if that is at all offensive to you, a bath is in order right then and there!

In good weather a Sammy can be kept clean by sprinkling with a little powder or corn starch and then brushing it out of the coat. You might also just stick the feet in a pan or pail of water and towel them dry after a walk outside. But neglected grooming, especially on a longhaired breed, is unforgiveable. Dogs which are allowed to run will be required to have baths to look and smell properly and to be happy with themselves. A bath when a dog is shedding will also help and hasten the process by washing away the dead hair and will stimulate the growth of the new hair.

SAMOYED BATHING AREA

Before you even reach for the soap and towels, be sure that you have a space set aside to confine the dog until he is completely dry. Otherwise the thick coat will pick up dust and dirt right from the moment he gets out of the tub. The best idea is to lift the dog right from the tub to a grooming table and brush dry under warm (not hot!) vacuum heat. Most vacuum cleaners have an attachment which is perfect for this. Since the Samoyed coat is supposed to stand straight out from the body naturally, brushing dry in the proper direction will enhance the appearance of the coat when it is completely dry. Hold the hose of the vacuum cleaner in one hand and the brush in the other and go over the entire body rather than directing the air stream and your effort in one particular spot until it is completely dry. This same procedure can apply when you give the dog a dry shampoo, or when you give "quick cleanups" with a spray of water or coat cleaner, or rub down with a wet towel, and brush dry with powder or corn starch.

THE ACTUAL BATH

Fill the tub half full with warm, almost hot, water and place the dog in the tub. The water should touch the stomach so that the heaviest concentrations of dirt on the legs and stomach, which constantly touch the ground, can be soaking in the water and getting through to the skin.

Using a pan or dish, pour water over the dog, or use a hose which can be attached to the faucet, and wet the dog down until he is saturated right to the skin. Save the head until last. Some put oil in the dog's eyes to prevent the soap from burning and put cotton in the ears, but once you are expert at bathing (and you will be if you intend to have a Sammy!) you will find this unnecessary. Use a wet face cloth to wash the face and ears, when the time comes.

Once the dog is thoroughly wet to the skin on all parts of the body, use the soap, which should not really be a soap at all, but rather a good commercial dog shampoo, since most soaps and detergents will irritate the skin, or perhaps even discolor the coat. Give the dog two complete and thorough latherings, working the suds down to the skin, and then two complete rinsings. Give a third rinsing if there is any doubt in your mind about soap suds being left in the fur or it will come out dull instead of shiny. Special care should be given to make sure that the vent area and the elbows and hocks have been cleaned completely.

Use a creme rinse to help ease the problem of tangles when drying, but you can help solve the problems of tangles by making sure your dog has the tangles combed out BEFORE bathing. Be sure that the creme rinse you use is not one for humans which tends to soften hair, but one of the canine variety made expressly for dogs with the Samoyed type of coat.

THE DRYING PROCESS

When the dog has been thoroughly rinsed and is on the table ready for drying, use large turkish towels and *squeeze*, don't rub, the excess water off the dog while the dryer is turned on and warming up in the meantime. Never allow that first cold blast of air from the dryer to hit the wet dog—and especially not a puppy!

Once the excess moisture is squeezed off the coat, your work really begins. Direct the current of air from the dryer slowly all over the body, brushing lightly at the same time, not so much to groom as to separate the hair and allow the stream of warm air to get through the coat down to the skin. The dryer should be held anywhere from six to twelve inches from the body, or enough distance for you to be able to brush the coat in the proper direction.

Ch. Pilot Frosty Mist of Top Acres being shown by owner Ruth Bates Young of Medway, Ohio.

Ch. Nakomis and Ch. Tonto with a young handler, Shellie Delmain, photographed by Bennett at a 1957 dog show.

If done properly and leisurely, the dog will actually enjoy the warmth and stimulation and attention. If he is fretful or restless, you are not doing it right! If the dog pants excessively, offer a drink of water now and then, since either nervousness or too much air around the face will dry out his mouth and a drink of water will prevent discomfort. Keep up this drying process until the dog is completely dry. If there is even a hint of dampness confine the dog in an area where he can't possibly get dirty. In either case, beware of drafts.

A gentle combing when dry and a few shakings on the part of the dog will put the finishing touches on the whole procedure.

GROOMING THE PUPPY

All of the preceding rules of order apply to your Samoyed puppy. However, it is not advisable to bathe a puppy any more than is absolutely necessary—especially in winter, and especially before six months of age. If there is a danger of staining the coat through some unforeseen accident or condition, a bath is in order. But this also means that grooming the puppy is more important than ever. Start early so he gets used to it and it becomes a part of his life pattern rather than an occasional experience.

Start grooming the very young puppy with a toothbrush. Then later switch to a soft-bristled baby's brush, and eventually work up to the stiff-bristled brush for the grown dog. It is also wise to have the

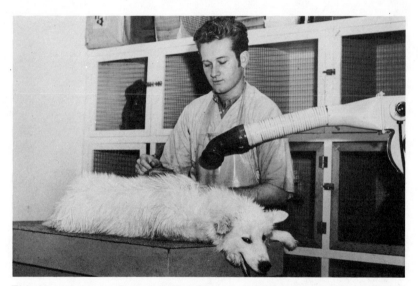

This is one way to dry out a dog after a bath. For owners who prefer to bathe their own Samoyeds, a towel or a small hand dryer could be more practical than the large professional unit shown at the right. Photo by Louise Van der Meid.

dog learn to be groomed either standing or lying on its side. Start by holding it on its back on your lap. This will make the grooming easier when he is full grown and there is a full coat to contend with.

The great beauty of the white Samoyed can be most fully appreciated only in the well groomed, clean specimen. The hard work you put into grooming your dog will bring you great reward if for no other reason than that he will be a happier dog for it.

As ye spin, so shall ye reap. . . and with Samoyeds it's a veritable harvest of coat combings which can be corded and spun into wool for material which is both warm and beautiful. More and more Sammy owners are doing this.

THE PROBLEM OF SHEDDING

The Samoyed male sheds once a year and sometimes in mid-season. Bitches shed twice a year, usually in the spring and fall, and other than during these two periods there is little problem of excessive hair on the furniture, carpets and clothes as there is with some of the other breeds. Excessive heat or cold or unusually high humidity may also affect the shedding schedule.

It is at the time of the shedding that extra grooming will not only avoid the problem of finding the hair around the house, but will actually speed up the shedding and encourage the growth of the new hair. Additionally, the dog will feel better; certainly the house will look better.

Mrs. William F. Conlon spinning cloth from Samoyed hair. This booth was a popular feature at the International Kennel Club show in Chicago in 1948 and was presented in conjunction with the Samoyed Specialty Show.

Mrs. Vincent Duffy with Dondianes Siberian Ranook and Dondianes Czaruke, pictured on a rug made from ten pounds of the wooly combings of the undercoat of her dogs. Mrs. Duffy had it spun into 4-ply yarn and tufted three-inch strands. Incidentally, Mrs. Duffy says the rug never shows dog hair!

The Samoyed has a double coat, and it is the undercoat which is "wooly" and lends itself so beautifully to being carded and spun and woven or knitted into magnificent material! It is not only beautiful but also soft and strong and warm. When you anticipate shedding, the undercoat should be combed out and saved if you care to have material made. Sometimes you will get basketfuls and, when you do, it is time to think about having it made into fabric.

Mrs. Vincent Duffy of Cincinnati, Ohio, made a magnificent 8 x 10 foot rug for her dining room several years ago out of the combings of her Dondianes Siberian Ranook and Dondianes Czaruke. A friend, Martha Humphries, spun the wool into 4-ply yarn which Lorna Duffy then tufted and inserted into awning canvas cut into octagonal shape to fit her dining room. After finishing the rug, she brushed liquid rubber on the back of the canvas to prevent slipping. She cleans it with a detergent or a dog coat cleaner, and Lorna says it never shows dog hair!

During the second half of the 1920's an article appeared in the *American Kennel Gazette* which suggested that our "Northern breed" be stripped during the warm months in the warmer climates. Since seemingly endless time is involved in stripping any breed—

much less a dog the size of the Samoyed—the idea met with much opposition.

The systematic removal of the shedding, loose undercoat is all that is necessary to be combed out for proper and sufficient grooming.

FOOT CARE

Every dog should have particular attention paid to his feet. Nails should be trimmed short enough so that they cannot be heard clicking on bare floors. They should be cut just in front of the vein. The vein can be judged in white nails by holding the nail up to the light. In black nails the vein cannot be seen in this way and extra care must be taken to cut back slowly and repeatedly so that too much isn't taken off. A veterinarian is the best teacher the first time you wish to attempt it. Later on, instinct will tell you. If you cut the vein, bleeding (and mess) will be excessive and will require smearing the end with Vaseline after pressing wet cotton to the end, or the application of a styptic pencil. Any repeated or painful experience like this is very likely to make a dog foot shy, which may go against him in the show ring.

Hair should be cut out from between the toes with blunt end scissors until it is even with the pads on the underside of the foot.

EYE CARE

Any white dog requires special care for the area around the eyes. Excessive watering or tearing will stain the area under the eyes and detract from the beauty and expression on the dog's face. Desitin ointment, commercial creams, sticks, and the like are available from veterinarians and pet shops. Prolonged tearing or watering should merit a visit to the vet for a more serious cause of the condition.

EAR CARE

All breeds of dogs seem prone to picking up dirt in their ears. With the Samoyed it is particularly important for the ears to stand erect, and there is nothing more certain to make a dog hold down his ears than an ear problem, perhaps from mites or an infection. Even scratching from excess wax or dirt can ruin the coat around the ear as well as make the dog miserable.

Start ear cleaning when the dog is still a puppy, using cotton tips or swabs. Clean the outside of the ear gently first rather than by digging right in. But when you clean down in the ear canal remember to keep the swab in a straight line with the dog's nose since that is the direction the ear canal runs. Be gentle and slow; use a twirling motion rather than a scraping motion. Do not try to probe deeper or "to go around corners." If this simple care is not enough, it is time to see the veterinarian.

Valkhi of Snow Shoe Hill, bred and owned by the late well-known Samoyed fancier Juliet Goodrich of Chicago, Illinois.

TEETH

If you are feeding your dog the proper diet there will be little work for you to do on his teeth. If drinking water in your area is bad, or if a particular health problem with your dog presents somewhat of a problem by discoloring his teeth, a toothbrush and baking soda are advised for brushing. Any tartar that forms should be removed by a veterinarian, since scaling the teeth with the scaler held at an improper angle can permanently damage the enamel on the teeth and lead to all sorts of problems. Care of the teeth is especially important with the old dog. Teeth are essential to proper digestion and therefore must be in good condition for the older dog to digest and benefit fully from the food he eats.

10. GENETICS

No one can guarantee the workings of nature. But, with facts and theories as guides, you can plan, at least on paper, a litter of puppies that should fulfill your fondest expectations. Since the ultimate purpose of breeding is to try to improve the breed, or maintain it at the highest possible standard, such planning should be earnestly done, no matter how uncertain particular elements may be.

There are a few terms with which you should become familiar to help you understand the breeding procedure and the workings of genetics. The first thing that comes to mind is a set of formulae known as Mendelian Laws. Gregor Mendel was an Austrian cleric and botanist born July 22, 1822 in what is now named Hyncice and is in Czechoslovakia. He developed his theories on heredity by working for several years with garden peas. A paper on his work was published in a scientific journal in 1866, but for many years it went unnoticed. Today the laws derived from these experiments are basic to all studies of genetics and are employed by horticulturists and animal breeders.

To use these laws as applicable to the breeding of dogs, it is necessary to understand the physical aspects of reproduction. First, dogs possess reproductive glands called gonads. The male gonads are the testicles and there are produced the sperms (spermatozoa) that impregnate the female. Eggs (ova) are produced in the female gonads (ovaries). When whelped, the bitch possesses in rudimentary form all the eggs that will develop throughout her life, whereas spermatozoa are in continual production within the male gonads. When a bitch is mature enough to reproduce, she periodically comes in heat (estrus). Then a number of eggs descend from the ovaries via the fallopian tubes and enter the two horns of the uterus. There they are fertilized by male sperm deposited in semen while mating, or they pass out if not fertilized.

In the mating of dogs, there is what is referred to as a tie, a period during which anatomical features bind the male and female together and about 600 million spermatozoa are ejected into the female to fertilize the ripened eggs. When sperm and ripe eggs meet, zygotes are created and these one-celled future puppies descend from the fallopian tubes, attach themselves to the walls of the uterus, and begin the developmental process of cell production known as mitosis. With all inherited characteristics determined as the zygote was formed, the

Ch. Frosty Ledge's Cheeta Dvina, owned by Juliette Chessor. Sire: Ch. Bon-Sitka-Lyn, C.D., dam: Ch. Frosty Ledge's Kola. Photo by Powell.

Ch. Czar of Belaya Sobaka, a New Zealand winner, owned by Mr. and Mrs. L.A.S. Aukram. Sire: Ch. Silver Hunter of Dudinka; dam: Lo of Te Whiti.

Ch. Dvina's Prince Loa-Tze, owned by Juliette Chessor. Sire: Silver Rocket of Wychwood; dam: Ch. Frosty Ledge's Cheeta Dvina. Photo by L.B. Englefield.

142

Champion Beta Sigma's Mufti pictured after winning Best of Breed at the Dayton Kennel Club Show in 1966. Mufti is owned by Ruth Bates Young of the Top Acres Kennel in Medway, Ohio.

dam then assumes her role as an incubator for the developing organisms. She has been bred and is in whelp; in these circumstances she also serves in the exchange of gases and in furnishing nourishment for the puppies forming within.

Let us take a closer look at what is happening during the breeding process. We know that the male deposits millions of sperms within the female and that the number of ripe eggs released by the female will determine the number of puppies in the litter. Therefore, those breeders who advertise a stud as a "producer of large litters" do not know the facts or are not sticking to them. The bitch determines the size of the litter; the male sperm determines the sex of the puppies. Half of the millions of sperm involved in a mating carry the characteristic that determines development of a male and the other half carry the factor which triggers development of a female, and distribution of sex is thus decided according to random pairings of sperms and eggs.

Each dog and bitch possesses 39 pairs of chromosomes in each body cell; these pairs are split up in the formation of germ cells so that each one carries half of the hereditary complement. The chromosomes carry the genes, approximately 150,000 like peas in a pod in each chromosome, and these are the actual factors that determine inherited characteristics. As the chromosomes are split apart and rearranged as to genic pairings in the production of ova and spermatozoa, every zygote formed by the joining of an egg and a sperm receives 39 chromosomes from each to form the pattern of 78 chromosomes inherited from dam and sire which will be reproduced in every cell of the developing individual and determine what sort of animal it will be.

To understand the procedure more clearly, we must know that there are two kinds of genes—dominant and recessive. A dominant gene is one of a pair whose influence is expressed to the exclusion of the effects of the other. A recessive gene is one of a pair whose influence is subdued by the effects of the other, and characteristics determined by recessive genes become manifest only when both genes of a pairing are recessive. Most of the important qualities we wish to perpetuate in our breeding programs are carried by the dominant genes. It is the successful breeder who becomes expert at eliminating recessive or undesirable genes and building up the dominant or desirable gene patterns.

There are many excellent books available which take you deeper into the fascinating subject of canine genetics. You can learn about your chances of getting so many black, so many white, or so many black-and-white puppies proportionally in a litter, and the ratio of other such expectations. Avail yourself of such information to put purpose into your breeding program.

We have merely touched upon genetics here to point out the importance of planned mating. Any librarian can help you find further information, or books may be purchased offering the very latest findings on canine genetics. It is a fascinating and rewarding program toward creating better dogs.

11. BREEDING YOUR SAMOYED

Let us assume the time has come for your dog to be bred, and you have decided you are in a position to enjoy producing a litter of puppies that you hope will make a contribution to the breed. The bitch you purchased is sound, her temperament is excellent and she is a most worthy representative of the breed.

You have taken a calendar and counted off the ten days since the first day of red staining and have determined the tenth to fourteenth day, which will more than likely be the best days for the actual mating. You have additionally counted off 65 to 63 days before the puppies are likely to be born to make sure everything necessary for their arrival will be in good order by that time.

From the moment the idea of having a litter occurred to you, your thoughts should have been given to the correct selection of a proper stud. Here again the novice would do well to seek advice on analyzing pedigrees and tracing bloodlines for your best breedings. As soon as the bitch is in season and you see color (or staining) and a swelling of the vulva, it is time to notify the owner of the stud you selected and make appointments for the breedings. There are several pertinent questions you will want to ask the stud owners after having decided upon the pedigree. The owners, naturally, will also have a few questions they wish to ask you. These questions will concern your bitch's bloodlines, health, age, how many previous litters if any, etc.

THE HEALTH OF THE BREEDING STOCK

Some of your first questions should concern whether or not the stud has already proved himself by siring a normal healthy litter. Also inquire as to whether or not the owners have had a sperm count made to determine just exactly how fertile or potent the stud is. Also ask whether he has been X-rayed for hip dysplasia and found to be clear. Determine for yourself whether the dog has two normal testicles.

When considering your bitch for this mating, you must take into consideration a few important points that lead to a successful breeding. You and the owner of the stud will want to recall whether she has had normal heat cycles, whether there were too many runts in the lit-

The charm of Samoyed puppies is dramatically highlighted by this attractive foursome, which appeared on a Christmas card received by Ruth Bates Young.

ter, and whether Caesarean section was ever necessary. Has she ever had a vaginal infection? Could she take care of her puppies by herself, or was there a milk shortage? How many surviving puppies were there from the litter, and what did they grow up to be in comparison to the requirements of the breed Standard?

Don't buy a bitch that has problem heats and has never had a litter. But don't be afraid to buy a healthy maiden bitch, since chances are, if she is healthy and from good stock, she will be a healthy producer. Don't buy a monorchid male, and certainly not a cryptorchid. If there is any doubt in your mind about his potency, get a sperm count from the veterinarian. Older dogs that have been good producers and are for sale are usually not too hard to find at good established kennels. If they are not too old and have sired quality show puppies, they can give you some excellent show stock from which to establish your own breeding lines.

THE DAY OF THE MATING

Now that you have decided upon the proper male and female combination to produce what you hope will be—according to the pedigrees—a fine litter of puppies, it is time to set the date. You have selected the two days (with a one day lapse in between) that you feel are best for the breeding, and you call the owner of the stud. The bitch always goes to the stud, unless, of course, there are extenuating circumstances. You set the date and the time and arrive with the bitch *and* the money.

Standard procedure is payment of a stud fee at the time of the first breeding, if there is a tie. For the stud fee, you are entitled to two breedings with ties. Contracts may be written up with specific conditions on breeding terms, of course, but this is general procedure. Often a breeder will take the pick of a litter to protect and maintain his bloodlines. This can be especially desirable if he needs an outcross for his breeding program or if he wishes to continue his own bloodlines if he sold you the bitch to start with, and this mating will continue his line-breeding program. This should all be worked out ahead of time and written and signed before the two dogs are bred. Remember that the payment of the stud fee is for the services of the stud—not for a guarantee of a litter of puppies. This is why it is so important to

Three of Laura and Leo Povier's Sammys pose with some of the trophies they captured at Canadian shows. Ch. Crystal is on the left, Champion Frosty is in the middle and Ch. Snow Blizzard is on the right. Ch. Crystal, mother of these two magnificent sons, was bred by Ruth Bates Young and her official name is Ch. Kola Snow Cloud.

Taking it easy at Top Acres. . .

Zik's Snow Chief of Obi at two and a half months of age, shown taking it easy under a tree on a hot summer afternoon with a litter sister.

A magnificent headstudy of Ch. Glazier of Singing Trees, owned by Jennette Gifford of Indianapolis. Glazier is a grandson of Ruth Bates Young's Ch. Frost Star, C.D.

make sure you are using a proven stud. Bear in mind also that the American Kennel Club will not register a litter of puppies sired by a male that is under eight months of age. In the case of an older dog, they will not register a litter sired by a dog over 12 years of age, unless there is a witness to the breeding in the form of a veterinarian or other responsible person.

Many studs over 12 years of age are still fertile and capable of producing puppies, but if you do not witness the breeding there is always the danger of a "substitute" stud being used to produce a litter. This brings up the subject of sending your bitch away to be bred if you cannot accompany her.

The disadvantages of sending a bitch away to be bred are numerous. First of all, she will not be herself in a strange place, so she'll be difficult to handle. Transportation if she goes by air, while reasonably safe, is still a traumatic experience, and there is the danger of her being put off at the wrong airport, not being fed or watered properly, etc. Some bitches get so upset that they go out of season and the trip, which may prove expensive, especially on top of a substantial stud fee, will have been for nothing.

If at all possible, accompany your bitch so that the experience is as comfortable for her as it can be. In other words, make sure before setting this kind of schedule for a breeding that there is no stud in the area that might be as good for her as the one that is far away. Don't sacrifice the proper breeding for convenience, since bloodlines are so important, but put the safety of the bitch above all else. There is always a risk in traveling, since dogs are considered cargo on a plane.

HOW MUCH DOES THE STUD FEE COST?

The stud fee will vary considerably—the better the bloodlines, the more winning the dog does at shows, the higher the fee. Stud service from a top winning dog could run up to $500.00. Here again, there may be exceptions. Some breeders will take part cash and then, say, third pick of the litter. The fee can be arranged by a private contract rather than the traditional procedure we have described.

Here again, it is wise to get the details of the payment of the stud fee in writing to avoid trouble.

THE ACTUAL MATING

It is always advisable to muzzle the bitch. A terrified bitch may fear-bite the stud, or even one of the people involved, and the wild bitch may snap or attack the stud, to the point where he may become discouraged and lose interest in the breeding. Muzzling can be done with a lady's stocking tied around the muzzle with a half knot, crossed under the chin and knotted at the back of the neck. There is enough "give" in the stocking for her to breathe or salivate freely and yet not open her jaws far enough to bite. Place her in front of her own-

This charming family scene, taken in their music room, pictured the Ruicks of Indianapolis with Cupid, Tish, Yendvik and Chuckles, with Strog majestically posed on the organ bench.

er, who holds onto her collar and talks to her and calms her as much as possible.

If the male will not mount on his own initiative, it may be necessary for the owner to assist in lifting him onto the bitch, perhaps even in guiding him to the proper place. But usually, the tie is accomplished once the male gets the idea. The owner should remain close at hand, however, to make sure the tie is not broken before an adequate breeding has been completed. After a while the stud may get bored and try to break away. This could prove injurious. It may be necessary to hold him in place until the tie is broken.

Samtara's Sugary N Spice, pictured at nine months of age in 1964. Bred and owned by Joyce Cain, Ripon, Wisconsin.

We must stress at this point that while some bitches carry on physically, and vocally, during the tie, there is no way the bitch can be hurt. However, a stud can be seriously or even permanently damaged by a bad breeding. Therefore the owner of the bitch must be reminded that she must not be alarmed by any commotion. All concentration should be devoted to the stud and a successful and properly executed service.

Many people believe that breeding dogs is simply a matter of placing two dogs, a male and a female, in close proximity, and letting nature take its course. While often this is true, you cannot count on it. Sometimes it is hard work, and in the case of valuable stock it is essential to supervise to be sure of the safety factor, especially if one or both of the dogs are inexperienced. If the owners are also inexperienced it may not take place at all!

ARTIFICIAL INSEMINATION

Breeding by means of artificial insemination is usually unsuccessful, unless under a veterinarian's supervision, and can lead to an infection for the bitch and discomfort for the dog. The American Kennel Club requires a veterinarian's certificate to register puppies from such a breeding. Although the practice has been used for over two decades, it now offers new promise, since research has been conducted to make it a more feasible procedure for the future.

Great dogs may eventually look forward to reproducing themselves years after they have left this earth. There now exists a frozen semen concept that has been tested and found successful. The study, headed by Dr. Stephen W.J. Seager, M.V.B., an instructor at the University of Oregon Medical School, has the financial support of the American Kennel Club, indicating that organization's interest in the work. The study is being monitored by the Morris Animal Foundation of Denver, Colorado.

Dr. Seager announced in 1970 that he had been able to preserve dog semen and to produce litters with the stored semen. The possibilities of selective world-wide breedings by this method are exciting. Imagine simply mailing a vial of semen to the bitch! The perfection of line-breeding by storing semen without the threat of death interrupting the breeding program is exciting, also.

As it stands today, the technique for artificial insemination requires the depositing of semen (taken directly from the dog) into the bitch's vagina, past the cervix and into the uterus by syringe. The correct temperature of the semen is vital, and there is no guarantee of success. The storage method, if successfully adopted, will present a new era in the field of purebred dogs.

THE GESTATION PERIOD

Once the breeding has taken place successfully, the seemingly endless waiting period of about 63 days begins. For the first ten days after the breeding, you do absolutely nothing for the bitch—just spin dreams about the delights you will share with the family when the puppies arrive.

Around the tenth day it is time to begin supplementing the diet of the bitch with vitamins and calcium. We strongly recommend that you take her to your veterinarian for a list of the proper or perhaps necessary supplements and the correct amounts of each for your particular bitch. Guesses, which may lead to excesses or insufficiencies, can ruin a litter. For the price of a visit to your veterinarian, you will be confident that you are feeding properly.

The bitch should be free of worms, of course, and if there is any doubt in your mind, she should be wormed now, before the third week of pregnancy. Your veterinarian will advise you on the necessity of this and proper dosage as well.

Ch. Bunky Junior of Lucky Dee winning at a California show under judge Anton Korbel. Owned by Hazel Dawes of Cupertino, California. A Joan Ludwig photo.

Ch. Sparkle Plenty, the dam of seven champions, owned by Ruth Bates Young of the Top Acres Kennel in Medway, Ohio.

PROBING FOR PUPPIES

Far too many breeders are overanxious about whether the breeding "took" and are inclined to feel for puppies or persuade a veterinarian to radiograph or X-ray their bitches to confirm it. Unless there is reason to doubt the normalcy of a pregnancy, this is risky. Certainly 63 days are not too long to wait, and why risk endangering the litter by probing with your inexperienced hands? Few bitches give no evidence of being in whelp, and there is no need to prove it for yourself by trying to count puppies.

ALERTING YOUR VETERINARIAN

At least a week before the puppies are due, you should telephone your veterinarian and notify him that you expect the litter and give him the date. This way he can make sure that there will be someone available to help, should there be any problems during the whelping. Most veterinarians today have answering services and alternate vets on call when they are not available themselves. Some veterinarians suggest that you call them when the bitch starts labor so that they may further plan their time, should they be needed. Discuss this matter with your veterinarian when you first take the bitch to him for her diet instructions, etc., and establish the method which will best fit in with his schedule.

DO YOU NEED A VETERINARIAN IN ATTENDANCE?

Even if this is your first litter, I would advise that you go through the experience of whelping without panicking and calling desperately for the veterinarian. Most animal births are accomplished without complications, and you should call for assistance only if you run into trouble.

When having her puppies, your bitch will appreciate as little interference and as few strangers around as possible. A quiet place, with her nest, a single familiar face and her own instincts are all that is necessary for nature to take its course. An audience of curious children squealing and questioning, other family pets nosing around, or strange adults should be avoided. Many a bitch which has been distracted in this way has been known to devour her young. This can be

Ch. Storm Way Victory of Top Acres. "Tory" finished for his title under Judge A. Peter Knoop at the Pensacola Dog Fanciers Association show in October, 1970 by going Best of Winners for a three-point major win. Tory is owned by Ellen Freeman of Waynesville, North Carolina.

All ready for a ride! Yasmin of Top Acres was named by the Shah of Iran while the Shah was a guest at General Allen's home in Fort Knox, Kentucky. The Shah gave all five sisters in this litter beautiful names of white flowers. The litter was bred by Ruth Bates Young.

the horrible result of intrusion into the bitch's privacy. There are other ways of teaching children the miracle of birth, and there will be plenty of time later for the whole family to enjoy the puppies. Let them be born under proper and considerate circumstances.

LABOR

Some litters—many first litters—do not run the full term of 63 days. So, at least a week before the puppies are actually due, and at the time you alert your veterinarian as to their arrival, start observing the bitch for signs of the commencement of labor. This will manifest itself in the form of ripples running down the sides of her body, which will come as a revelation to her as well. It is most noticeable when she is lying on her side—and she will be sleeping a great deal as

What could be cuter than a Sammy puppy? Only *two* Sammy puppies. These seven-month-old pups belong to Joyce Cain of Ripon, Wisconsin.

the arrival date comes closer. If she is sitting or walking about, she will perhaps sit down quickly or squat peculiarly. As the ripples become more frequent, birth time is drawing near; you will be wise not to leave her. Usually within 24 hours before whelping, she will stop eating, and as much as a week before she will begin digging a nest. The bitch should be given something resembling a whelping box with layers of newspaper (black and white only) to make her nest. She will dig more and more as birth approaches, and this is the time to begin making your promise to stop interfering unless your help is specifically required. Some bitches whimper and others are silent, but whimpering does not necessarily indicate trouble.

THE ARRIVAL OF THE PUPPIES

The sudden gush of green fluid from the bitch indicates that the water or fluid surrounding the puppies has "broken" and they are about to start down the canal and come into the world. When the

Ch. Cotton Fluff of Top Acres, dam of three champions. Fluff is owned by Ruth Bates Young of Medway, Ohio.

water breaks, birth of the first puppy is imminent. The first puppies are usually born within minutes to a half hour of each other, but a couple of hours between the later ones is not uncommon. If you notice the bitch straining constantly without producing a puppy, or if a puppy remains partially in and partially out for too long, it is cause for concern. Breech births (puppies born feet first instead of head first) can often cause delay or hold things up, and this is often a problem which requires veterinarian assistance.

FEEDING THE BITCH BETWEEN BIRTHS

Usually the bitch will not be interested in food for about 24 hours before the arrival of the puppies, and perhaps as long as two or three days after their arrival. The placenta which she cleans up after each puppy is high in food value and will be more than ample to sustain her. This is nature's way of allowing the mother to feed herself and her babies without having to leave the nest and hunt for food during the first crucial days. The mother always cleans up all traces of birth in the wilds so as not to attract other animals to her newborn babies.

However, there are those of us who believe in making food available should the mother feel the need to restore her strength during or after delivery—especially if she whelps a large litter. Raw chopmeat, beef boullion, and milk are all acceptable and may be placed near the whelping box during the first two or three days. After that, the mother will begin to put the babies on a sort of schedule. She will leave the whelping box at frequent intervals, take longer exercise periods, and begin to take interest in other things. This is where the fun begins for you. Now the babies are no longer soggy little pinkish blobs. They begin to crawl around and squeal and hum and grow before your very eyes!

It is at this time, if all has gone normally, that the family can be introduced gradually and great praise and affection given to the mother.

BREECH BIRTHS

Puppies normally are delivered head first. However, some are presented feet first, or in other abnormal positions, and this is referred to as a "breech birth." Assistance is often necessary to get the puppy out of the canal, and great care must be taken not to injure the puppy or the dam.

Aid can be given by grasping the puppy with a piece of turkish toweling and pulling gently during the dam's contractions. Be careful not to squeeze the puppy too hard; merely try to ease it out by moving it gently back and forth. Because even this much delay in delivery may mean the puppy is drowning, do not wait for the bitch to remove the sac. Do it yourself by tearing the sac open to expose the face and head. Then cut the cord anywhere from one-half to three-quarters of an inch away from the navel. If the cord bleeds excessively, pinch the end of it with your fingers and count five. Repeat if necessary. Then pry open the mouth with your finger and hold the puppy upside-down for a moment to drain any fluids from the lungs. Next, rub the puppy briskly with turkish or paper toweling. You should get it wriggling and whimpering by this time.

Who goes there?. . . two of Ruth Bates Young's Sammys on guard at the gate!

If the litter is large, this assistance will help conserve the strength of the bitch and will probably be welcomed by her. However, it is best to allow her to take care of at least the first few herself to preserve the natural instinct and to provide the nutritive values obtained by her consumption of the afterbirths.

DRY BIRTHS

Occasionally the sac will break before the delivery of a puppy and will be expelled while the puppy remains inside, thereby depriving the dam of the necessary lubrication to expel the puppy normally.

Inserting vaseline or mineral oil via your finger will help the puppy pass down the birth canal. This is why it is essential that you be present during the whelping so that you can count puppies and afterbirths and determine when and if assistance is needed.

THE TWENTY-FOUR-HOUR CHECKUP

It is smart to have a veterinarian check the mother and her puppies within 24 hours after the last puppy is born. The vet can check the puppies for cleft palates or umbilical hernia and may wish to give the dam—particularly if she is a show dog—an injection of Pituitin to make sure of the expulsion of all afterbirths and to tighten up the uterus. This can prevent a sagging belly after the puppies are weaned and the bitch is being readied for the show ring.

FALSE PREGNANCY

The disappointment of a false pregnancy is almost as bad for the owner as it is for the bitch. She goes through the gestation period with all the symptoms—swollen stomach, increased appetite, swollen nipples—even makes a nest when the time comes. You may even take an oath that you noticed the ripples on her body from the labor pains. Then, just as suddenly as you made up your mind that she was definitely going to have puppies, you will know that she definitely is not! She may walk around carrying a toy as if it were a puppy for a few days, but she will soon be back to normal and acting just as if nothing happened—and nothing did!

CAESAREAN SECTION

Should the whelping reach the point where there is complication, such as the bitch's not being capable of whelping the puppies herself, the "moment of truth" is upon you and a Caesarean section may be necessary. The bitch may be too small or too immature to expel the puppies herself; or her cervix may fail to dilate enough to allow the young to come down the birth canal; or there may be torsion of the uterus, a dead or monster puppy, a sideways puppy blocking the canal, or perhaps toxemia. A Caesarean section will be the only solution. No matter what the cause, get the bitch to the veterinarian immediately to insure your chances of saving the mother and/or puppies.

The Caesarean section operation (the name derived from the idea that Julius Caesar was delivered by this method) involves the removal of the unborn young from the uterus of the dam by surgical incision into the walls through the abdomen. The operation is performed when it has been determined that for some reason the puppies cannot be delivered normally. While modern surgical methods have made the operation itself reasonably safe, with the dam being per-

Suffolk Nicholas Nikita, owned by Mrs. Claire Wolff of Sayville, Long Island, New York, won his first points toward championship at seven months of age. Sire was Ch. Snowflakes Sam *ex* Princess Kirin. Handled by Claire Wolff to this Best Senior Puppy win early in his career at ten months.

fectly capable of nursing the puppies shortly after the completion of the surgery, the chief danger lies in the ability to spark life into the puppies immediately upon their removal from the womb. If the mother dies, the time element is even more important in saving the young, since the oxygen supply ceases upon the death of the dam, and the difference between life and death is measured in seconds.

After surgery, when the bitch is home in her whelping box with the babies, she will probably nurse the young without distress. You must be sure that the sutures are kept clean and that no redness or swelling or ooze appears in the wound. Healing will take place naturally, and no salves or ointments should be applied unless prescribed by the veterinarian, for fear the puppies will get it into their systems. If there is any doubt, check the bitch for fever, restlessness (other than the natural concern for her young) or a lack of appetite, but do not anticipate trouble.

EPISIOTOMY

Even though large dogs are generally easy whelpers, any number of reasons might occur to cause the bitch to have a difficult birth. Before automatically resorting to Caesarean section, many veterinarians are now trying the technique known as episiotomy.

Used rather frequently in human deliveries, episiotomy (pronounced A-PEASE-E-*OTT*-O-ME) is the cutting of the membrane between the rear opening of the vagina back almost to the opening of the anus. After delivery it is stitched together, and barring complications, heals easily, presenting no problem in future births.

SOCIALIZING YOUR PUPPY

The need for puppies to get out among other animals and people cannot be stressed enough. Kennel-reared dogs are subject to all sorts of idiosyncrasies and seldom make good house dogs or normal members of the world around them when they grow up.

The crucial age, which determines the personality and general behavior patterns which will predominate during the rest of the dog's life, are formed between the ages of three and ten weeks. This is particularly true during the 21st to 28th day. It is essential that the puppy be socialized during this time by bringing him into family life as much as possible. Floor surfaces, indoor and outdoor, should be experienced; handling by all members of the family and visitors is important; preliminary grooming gets him used to a lifelong necessity; light training, such as setting him up on tables and cleaning teeth and ears and cutting nails, etc., has to be started early if he is to become a show dog. The puppy should be exposed to car riding, shopping tours, a leash around its neck, children—your own and others—and in all possible ways develop relationships with humans.

It is up to the breeder, of course, to protect the puppy from harm or injury during this initiation into the outside world. The benefits

Samoyed owners have found that their pet's combings can be woven into beautiful and luxurious articles of apparel. Here Mrs. Lester Ellis models a coat and frock made of Samoyed wool. With her is Prince Valiant.

reaped from proper attention will pay off in the long run with a well-behaved, well-adjusted grown dog capable of becoming an integral part of a happy family.

REARING THE FAMILY

Needless to say, even with a small litter there will be certain considerations which must be adhered to in order to insure successful rearing of the puppies. For instance, the diet for the mother should be appropriately increased as the puppies grow and take more and more nourishment from her. During the first few days of rest while the bitch just looks over her puppies and regains her strength, she should be left pretty much alone. It is during these first days that she begins to put the puppies on a feeding schedule and feels safe enough about

Above and left:
American and
Canadian Ch.
Oakwood
Farm's Kari J'Go
Diko with
breeder-owner
Joan Lueck of
Oxford,
Michigan.

Yake-Sea Bidushka, owned by Connie Brotherton of Short Hills, New Jersey. The sire was Snowdrift of Kobe *ex* Yate-Sea's Bubka.

Ch. Kondako's Kimba of Karalot is pictured with Mary R. Fryer who co-owns Marcliff Samoyeds with Clifton Fryer, Paradise, Pennsylvania.

them to leave the whelping box long enough to take a little extended exercise.

It is cruel, however, to try and keep the mother away from the puppies any longer than she wants to be because you feel she is being too attentive or to give the neighbors a chance to peek in at the puppies. The mother should not have to worry about harm coming to her puppies for the first few weeks. The veterinary checkup will be enough of an experience for her to have to endure until she is more like herself once again.

Samoyed puppies will have short white coats and pink skin all over. However, do not panic and think that your litter has bad pigmentation. The black around the eye rims and the nose will not appear until after a few days. For those of you who like to keep weight records, have the baby scale ready. They should weigh anywhere from ten to 20 ounces. Weighing can be fun, since working breeds seem to grow by leaps and bounds!

Eyes will open about the tenth day, and usually a little at a time. The color will be blue at first and darken quickly. The black pigmentation will be appearing more obviously now on the nose and eyerims and the puppy will begin to hear. The little ears which are plastered down flat against their heads when they are born begin to stick out, and the puppies begin to be aware of a world outside the whelping box. Their weight should have doubled by now.

Four-week-old Samoyed puppies bred and owned by the Clifton Fryers, Marcliff Samoyeds, Paradise, Pennsylvania. Sire was Ch. Gentle Giant of Snow Country *ex* Ch. Kondako's Fryers' Snow White.

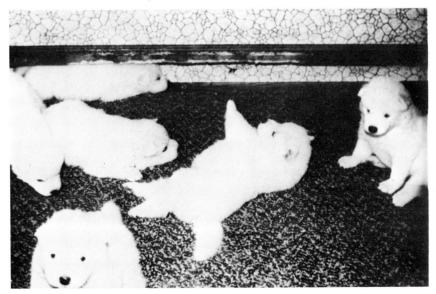

Mobbed by a litter of eleven puppies! The sire Ch. Kymric Taz of Top Acres, the dam Frostar's Kaouli Karin. Owned by E. Beckman, Clayton, Illinois.

As the puppies continue to thrive and grow, you will notice that they take on individual characteristics. If you are going to keep and show one of the puppies, this is the time to start observing them for various outstanding characteristics.

EVALUATING THE LITTER

A show puppy prospect should be outgoing, (probably the first one to fall out of the whelping box!) and all efforts should be made to socialize the puppy which appears to be the most shy. Once the puppies are about three weeks old, they can and should be handled a great deal by friends and members of the family.

During the third week they begin to try to walk instead of crawl, but they are unsteady on their feet. Tails are used for balancing, and they begin to make sounds. The pigment is even more noticeable, and weight is somewhere around four pounds.

The crucial period in a puppy's life occurs when the puppy is from 21 to 28 days old, so all the time you can devote to them at this time will reap rewards later on in life. This is the age when several other important steps must be taken in a puppy's life. Weaning should start if it hasn't already, and it is the time to check for worms. Do not worm unnecessarily. A veterinarian should advise on worming and appropriate dosage and can also discuss with you at this time the schedule for serum or vaccination, which will depend on the size of the puppies as well as their age.

Exercise and grooming should be started at this time, with special care and consideration given to the diet. You will find that the dam will help you wean the puppies, leaving them alone more and more as she notices that they are eating well on their own. Begin by

Suffolk Kirin's White Frost pictured with handler Jack Price. Frost is by Ch. Snowflake *ex* Suffolk Princess Kirin. Owned by George Price of Oakdale, New York.

Ch. Bubbles La Rue of Oakwood photographed as Best of Winners at seven months of age on the way to her championship. This Somerset Hills Kennel Club show was judged by George Head of Australia. Bubbles was sired by Park Cliffe Kris Kringle *ex* Suffolk Princess Kirin and is owned by Jack Price of Oakdale, New York.

BEST OF WINNERS

GILBERT PHOTO

leaving them with her during the night for comfort and warmth; eventually, when she shows less interest, keep them separated entirely.

By the time the fifth week of their lives arrives you will already be in love with every one of them and desperately searching for reasons to keep them all. They recognize you—which really gets to you!—and they box and chew on each other and try to eat your finger and a million other captivating antics which are special with puppies. Their stomachs seem to be bottomless pits, and their weight will rise to about six pounds.

At eight to ten weeks, the puppies will be weaned and ready to go. The pigment should be filled in by now and tails carried up over their backs. Weight will be about ten to fifteen pounds during this period.

SPAYING AND CASTRATING

A wise old philosopher once said, "Timing in life is everything!" No statement could apply more readily to the age-old question which every dog owner is faced with sooner or later. . . to spay or not to spay.

For the one-bitch pet owner, spaying is the most logical answer, for it solves many problems. The pet is usually not of top breeding quality, and therefore there is no great loss to the bloodline; it takes the pressure off the family if the dog runs free with children and certainly eliminates the problem of repeated litters of unwanted puppies or a backyard full of eager males twice a year.

But for the owner or breeder, the extra time and protection which must be afforded a purebred quality bitch can be most worthwhile—even if it is only until a single litter is produced after the first heat. It is then not too late to spay, the progeny can perpetuate the bloodline, the bitch will have been fulfilled—though it is merely an old wives' tale that bitches should have at least one litter to be "normal"—and she may then be retired to her deserved role as family pet once again.

With spaying the problem of staining and unusual behavior around the house is eliminated without the necessity of having to keep her in "pants" or administering pills, sprays, or shots. . . which most veterinarians do not approve of anyway.

In the case of males, castration is seldom contemplated, which to me is highly regrettable. The owner of the male dog merely overlooks the dog's ability to populate an entire neighborhood, since they do not have the responsibility of rearing and disposing of the puppies. But when you take into consideration all the many females the male dog can impregnate it is almost more essential that the males be taken out of circulation than that the female be. The male dog will still be inclined to roam but will be less frantic about leaving the grounds, and you will find that a lot of the wanderlust has left him.

One of the breed's top sires, Ch. Omak, owned by Pat Morehouse of Los Angeles, California. Omak sired Ch. Yurok.

Oakwood Farm's Diko Vjeda pictured winning Best of Breed from the puppy class under judge Winifred Heckman in September, 1974. Vjeda is handled here by William Trainor for owner Joan Lueck, Oakwood Farm, Oxford, Michigan. Vjeda was sired by Amer. and Can. Ch. Oakwood Farm's Kari J'Go Diko ex Oakwood Farm's Silva Image.

Sobaka II, pictured winning first in the Novice Class at one year of age at the 1973 S.C.A. Specialty Show in San Leandro, California. The sire was Ch. Karasam's Cowboy of Misty Way *ex* Country Boy's Tasha. Owner Peggy McCarthy of Eugene, Oregon.

STERILIZING FOR HEALTH

When considering the problem of spaying or castrating, the first consideration after the population explosion should actually be the health of the dog or bitch. Males are frequently subject to urinary diseases, and sometimes castration is a help. Your veterinarian can best advise you on this problem. Another aspect to consider is the kennel dog which is no longer being used at stud. It is unfair to keep him in a kennel with females in heat when there is no chance for him to be used. There are other more personal considerations for both kennel and one-dog owners, but when making the decision remember that it is final. You can always spay or castrate, but once the deed is done there is no return!

THE POWER OF PEDIGREES

Someone in the dog fancy once remarked that the definition of a show prospect puppy is one third the pedigree, one third what you see, and one third what you *hope* it will be! Well, no matter how you break down your qualifying fractions, we all quite agree that good breeding is essential if you have any plans at all for a show career for

Three of the Swensons' children with their Sammy puppy. The Swensons are from Worthington, Ohio.

Group Second in Brace Class at the January, 1974 Orange Empire Kennel Club Show under judge Ruth Schrieffer was Ch. Sam O'Khan's Kubla Khan (on the right) and his young son, Kubla Khan's Yogi Bear. Bred and owned by Patricia Morehouse of the Kubla Khan Kennels in Los Angeles, California.

Ch. Suffolk Czar Nicholas pictured winning Best of Breed at the 1971 Hatboro Kennel Club show. Czar, sired by Ch. Snowflake's Sam *ex* Suffolk Countess Kirovakan, was Best of Winners at the 1971 Westminster Kennel Club Show in 1971 under judge Lorna Demidoff. Bred by George Price.

Three-month-old winner! Future Ch. Bubbles La Rue of Oakwood wins at a 1973 Match Show with owner-handler Jack Price of Oakwood, New York.

BROOKHAVEN K.C.
MAY 13, 1973
BEST PUPPY
WORKING
GROUP
A BUSHMAN PHOTO

The Samoyed's destiny: Sams were originally bred as sled dogs in Arctic regions. This team, owned by Miss Shirley Keepers, proves that the breed can still give a good account of itself in harness. Photo by Edison.

your dog! Many breeders will buy on pedigree alone, counting largely on what they can do with the puppy themselves by way of feeding, conditioning and training. Needless to say, that very important piece of paper commonly referred to as "the pedigree" is mighty reassuring to a breeder or buyer new at the game or to one who has a breeding program in mind and is trying to establish his own bloodline.

One of the most fascinating aspects of tracing pedigrees is the way the names of the really great dogs of the past keep appearing in the pedigrees of the great dogs of today. . . positive proof of the strong influence of heredity, and witness to a great deal of truth in the statement that great dogs frequently reproduce themselves, though not necessarily in appearance only. A pedigree represents something of value when one is dedicated to breeding better dogs.

To the novice buyer or one who is perhaps merely switching to another breed and sees only a frolicking, leggy, squirming bundle of energy in a fur coat, a pedigree can mean *everything*! To those of us who believe in heredity, a pedigree is more like an insurance policy . . . so read it carefully and take heed!

12. TRAINING AND OBEDIENCE FOR YOUR SAMOYED

There are few things in the world a dog would rather do than please his master. Therefore, obedience training, or even the initial basic training, will be a pleasure for your dog, if taught correctly, and will make him a much nicer animal to live with for the rest of his life.

WHEN TO START TRAINING

The most frequently asked question by those who consider training their dog is, naturally, "What is the best age to begin training?" The answer is "not before six months." A dog simply cannot be sufficiently or permanently trained before this age and be expected to retain all he has been taught. If too much is expected of him, he can become frustrated and it may ruin him completely for any serious training later on, or even jeopardize his disposition. Most things a puppy learns and repeats before he is six months of age should be considered habit rather than training.

THE REWARD METHOD

The only proper and acceptable kind of training is the kindness and reward method which will build a strong bond between dog and owner. A dog must have confidence in and respect for his teacher. The most important thing to remember in training any dog is that the quickest way to teach, especially the young dog, is through repetition. Praise him when he does well, and scold him when he does wrong. This will suffice. There is no need or excuse for swinging at a dog with rolled up newspapers, or flailing hands which will only tend to make the dog hand shy the rest of his life. Also, make every word count. Do not give a command unless you intend to see it through. Pronounce distinctly with the fewest possible words, and use the same words for the same command every time.

Include the dog's name every time to make sure you have his undivided attention at the beginning of each command. Do not go on to another command until he has successfully completed the previous

Reins Lady of Silver Snow pictured going Best of Winners and Best of Opposite Sex over a Special. The handler is Sue Wholey for owner Stuart J. Rein of Bowie, Maryland.

Photographer Harold McLaughlin's beautiful puppy illustrates perfect stance (above) and over-all charm of the breed.

one and is praised for it. Of course, you should not mix play with the serious training time. Make sure the dog knows the difference between the two.

In the beginning, it is best to train without any distractions whatsoever. After he has learned to concentrate and is older and more proficient, he should perform the exercises with interference, so that the dog learns absolute obedience in the face of all distractions. Needless to say, whatever the distractions, you never lose control. You must be in command at all times to earn the respect and attention of your dog.

HOW LONG SHOULD THE LESSONS BE?

The lessons should be brief with a young dog, starting at five minutes, and as the dog ages and becomes adept in the first lessons, increase the time all the way up to one-half hour. Public training classes are usually set for one hour, and this is acceptable since the full hour of concentration is not placed on your dog alone. Working under these conditions with other dogs, you will find that he will not be as intent as he would be with a private lesson where the commands are directed to him alone for the entire thirty minutes.

If you should notice that your dog is not doing well, or not keeping up with the class, consider putting off training for awhile. Animals, like children, are not always ready for schooling at exactly the same age. It would be a shame to ruin a good obedience dog because you insist on starting his training at six months rather than at, say, nine months, when he would be more apt to be receptive both physically and mentally. If he has particular difficulty in learning one exercise, you might do well to skip to a different one and come back to it again at another session. There are no set rules in this basic training, except, "don't push!"

WHAT YOU NEED TO START TRAINING

From three to six months of age, use the soft nylon show leads, which are the best and safest. When you get ready for the basic training at six months of age, you will require one of the special metal-link choke chains sold for exactly this purpose. Do not let the word "choke" scare you. It is a soft, smooth chain and should be held slack whenever you are not actually using it to correct the dog. This chain should be put over the dog's head so that the lead can be attached over the dog's neck rather than underneath against his throat. It is wise when you buy your choke collar to ask the sales person to show you how it is put on. Those of you who will be taking your dog to a training class will have an instructor who can show you.

To avoid undue stress on the dog, use both hands on the lead. The dog will be taught to obey commands at your left side, and therefore, your left hand will guide the dog close to his collar on a six-foot train-

Ch. Ninna Nanna Nordica, C.D., owned by her breeder, Mrs. Vera R. Micele of the Bonaventura Farm in Fort Wayne, Indiana.

First time in Best of Breed competition at just one year and one week old, Ch. Bubbles La Rue of Oakwood won Best of Opposite Sex at the 1974 Westminster Kennel Club show at Madison Square Garden under judge Charles Hamilton. Bubbles is by Park Cliffe Kris Kringle *ex* Suffolk Princess Kirin. She is owned and handled by Jack Price of Oakdale, New York and has a Best of Winners award at the Potomac Valley Samoyed Club Specialty Show to her credit as well.

T OF
OSITE

GILBERT PHOTO

Am. and Can. Ch. Kipperic Kandu of Suruka Orr, C.D.—the only female in the history of the breed in the U.S.A. to have won both an all-breed Best In Show and a Samoyed Specialty. Kandi is pictured here winning Best of Breed at the 1973 Samoyed Club of America National Specialty in competition with 243 Samoyeds, the largest Specialty ever held. The judge is Phil Marsh; Kandi's owners are Mr. and Mrs. Donald Hodges of Columbus, Wisconsin. She was bred by Mr. and Mrs. J.M. Laskey of Madison, Wisconsin. Her sire was the Samoyed Club of America Stud Dog Trophy winner Ch. Nachalnik of Drayalene, and her dam is Am. and Can. Ch. Kuei of Suruka Orr, C.D. Kandi has also won a number of Working Group Firsts, including the March, 1974 Group at the Chicago International Show.

ing lead. The balance of the lead will be held in your right hand. Learn at the very beginning to handle your choke collar and lead correctly. It is as important in training a dog as is the proper equipment for riding a horse.

WHAT TO TEACH FIRST

The first training actually should be to teach the dog to know his name. This, of course, he can learn at an earlier age than six months, just as he can learn to walk nicely on a leash or lead. Many puppies will at first probably want to walk around with the leash in their mouths. There is no objection to this if the dog will walk while doing it. Rather than cultivating this as a habit, you will find that if you don't make an issue of it, the dog will soon realize that carrying the lead in his mouth is not rewarding and he'll let it fall to his side where it belongs.

We also let the puppy walk around by himself for a while with the lead around his neck. If he wishes to chew on it a little, that's all right too. In other words, let it be something he recognizes and associates with at first. Do not let the lead start out being a harness.

If the dog is at all bright, chances are he has learned to come on command when you call him by name. This is relatively simple with sweet talk and a reward. On lead, without a reward, and on command

After the big snow: the obedience-titled Ch. Frost Star, C.D., looks things over.

One of the early C.D.X. obedience degree winners in the breed. . . Ch. Major Bee, photographed in May, 1965. Bred and owned by Mrs Marjorie Von Ornum of Cincinnati, Ohio.

without a lead is something else again. If there has been, or is now, a problem, the best way to correct it is to put on the choke collar and the six-foot lead. Then walk away from the dog, and call him, "Pirate, come!" and gently start reeling him in until the dog is in front of you. Give him a pat on the head and/or reward.

Walking, or heeling, next to you is also one of the first and most important things for him to learn. With the soft lead training starting very early, he should soon take up your pace at your left side. At the command to "heel" he should start off with you and continue alongside until you stop. Give the command, "Pirate, sit!" This is taught by leaning over and pushing down on his hindquarters until he sits next to you, while pulling up gently on the collar. When you have this down pat on the straightaway, then start practicing it in circles, with turns and figure eights. When he is an advanced student, you can look forward to the heels and sits being done neatly, spontaneously, and off lead as well.

Silver Frost's Crystal Holly, owned by Nancy Brotherton of Short Hills, New Jersey. This three-month-old puppy was sired by Canadian Ch. Snowflake's Perdita *ex* Deablo Siber Star.

The magnificent American and Canadian Ch. Oakwood Farm's Kari J'Go Diko, bred and owned by Joan Lueck of Oxford, Michigan.

Four-week-old puppies sired by Ch. Gentle Giant of Snow Country *ex* Ch. Kondako's Fryer's Snowwhite. Bred and owned by Clifton and Mary Fryer, Marcliff Samoyeds, Paradise, Pa.

A young son of the great Silver Flare of Wychwood, bred by Bernice Ashdown of Long Island, New York.

Four-year-old Chip and his six-month-old Samuel Samoyed.

THE "DOWN" COMMAND

One of the most valuable lessons or commands you can teach your dog is to lie down on command. Some day it may save his life, and is invaluable when traveling with a dog or visiting, if behavior and manners are required even beyond obedience. While repeating the words, "Pirate, down!" lower the dog from a sitting position in front of you by gently pulling his front legs out in front of him. Place your full hand on him while repeating the command, "Pirate, down!" and hold him down to let him know you want him to *stay* down. After he gets the general idea, this can be done from a short distance away on a lead along with the command, by pulling the lead down to the floor. Or perhaps you can slip the lead under your shoe (between the heel and sole) and pull it directly to the floor. As the dog progresses in training, a hand signal with or without verbal command, or with or without lead, can be given from a considerable distance by raising your arm and extending the hand palm down.

THE "STAY" COMMAND

The stay command eventually can be taught from both a sit and a down position. Start with the sit. With the dog on your left side in the sitting position give the command, "Pirate, stay!" Reach down with the left hand open and palm side to the dog and sweep it in close to his nose. Then walk a short distance away and face him. He will at first, having learned to heel immediately as you start off, more than likely start off with you. The trick in teaching this is to make sure he hears "stay" before you start off. It will take practice. If he breaks, sit him down again, stand next to him, and give the command all over again. As he masters the command, let the distance between you and your dog increase while the dog remains seated. Once the command is learned, advance to the stay command from the down position.

THE STAND FOR EXAMINATION

If you have any intention of going on to advanced training in obedience with your dog, or if you have a show dog which you feel you will enjoy showing yourself, a most important command which should be mastered at six months of age is the stand command. This is essential for a show dog since it is the position used when the show judge goes over your dog. This is taught in the same manner as the stay command, but this time with the dog remaining up on all four feet. He should learn to stand still, without moving his feet and without flinching or breaking when approached by either you or strangers. The hand with palm open wide and facing him should be firmly placed in front of his nose with the command, "Pirate, stand!" After he learns the basic rules and knows the difference between stand and stay, ask friends, relatives, and strangers to assist you with this exercise by walking up to the dog and going over him. He should not react physically to their touch. A dog posing in this stance should show all the beauty and pride of being a sterling example of his breed.

FORMAL SCHOOL TRAINING

We mentioned previously about the various training schools and classes given for dogs. Your local kennel club, newspaper, or the yellow pages of the telephone book will put you in touch with organizations in your area where this service is performed. You and your dog will learn a great deal from these classes. Not only do they offer formal training, but the experience for you and your dog in public, with other dogs of approximately the same age and with the same purpose in mind, is excellent. If you intend to show your dog, this training is valuable ring experience for later on. If you are having difficulty with the training, remember, it is either too soon to start—or YOU are doing something wrong!

The magnificence of a Samoyed at work: Rimsky of Norka captured in action by photographer Percy T. Jones. The author used this great photograph as a cover on *Popular Dogs* magazine.

A litter of seven-week-old Samoyed puppies bred by Sharon Eggiman; four grew up to be champions! They were sired by Ch. Sam O'Khan's Kubla Khan *ex* Frost River's Tsari of Orion.

Suffolk Kirin's Snow Bunny, ten-month-old bitch handled to this class win by Jack Price. Owner-bred by Mr. and Mrs. George Price.

Ch. Frost Star, C.D. being shown under the late judge Colonel McQuown several years ago with owner-handler Ruth Bates Young. Star was the first Samoyed and the first dog in the Dayton, Ohio area to win both his championship and obedience titles at the same time. Mrs. Young had been told it couldn't be done, and she set out to prove that it could!

ADVANCED TRAINING AND OBEDIENCE TRIALS

The A.K.C. obedience trials are divided into three classes: Novice, Open and Utility.

In the Novice Class, the dog will be judged on the following basis:

TEST	MAXIMUM SCORE
Heel on lead	35
Stand for examination	30
Heel free—on lead	45
Recall (come on command)	30
One-minute sit (handler in ring)	30
Three-minute down (handler in ring)	30
Maximum total score	200

If the dog "qualifies" in three shows by earning at least 50% of the points for each test, with a total of at least 170 for the trial, he has earned the Companion Dog degree and the letters C.D. (Companion Dog) are entered after his name in the A.K.C. records.

After the dog has qualified as a C.D., he is eligible to enter the Open Class competition, where he will be judged on this basis:

Donder, C.D., owned by Dan Nian of Huntington Station, Long Island, New York, is pictured with some of the trophies won on the way toward her Companion Dog obedience title.

Ch. Frostar's Tundra Star Frost, owned by Louis and Joyce Cain. Sire: Ch. Kusang of Northern Frost; dam: Tundra Princess Starya. This is one of the top winning Samoyed bitches in the United States.

Smo-Bilt's Susie Snoflake, C.D., obedience title holder and brood bitch at Anne Copeland's Celestial Samoyed kennel in Palatine, Illinois. Susie was bred by John and Jodine Vertuno; her sire was Joli Rainie *ex* Ch. Zan Zelda Noel, C.D.X. Susie was whelped in 1965 and is still going strong . . . and notice the typical Sammy smile!

Jola at five weeks of age. This beautiful puppy is a son of Ch. Major Bee, C.D.X., owned by Marjorie Van Ornum.

TEST	MAXIMUM SCORE
Heel free	40
Drop on Recall	30
Retrieve (wooden dumbbell) on flat	25
Retrieve over obstacle (hurdle)	35
Broad jump	20
Three-minute sit (handler out of ring)	25
Five-minute down (handler out of ring)	25
maximum total score	200

Again he must qualify in three shows for the C.D.X. (Companion Dog Excellent) title and then is eligible for the Utility Class, where he can earn the Utility Dog (U.D.) degree in these rugged tests:

TEST	MAXIMUM SCORE
Scent discrimination (Article #1)	30
Scent discrimination (Article #2)	30
Directed retrieve	30
Signal exercise (heeling, etc., on hand signal)	35
Directed jumping (over hurdle and bar jump)	40
Group examination	35
Maximum total score	200

For more complete information about these obedience trials, write for the American Kennel Club's *Regulations and Standards for Obedience Trials*. Dogs that are disqualifed from breed shows because of alteration or physical defects are eligible to compete in these trials.

THE COMPANION DOG EXCELLENT DEGREE

There are seven exercises which must be executed to achieve the C.D.X. degree, and the percentages for achieving these are the same as for the U.D. degree. Candidates must qualify in three different obedience trials and under three different judges and must have received scores of more than 50% of the available points in each exercise, with a total of 170 points or more out of the possible 200. At that time they may add the letters C.D.X. after their name.

THE UTILITY DOG DEGREE

The Utility Dog degree is awarded to dogs which have qualified by successfully completing six exercises under three different judges

Ch. Moonlighter's Celestial Hipy, American and Canadian Companion Dog title holder, is pictured here winning under judge Ramona Van Court with handler Mrs. Joan Scovin. Hipy was bred by Jeanne and Wayne Nonhof and is owned by Anne Copeland of Palatine, Illinois. The sire was Ch. Saroma's Polar Prince *ex* Moonlighter's Altai Star Mist. Hipy is the first offspring of the late great Polar Prince to achieve both a championship and obedience title.

Ch. Major Bee, C.D.X., pictured in Chicago in 1965. Major was bred and owned by Marjorie Van Ornum of Kentucky.

at three different obedience trials, with a score of more than 50% of available points in each exercise, and with a score of 170 or more out of a possible 200 points.

These six exercises consist of Scent Discrimination, with two different articles for which they receive thirty points each if successfully completed; Direct Retrieving, for 30 points; Signal Exercise for 35 points; Directed Jumping for 40 points and a Group Examination for 35 points.

THE TRACKING DOG DEGREE

The Tracking Dog trials are not held, as the others are, with the dog shows, and need be passed only once.

The dog must work continuously on a strange track at least 440 yards long and with two right angle turns. There is no time limit, and the dog must retrieve an article laid at the other end of the trail. There is no score given; the dog either earns the degree or fails. The dog is worked by his trainer on a long leash, usually in harness.

There are comparatively few dogs in any breed which attain this degree, so the Samoyeds which have earned it are to be especially commended.

A lovely informal photograph of Ch. Glazier of Singing Trees, owned by Jennette Gifford of Carmel, Indiana.

THE SAMOYED IN OBEDIENCE

The first Companion Dog title was won in 1937 by Ch. Alstasia's Rukavitza, owned by Mrs. Anastasia McBain, a breeder-judge of renown. Rukavitza not only made his mark in the obedience ring but also distinguished himself in the show ring by gaining a championship title and a record of 33 Bests of Breed, 13 Group placings, and the Best of Breed win at the 1941 Samoyed Club of America Specialty held in conjunction with the Morris and Essex show over an entry of 29 under judge C.H. Chamberlain.

Mrs. McBain's Ch. Marina of Wychwood (Rukavitz's granddaughter) was the first bitch to earn a Companion Dog title and also the first bitch to win a Companion Dog Excellent title. At the same time she was earning her championship points. A mating between Rukavitza and Marina produced a litter which contained four C.D. title-holders, all of which goes a long way to prove that the innate desire to please and excel in the obedience ring depends a lot on heredity!

Six-year-old Ch. Samoyland's Vojak, U.D., owned by the Thomas Witchers of San Francisco, was the first Sammy to earn a dual championship and was one leg away from earning his Tracking title when he met an untimely death. Just as his father before him, Soldier Frosty of Rimini, commissioned a colonel in the Army Reserve K-9 Corps for work during Word War II in Attu, Iceland and Greenland, Vojak also visited hospitals to entertain for the March of Dimes and other organizations, and appeared on television.

Rimsky of Norka was the third Samoyed to earn a C.D. title and went on to C.D.X. and all the way to Utility Dog, Tracker. While working toward this top-most obedience title he was also racking up championship points which brought him the permanent honor of being the first Samoyed champion with the U.D.T. title.

13. SHOWING YOUR SAMOYED

Let us assume that after a few months of tender loving care, you realize your dog is developing beyond your wildest expectations and that the dog you selected is very definitely a show dog! Of course, every owner is prejudiced. But if you are sincerely interested in going to dog shows with your dog and making a champion of him, now is the time to start casting a critical eye on him from a judge's point of view.

There is no such thing as a perfect dog. Every dog has some faults, perhaps even a few serious ones. The best way to appraise your dog's degree of perfection is to compare him with the Standard for the breed, or before a judge in a show ring.

MATCH SHOWS

For the beginner there are "mock" dog shows, called Match Shows, where you and your dog go through many of the procedures of a regular dog show, but do not gain points toward championship. These shows are usually held by kennel clubs, annually or semiannually, and much ring poise and experience can be gained there. The age limit is reduced to two months at match shows to give puppies four months of training before they compete at the regular shows when they reach six months of age. Classes range from two to four months; four to six months; six to nine months; and nine to twelve months. Puppies compete with others of their own age for comparative purposes. Many breeders evaluate their litters in this manner, choosing which is the most outgoing, which is the most poised, the best showman, etc.

For those seriously interested in showing their dogs to full championship, these match shows provide important experience for both the dog and the owner. Class categories may vary slightly, according to number of entries, but basically include all the classes that are included at a regular point show. There is a nominal entry fee and, of course, ribbons and usually trophies are given for your efforts as well. Unlike the point shows, entries can be made on the day of the show right on the show grounds. They are unbenched and provide an informal, usually congenial atmosphere for the amateur, which helps to make the ordeal of one's first adventures in the show ring a little less nerve-wracking.

THE POINT SHOWS

It is not possible to show a puppy at an American Kennel Club sanctioned point show before the age of six months. When your dog reaches this eligible age, your local kennel club can provide you with the names and addresses of the show-giving superintendents in your area who will be staging the club's dog show for them, and where you must write for an entry form.

Ch. Jan Mayen of Top Acres, a winner several years ago, owned by Ruth Bates Young of Medway, Ohio, owner of the famous Top Acres Samoyed Kennels.

Ch. Pinehills Pixie O'Whytekrest, photographed by Gilbert, winning Winners Bitch at a show on the way to her championship. Owners are Barbara and Mary Telychan of Edison, New Jersey.

Ch. Jomay of Singing Trees, owned by Jennette Gifford of Carmel, Indiana.

Nimrod of Nottingham photographed as a puppy called "Pudge!" Owned by Mrs. Ada L. Westcott of the Snowlands Kennels in Devon, England.

The forms are mailed in a pamphlet called a premium list. This also includes the names of the judges for each breed, a list of the prizes and trophies, the name and address of the show-giving club and where the show will be held, as well as rules and regulations set up by the American Kennel Club which must be abided by if you are to enter.

A booklet containing the complete set of show rules and regulations may be obtained by writing to the American Kennel Club, Inc., 51 Madison Avenue, New York, N.Y., 10010.

When you write to the Dog Show Superintendent, request not only your premium list for this particular show, but ask that your name be added to their mailing list so that you will automatically receive all premium lists in the future. List your breed or breeds and they will see to it that you receive premium lists for Specialty shows as well.

Unlike the match shows where your dog will be judged on ring behavior, at the point shows he will be judged on conformation to the breed Standard. In addition to being at least six months of age (on the

Whitecliff's Erin of Misty Way, just three months old and winner of Best in Match. Sired by Ch. Sho-Offs Dorok of Whitecliff *ex* Ch. Silver Trinkets of Misty Way. Owned by the Misty Way Kennels.

American and Canadian Ch. Oakwood Farm's Silver Pada and her dam, American and Canadian Ch. Silveracres Tsaritsa, owned by Joan Lueck, Oakwood Farm, Oxford, Michigan.

day of the show) he must be a purebred for a point show. This means both of his parents and he are registered with the American Kennel Club. There must be no alterations or falsifications regarding his appearance. Females cannot have been spayed and males must have both testicles in evidence. No dyes or powders may be used to enhance the appearance, and any lameness or deformity or major deviation from the Standard for the breed constitutes a disqualification.

With all these things in mind, groom your dog to the best of your ability in the specified area for this purpose in the show hall and walk into the show ring with great pride of ownership and ready for an appraisal of your dog by the judge.

The presiding judge on that day will allow each and every dog a certain amount of time and consideration before making his decisions. It is never permissible to consult the judge regarding either

Ch. Moonlighter's Hallmark finished at fifteen months with all majors and a Best of Breed over Specials including a Best In Show winner. Owner-handled from Puppy and Bred by Exhibitor Class. Sire was American and Canadian Ch. Saroma's Polar Prince (a Best in Show winner) *ex* Moonlighter's Altai Star Mist. Owned by Wayne and Jeanne Nonhof of Moonlighter Kennels, Waldo, Wisconsin.

your dog or his decision while you are in the ring. An exhibitor never speaks unless spoken to, and then only to answer such questions as the judge may ask—the age of the dog, the dog's bite, or to ask you to move your dog around the ring once again.

However, before you reach the point where you are actually in the ring awaiting the final decisions of the judge, you will have had to decide in which of the five classes in each sex your dog should compete.

Point Show Classes

The regular classes of the AKC are: Puppy, Novice, Bred-by-Exhibitor, American-Bred, Open; if your dog is undefeated in any of the regular classes (divided by sex) in which it is entered, he or she is *required* to enter the Winners Class. If your dog is placed second in the class to the dog which won Winners Dog or Winners Bitch, hold the dog or bitch in readiness as the judge must consider it for Reserve Winners.

PUPPY CLASSES shall be for dogs which are six months of age and over but under twelve months, which were whelped in the U.S.A. or Canada, and which are not champions. Classes are often divided 6 and (under) 9, and 9 and (under) 12 months. The age of a dog shall be calculated up to and inclusive of the first day of a show. For example, a dog whelped on Jan. 1st is eligible to compete in a puppy class on July 1st, and may continue to compete up to and including Dec. 31st of the same year, but is not eligible to compete Jan. 1st of the following year.

THE NOVICE CLASS shall be for dogs six months of age or over, whelped in the U.S.A. or Canada which have not, prior to the closing of entries, won three first prizes in the Novice Class, a first prize in Bred-by-Exhibitor, American-Bred or Open Class, nor one or more points toward a championship title.

THE BRED-BY-EXHIBITOR CLASS shall be for dogs whelped in the U.S.A. which are six months of age and over, which are not champions, and which are owned wholly or in part by the person or by the spouse of the person who was the breeder or one of the breeders of record. Dogs entered in the BBE Class must be handled by an owner or by a member of the immediate family of an owner, i.e., the husband, wife, father, mother, son, daughter, brother or sister.

THE AMERICAN-BRED CLASS is for all dogs (except champions) six months of age or over, whelped in the U.S.A. by reason of a mating that took place in the U.S.A.

THE OPEN CLASS is for any dog six months of age or over, except in a member specialty club show held for only American-Bred dogs, in which case the class is for American-Bred dogs only.

Kubla Khan Silver Moon, top bitch at Pat Morehouse's Kubla Khan Kennels in Los Angeles, is pictured here at one and a half years of age. Photograph by Joan Ludwig.

WINNERS DOG and WINNERS BITCH: After the above male classes have been judged, the first-place winners are then *required* to compete in the ring. The dog judged "Winners Dog" is awarded the points toward his championship title.

RESERVE WINNERS are selected immediately after the Winners Dog. In case of a disqualification of a win by the AKC, the Reserve Dog moves up to "Winners" and receives the points. After all male classes are judged, the bitch classes are called.

BEST OF BREED OR BEST OF VARIETY COMPETITION is limited to Champions of Record or dogs (with newly acquired points, for a 90-day period prior to AKC confirmation) which have completed championship requirements, and Winners Dog and Winners Bitch (or the dog awarded Winners if only one Winners prize has been awarded), together with any undefeated dogs which have been shown only in non-regular classes; all compete for Best of Breed or Best of Variety (if the breed is divided by size, color, texture or length of coat hair, etc.).

BEST OF WINNERS: If the WD or WB earns BOB or BOV, it automatically becomes BOW; otherwise they will be judged together for BOW (following BOB or BOV judging).

BEST OF OPPOSITE SEX is selected from the remaining dogs of the opposite sex to Best of Breed or Best of Variety.

OTHER CLASSES may be approved by the AKC: STUD DOGS, BROOD BITCHES, BRACE CLASS, TEAM CLASS; classes consist-

Ch. Barney Boy, noted sire of Ruth Bates Young's Victor of Top Acres, top Samoyed several years ago.

Ch. Sam O'Khan's Tsari of Khan, sired by American and Canadian Ch. Zayzan of Krisland, C.D. *ex* Ch. White Cliffs Polar Dawn, a Top Brood Bitch for 1965 according to the Phillips System. Bred and owned by Francis and George FitzPatrick, Tsari was winner of the Tucker Brood Bitch Award for 1966, 1967 and 1968 and the Juliet Goodrich Fund Trophy for Top Producing Bitch for 1970. She is pictured going Best of Breed over Group and Best In Show Samoyeds under the late judge Alva Rosenberg. She has produced eight champions, two of which are Best In Show winners; six have Group Placements. One of her sons has been named a Top Sire in the breed as well. In one litter there were two Best In Show dogs.

ing of local dogs and bitches may also be included in a show if approved by the AKC (special rules are included in the AKC Rule Book).

The MISCELLANEOUS CLASS shall be for purebred dogs of such breeds as may be designated by the AKC. No dog shall be eligible for entry in this class unless the owner has been granted an Indefinite Listing Privilege (ILP) and unless the ILP number is given on the entry form. Application for an ILP shall be made on a form provided by the AKC and when submitted must be accompanied by a fee set by the Board of Directors.

All Miscellaneous Breeds shall be shown together in a single class except that the class may be divided by sex if so specified in the premium list. There shall be *no* further competition for dogs entered in this class. Ribbons for 1st, 2nd, 3rd and 4th shall be Rose, Brown, Light Green and Gray, respectively. This class is open to the following Miscellaneous Breeds: _ _ _ _ _ _ Australian Cattle Dogs, Australian Kelpies, Border Collies, Cavalier King Charles Spaniels, Ibizan Hounds, Miniature Bull Terriers, and Spinoni Italiani.

If Your Dog Wins a Class. . .

Study the classes to make certain your dog is entered in a proper class for his or her qualifications. If your dog wins his class, the rule states: *You are required* to enter classes for Winners, Best of Breed and Best of Winners (no additional entry fees). The rule states, "No eligible dog may be withheld from competition." It is not mandatory that you stay for group judging. *If your dog wins a group*, however, *you must stay for Best-in-Show competition.*

THE PRIZE RIBBONS AND WHAT THEY STAND FOR

No matter how many entries there are in each class at a dog show, if you place first through fourth position you will receive a ribbon. These ribbons commemorate your win and can be impressive when collected and displayed to prospective buyers when and if you have puppies for sale, or if you intend to use your dog at public stud.

All ribbons from the American Kennel Club licensed dog shows will bear the American Kennel Club seal, the name of the show, the date and the placement. In the classes the colors are blue for first, red for second, yellow for third, and white for fourth. Winners Dog or Winners Bitch ribbons are purple, while Reserve Dog and Reserve Bitch ribbons are purple and white. Best of Winners ribbons are blue and white; Best of Breed, purple and gold; and Best of Opposite Sex ribbons are red and white.

In the six groups, first prize is a blue rosette or ribbon, second placement is red, third yellow, and fourth white. The Best In Show rosette is either red, white and blue, or incorporates the colors used in the show-giving club's emblem.

QUALIFYING FOR CHAMPIONSHIP

Championship points are given for Winners Dog and Winners Bitch in accordance with a scale of points established by the American Kennel Club based on the popularity of the breed in entries, and the number of dogs competing in the classes. This scale of points varies in different sections of the country, but the scale is published in the front of each dog show catalog. These points may differ between the dogs and the bitches at the same show. You may, however, win additional points by winning Best of Winners, if there are fewer dogs than bitches entered, or vice versa. Points never exceed five at any one show, and a total of fifteen points must be won to constitute a championship. These fifteen points must be won under at least three different judges, and you must acquire at least two major wins. Anything from a three to five point win is a major, while one and two point wins are minor wins. Two major wins must be won under two different judges to meet championship requirements.

OBEDIENCE TRIALS

Some shows also offer Obedience Trials, which are considered as separate events. They give the dogs a chance to compete and score on performing a prescribed set of exercises intended to display their training in doing useful work.

There are three obedience titles for which they may compete. First, the Companion Dog or C.D. title; second, the Companion Dog Excellent or C.D.X.; and third, the Utility Dog or U.D. Detailed information on these degrees is contained in a booklet entitled Official Obedience Regulations and may be obtained by writing to the American Kennel Club.

JUNIOR SHOWMANSHIP COMPETITION

Junior Showmanship Competition is for boys and girls in different age groups handling their own dogs or one owned by their immediate family. There are four divisions: Novice A, for the ten to 12 year olds; Novice B, for those 13 to 16 years of age, with no previous junior showmanship wins; Open C, for ten to 12 year olds; and Open D, for 13 to 16 year olds who have earned one or more JS awards.

As Junior Showmanship at the dog shows increased in popularity, certain changes and improvements had to be made. As of April 1, 1971, the American Kennel Club issued a new booklet containing the Regulations for Junior Showmanship which may be obtained by writing to the A.K.C. at 51 Madison Avenue, New York, N.Y. 10010.

This full-body photograph by Joan Ludwig of the beautiful Ch. Sam O'Khan's Kubla Khan appeared on the cover of the June, 1973 *American Kennel Club Gazette* and was featured in a 1972 club calendar. Whelped in 1967, he was 1971 Top Sire in *Kennel Review* magazine and a Specialty Show Stud Dog Class winner in both 1972 and 1973. His sire was American and Canadian Ch. Noatak of Silver Moon and his dam American and Canadian Ch. Sam O'Khan Tsari O'Khan. Khan, in addition to being a beautiful show dog, has also run at wheel position on many long distance sled races to prove himself a top working dog as well. Owned by Patricia Morehouse, Kubla Khan Kennels, Los Angeles, California.

DOG SHOW PHOTOGRAPHERS

Every show has at least one official photographer who will be more than happy to take a photograph of your dog with the judge, ribbons and trophies, along with you or your handler. These make marvelous remembrances of your top show wins and are frequently framed along with the ribbons for display purposes. Photographers can be paged at the show over the public address system, if you wish to obtain this service. Prices vary, but you will probably find it costs little to capture these happy moments, and the photos can always be used in the various dog magazines to advertise your dog's wins.

TWO TYPES OF DOG SHOWS

There are two types of dog shows licensed by the American Kennel Club. One is the all-breed show which includes classes for all the recognized breeds, and groups of breeds; i.e., all terriers, all toys, etc. Then there are the specialty shows for one particular breed which also offer championship points.

Marie Gillette of California sharing an intimate moment with her Ch. Jomay of Singing Trees.

Polar Star's Nika Chum (on left) and his brother Polar Star's Akrum. These sled dogs, owned by Georgia Gleason, are ancestral to the famous American and Canadian Ch. Noatak of Silver Moon and are descendants of Ch. Stormy Weather of Betty Blue, a top sire and most important stud force in the Pacific Northwest years ago.

BENCHED OR UNBENCHED DOG SHOWS

The show-giving clubs determine, usually on the basis of what facilities are offered by their chosen show site, whether their show will be benched or unbenched. A benched show is one where the dog show superintendent supplies benches (cages for toy dogs). Each bench is numbered and its corresponding number appears on your entry identification slip which is sent to you prior to the show date. The number also appears in the show catalog. Upon entering the show you should take your dog to the bench where he should remain until it is time to groom him before entering the ring to be judged. After judging, he must be returned to the bench until the official time of dismissal from the show. At an unbenched show the club makes no provision whatsoever for your dog other than an enormous tent (if an outdoor show) or an area in a show hall where all crates and grooming equipment must be kept.

American and Canadian Ch. Noatak of Silver Moon, whelped in 1960 and sired by Canadian Ch. Polar Star's Nika Tillicum *ex* Ch. Silver Moon. Bred and owned by Mr. and Mrs. Robert Bowles, Noatak was a Top Sire according to *Popular Dogs* magazine in 1968, winner of the A.E. Mason Trophy for Top Winning Samoyed for 1963 and winner of the Wimundstrev Stud Dog Trophy for 1965, 1966, and 1967. He is also the sire of the most Group Placing and Best In Show Samoyeds ever. Twice he sired two Best In Show dogs in litters from two different bitches.

Benched or unbenched, the moment you enter the show grounds you are expected to look after your dog and have it under complete control at all times. This means short leads in crowded aisles or getting out of cars. In the case of a benched show, a "bench chain" is needed. It should allow the dog to move around, but not get down off the bench. It is also not considered "cute" to have small tots leading enormous dogs around a dog show where the child might be dragged into the middle of a dog fight.

PROFESSIONAL HANDLERS

If you are new in the fancy and do not know how to handle your dog to his best advantage, or if you are too nervous or physically unable to show your dog, you can hire a licensed professional handler who will do it for you for a specified fee. The more successful or well-known handlers charge slightly higher rates, but generally speaking there is a pretty uniform charge for this service. As the dog progresses with his wins in the show ring, the fee increases proportionately. Included in this service is professional advice on when and where to show your dog, grooming, a statement of your wins at each show, and all trophies and ribbons that the dog accumulates. Any cash award is kept by the handler as a sort of "bonus."

When engaging a handler, it is advisable to select one that does not take more dogs to a show than he can properly and comfortably handle. You want your dog to receive his individual attention and not

Moonlighter's Altai Star Mist, Wisconsin's top-producing Samoyed bitch for 1971 and 1972. Star Mist had major points toward championship until her jaw was fractured and she lost three teeth in a shipping accident. She is the dam of Ch. Moonlighter's Hallmark, Ch. Moonlighter's Celestial Hipy and several other pointed Sammies. Owned by Wayne and Jeanne Nonhof of Waldo, Wisconsin.

The beautiful Ch. Dmitri of Kobe.

be rushed into the ring at the last moment because the handler has been busy with too many other dogs in other rings. Some handlers require that you deliver the dog to their establishment a few days ahead of the show so they have ample time to groom and train him. Others will accept well-behaved and previously trained and groomed dogs at ringside, if they are familiar with the dog and the owner. This should be determined well in advance of the show date. NEVER expect a handler to accept a dog at ringside that is not groomed to perfection!

There are several sources for locating a professional handler. Dog magazines carry their classified advertising; a note or telephone call to the American Kennel Club will put you in touch with several in your area. Usually, you will be billed after the day of the show.

DO YOU REALLY NEED A HANDLER?

The answer to the above question is sometimes yes! However, the answer most exhibitors give is, "But I can't *afford* a professional handler!" or, "I want to show my dog myself. Does that mean my dog will never do any big winning?"

Do you *really* need a handler to win? If you are mishandling a good dog that should be winning and isn't, because it is made to look simply terrible in the ring by its owner, the answer is yes. If you don't know how to handle a dog properly, why make your dog look bad when a handler could show it to its best advantage?

Some owners simply cannot handle a dog well and still wonder why their dogs aren't winning in the ring, no matter how hard they try. Others are nervous and this nervousness travels down the leash to the dog and the dog behaves accordingly. Some people are extroverts by nature, and these are the people who usually make excellent handlers. Of course, the biggest winning dogs at the shows usually have a lot of "show off" in their nature, too, and this helps a great deal.

THE COST OF CAMPAIGNING A DOG WITH A HANDLER

Many Samoyed champions are shown an average of 25 times before completing a championship. In entry fees at today's prices, that adds up to about $200. This does not include motel bills, traveling expenses, or food. There have been dog champions finished in fewer shows, say five to ten shows, but this is the exception rather than the rule. When and where to show should be thought out carefully so that you can perhaps save money on entries. Here is one of the services a professional handler provides that can mean a considerable saving. Hiring a handler can save money in the long run if you just wish to make a champion. If your dog has been winning reserves and not taking the points and a handler can finish him in five to ten shows, you would be ahead financially. If your dog is not really top quality, the length of time it takes even a handler to finish it (depending upon competition in the area) could add up to a large amount of money.

Campaigning a show specimen that not only captures the wins in his breed but wins group and Best in Show awards gets up into the big money. To cover the nation's major shows and rack up a record as one of the top dogs in the nation usually costs an owner between ten and fifteen thousand dollars a year. This includes not only the professional handler's fee for taking the dog into the ring, but the cost of conditioning and grooming, board, advertising in the dog magazines, photographs, etc.

There is great satisfaction in winning with your own dog, especially if you have trained and cared for it yourself. With today's enormous entries at the dog shows and so many worthy dogs competing for top wins, many owners who said "I'd rather do it myself!" and meant it became discouraged and eventually hired a handler anyway.

However, if you really are in it just for the sport, you can and should handle your own dog if you want to. You can learn the tricks by

Ch. Suruka Sira Jandu O'Kubla Khan, owned and shown by Maureen Ingham, bred by Pat Morehouse. The sire was Sam O'Khan's Kubla Khan *ex* Ch. Icelandic Princess Zoe. Jandu is pictured winning Best of Breed over four male Specials, including Westminster Breed and Specialty winners, owner-handled under breeder-judge Katheryn Tagliaferri.

The lovely Mikelo of York, owned by Robert Faulkner of Dayton, Ohio. Mikelo is a son of Ch. Silver Flare of Wychwood.

attending training classes, and you can learn a lot by carefully observing the more successful professional handlers as they perform in the ring. Model yourself after the ones that command respect as being the leaders in their profession. But, if you find you'd really rather be at ringside looking on, then do get a handler so that your worthy dog gets his deserved recognition in the ring. To own a good dog and win with it is a thrill, so good luck, no matter how you do it.

14. FEEDING AND NUTRITION

FEEDING PUPPIES

There are many diets today for young puppies, including all sorts of products on the market for feeding the newborn, for supplementing the feeding of the young and for adding this or that to diets, depending on what is lacking in the way of a complete diet.

When weaning puppies, it is necessary to put them on four meals a day, even while you are tapering off with the mother's milk. Feeding at six in the morning, noontime, six in the evening and midnight is about the best schedule, since it fits in with most human eating plans. Meals for the puppies can be prepared immediately before or after your own meals, without too much of a change in your own schedule.

6 A.M.

Two meat and two milk meals serve best and should be served alternately, of course. Assuming the 6 A.M. feeding is a milk meal, the contents should be as follows: Goat's milk is the very best milk to feed puppies but is expensive and usually available only a drug stores, unless you live in farm country where it could be readily available fresh and still less expensive. If goat's milk is not available, use evaporated milk (which can be changed to powdered milk later on) diluted two parts evaporated milk and one part water, along with raw egg yoke, honey or Karo syrup, sprinkled with high-protein baby cereal and some wheat germ. As the puppies mature, cottage cheese may be added or, at one of the two milk meals, it can be substituted for the cereal.

NOONTIME

A puppy chow which has been soaked in warm water or beef broth according to the time specified on the wrapper should be mixed with raw or simmered chopped meat in equal proportions with vitamin powder added.

6 P.M.

Repeat the milk meal—perhaps varying the type of cereal from wheat to oats, or corn or rice.

MIDNIGHT

Repeat the meat meal. If raw meat was fed at noon, the evening meal might be simmered.

Please note that specific proportions on this suggested diet are not given. However, it's safe to say that the most important ingredients are the milk and cereal, and the meat and puppy chow which forms the basis of the diet. Your veterinarian can advise on the portion sizes if there is any doubt in your mind as to how much to use.

If you notice that the puppies are cleaning their plates you are perhaps not feeding enough to keep up with their rate of growth. Increase the amount at the next feeding. Observe them closely; puppies should each "have their fill," because growth is very rapid at this age. If they have not satisfied themselves, increase the amount so that they do not have to fight for the last morsel. They will not overeat if they know there is enough food available. Instinct will usually let them eat to suit their normal capacity.

A mother Samoyed and her seven puppies, owned by Harold McLaughlin, Silveracres Samoyed Kennels, Morrison, Colorado.

If there is any doubt in your mind as to any ingredient you are feeding, ask yourself, "Would I give it to my own baby?" If the answer is no, then don't give it to your puppies. At this age, the comparison between puppies and human babies can be a good guide.

If there is any doubt in your mind, I repeat: ask your veterinarian to be sure.

Many puppies will regurgitate their food, perhaps a couple of times, before they manage to retain it. If they do bring up their food, allow them to eat it again, rather than clean it away. Sometimes additional saliva is necessary for them to digest it, and you do not want them to skip a meal just because it is an unpleasant sight for you to observe.

This same regurgitation process holds true sometimes with the bitch, who will bring up her own food for her puppies every now and then. This is a natural instinct on her part which stems from the days when dogs were giving birth in the wilds. The only food the mother could provide at weaning time was too rough and indigestible for her puppies. Therefore, she took it upon herself to pre-digest the food until it could be taken and retained by her young. Bitches today will sometimes resort to this, especially bitches which love having litters and have a strong maternal instinct. Some dams will help you wean their litters and even give up feeding entirely once they see you are taking over.

WEANING THE PUPPIES

When weaning the puppies the mother is kept away from the little ones for longer and longer periods of time. This is done over a period of several days. At first she is separated from the puppies for several hours, then all day, leaving her with them only at night for comfort and warmth. This gradual separation aids in helping the mother's milk to dry up gradually, and she suffers less distress after feeding a litter.

If the mother continues to carry a great deal of milk with no signs of its tapering off, consult your veterinarian before she gets too uncomfortable. She may cut the puppies off from her supply of milk too abruptly if she is uncomfortable, before they should be completely on their own.

There are many opinions on the proper age to start weaning puppies. If you plan to start selling them between six and eight weeks, weaning should begin between two and three weeks of age. Here again, each bitch will pose a different situation. The size and weight of the litter should help determine the time, and your veterinarian will have an opinion, as he determines the burden the bitch is carrying by the size of the litter and her general condition. If she is being pulled down by feeding a large litter, he may suggest that you start at two weeks. If she is glorying in her motherhood without any apparent

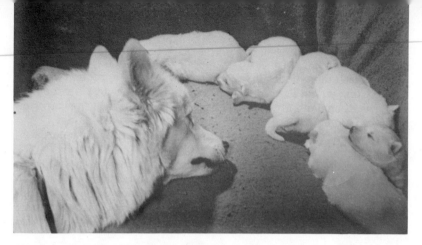

An anxious mother keeps an eye on her newborn babies. Bred by Marjorie Van Ornum of Cincinnati, Ohio.

taxing of her strength, he may suggest three to four weeks. You and he will be the best judges. But remember, there is no substitute that is as perfect as mother's milk—and the longer the puppies benefit from it, the better. Other food yes, but mother's milk first and foremost for the healthiest puppies!

FEEDING THE ADULT DOG

The puppies' schedule of four meals a day should drop to three by six months and then to two by nine months; by the time the dog reaches one year of age, it is eating one meal a day.

The time when you feed the dog each day can be a matter of the dog's preference or your convenience, so long as once in every 24 hours the dog receives a meal that provides him with a complete, balanced diet. In addition, of course, fresh clean water should be available at all times.

There are many brands of dry food, kibbles and biscuits on the market which are all of good quality. There are also many varieties of canned dog food which are of good quality and provide a balanced diet for your dog. But, for those breeders and exhibitors who show their dogs, additional care is given to providing a few "extras" which enhance the good health and good appearance of show dogs.

A good meal or kibble mixed with water or beef broth and raw meat is perhaps the best ration to provide. In cold weather many breeders add suet or corn oil (or even olive or cooking oil) to the mixture and others make use of the bacon fat after breakfast by pouring it over the dog's food.

Salting a dog's food in the summer helps replace the salt he "pants away" in the heat. Many breeders sprinkle the food with garlic powder to sweeten the dog's breath and prevent gas, especially in breeds that gulp or wolf their food and swallow a lot of air. I prefer garlic powder; the salt is too weak and the clove is too strong.

There are those, of course, who cook very elaborately for their dogs, which is not necessary if a good meal and meat mixture is provided. Many prefer to add vegetables, rice, tomatoes, etc., in with everything else they feed. As long as the extras do not throw the nutritional balance off, there is little harm, but no one thing should be fed to excess. Occasionally liver is given as a treat at home. Fish, which

Ch. Icelandic Princess Zoe, photographed by Joan Ludwig finishing for her championship in September, 1968 at the Samoyed Club of Los Angeles Specialty show under breeder-judge Anastasia McBain. The following month Zoe won Best of Opposite Sex at the Arctic Breed Olympiad in San Fernando, California. Zoe is the dam of four champions and three other Samoyeds which are pointed to date. She is owned by Patricia Morehouse of the Kubla Khan Kennels in Los Angeles, California.

Mr. and Mrs. Jan Mitchell pose in front of the fountain in front of the New York City Plaza Hotel with the two Samoyeds they owned at the time. Mr. Mitchell is the owner of the famous German restaurant Luchow's, on 14th Street in New York City, where for many years the Dog Fanciers Club held monthly luncheons and meetings.

most veterinarians no longer recommend even for cats, is fed to puppies, but should not be given in excess of once a week. Always remember that no one thing should be given as a total diet. Balance is most important; a 100 per cent meat diet can kill a dog.

THE ALL MEAT DIET CONTROVERSY

In March of 1971, the National Research Council investigated a great stir in the dog fancy about the all-meat dog-feeding controversy. It was established that meat and meat by-products constitute a complete balanced diet for dogs only when it is further fortified with vitamins and minerals.

Therefore, a good dog chow or meal mixed with meat provides the perfect combination for a dog's diet. While the dry food is a complete diet in itself, the fresh meat additionally satisfies the dog's anatomically and physiologically meat-oriented appetite. While dogs are actually carnivores, it must be remembered that when they were feeding themselves in the wild they ate almost the entire animal they captured, including its stomach contents. This provided some of the vitamins and minerals we must now add to the diet.

In the United States, the standard for diets which claim to be "complete and balanced" is set by the Subcommittee on Canine Nutrition of the National Research Council (NRC) of the National Academy of Sciences. This is the official agency for establishing the nutritional requirements of dog foods. Most foods sold for dogs and cats meet these requirements, and manufactuers are proud to say so on their labels, so look for this when you buy. Pet food labels must be approved by the Association of American Feed Control Officials, Pet Foods Committee. Both the Food and Drug Administration and the Federal Trade Commission of the AAFCO define the word "balanced" when referring to dog food as:

"Balanced is a term which may be applied to pet food having all known required nutrients in a proper amount and proportion based upon the recommendations of a recognized authority (The National Research Council is one) in the field of animal nutrition, for a given set of physiological animal requirements."

With this much care given to your dog's diet, there can be little reason for not having happy well-fed dogs in proper weight and proportions for the show ring.

OBESITY

As we mentioned before, there are many "perfect" diets for your dogs on the market today. When fed in proper proportions, they should keep your dogs in "full bloom." However, there are those owners who, more often than not, indulge their own appetites and are inclined to overfeed their dogs as well. A study in Great Britain in the early 1970's found that a major percentage of obese people also had obese dogs. The entire family was overfed and all suffered from the same condition.

Obesity in dogs is a direct result of the animal's being fed more food that he can properly "burn up" over a period of time, so it is stored as fat or fatty tissue in the body. Pet dogs are more inclined to become obese than show dogs or working dogs, but obesity also is a factor to be considered with the older dog, since his exercise is curtailed.

A lack of "tuck up" on a dog, or not being able to feel the ribs, or great folds of fat which hang from the underside of the dog can all be considered as obesity. Genetic factors may enter into the picture, but usually the owner is at fault.

The life span of the obese dog is decreased on several counts. Excess weight puts undue stress on the heart as well as the joints. The dog becomes a poor anesthetic risk and has less resistance to viral or bacterial infections. Treatment is seldom easy or completely effective, so emphasis should be placed on not letting your dog get FAT in the first place!

ORPHANED PUPPIES

The ideal solution to feeding orphaned puppies is to be able to put them with another nursing dam who will take them on as her own. If this is not possible within your own kennel, or a kennel that you know of, it is up to you to care for and feed the puppies. Survival is possible but requires a great deal of time and effort on your part.

Your substitute formula must be precisely prepared, always served heated to body temperature and refrigerated when not being fed. Esbilac, a vacuum-packed powder, with complete feeding instructions on the can, is excellent and about as close to mother's milk as you can get. If you can't get Esbilac, or until you do get Esbilac, there are two alternative formulas that you might use.

Mix one part boiled water with five parts of evaporated milk and add one teaspoonful of di-calcium phosphate per quart of formula. Di-calcium phosphate can be secured at any drug store. If they have it in tablet form only, you can powder the tablets with the back part of a tablespoon. The other formula for newborn puppies is a combination of eight ounces of homogenized milk mixed well with two egg yolks.

You will need baby bottles with three-hole nipples. Sometimes doll bottles can be used for the newborn puppies, which should be fed at six-hour intervals. If they are consuming sufficient amounts, their stomachs should look full, or slightly enlarged, though never distended. The amount of formula to be fed is proportionate to the size, age, growth and weight of the puppy, and is indicated on the can of Esbilac or on the advice of your veterinarian. Many breeders like to keep a baby scale nearby to check the weight of the puppies to be sure they are thriving on the formula.

A pair of Samoyeds waiting at ringside with their owner, ready to compete in brace competition at the Bermuda Kennel Club Show in 1971. Bermuda News Bureau photograph.

At two to three weeks you can start adding Pablum or some other high protein baby cereal to the formula. Also, baby beef can be licked from your finger at this age, or added to the formula. At four weeks the surviving puppies should be taken off the diet of Esbilac and put on a more substantial diet, such as wet puppy meal or chopped beef. However, Esbilac powder can still be mixed in with the food for additional nutrition. The jarred baby foods of pureed meats make for a smooth changeover also, and can be blended into the diet.

HOW TO FEED THE NEWBORN PUPPIES

When the puppy is a newborn, remember that it is vitally important to keep the feeding procedure as close to the natural mother's routine as possible. The newborn puppy should be held in your lap in

Mrs. George Brown gives Ch. Vicklutna Charm of Top Acres a few last-minute instructions for the ring at a summer outdoor dog show. "Klute" seems to be listening to every word.

Kolya of Snow Shoe Hill pictured at nine months of age. Owned by Juliet Goodrich.

your hand in an almost upright position with the bottle at an angle to allow the entire nipple area to be full of the formula. Do not hold the bottle upright so the puppy's head has to reach straight up toward the ceiling. Do not let the puppy nurse too quickly or take in too much air and possibly get the colic. Once in a while, take the bottle away and let him rest a while and swallow several times. Before feeding, test the nipple to see that the fluid does not come out too quickly, or by the same token, too slowly so that the puppy gets tired of feeding before he has had enough to eat.

When the puppy is a little older, you can place him on his stomach on a towel to eat, and even allow him to hold on to the bottle or to "come and get it" on his own. Most puppies enjoy eating and this will be a good indication of how strong an appetite he has and his ability to consume the contents of the bottle.

It will be necessary to "burp" the puppy. Place a towel on your shoulder and hold the puppy on your shoulder as if it were a human baby, patting and rubbing it gently. This will also encourage the puppy to defecate. At this time, you should observe for diarrhea or other intestinal disorders. The puppy should eliminate after each feeding with occasional eliminations between times as well. If the puppies do not eliminate on their own after each meal, massage their stomachs and under their tails gently until they do.

You must keep the puppies clean. If there is diarrhea or if they bring up a little formula, they should be washed and dried off. Under no circumstances should fecal matter be allowed to collect on their skin or fur.

All this—plus your determination and perseverance—might save an entire litter of puppies that would otherwise have died without their real mother.

Samoyed fancier Lucy Forbes of Chicago photographed several years ago with Ch. Pratikas Pilot as a puppy.

GASTRIC TORSION

Gastric torsion, or bloat, sometimes referred to simply as "twisted stomach," has become more and more prevalent. Many dogs that in the past had been thought to die of blockage of the stomach or intestines because they had swallowed toys or other foreign objects are now suspected of having been the victims of gastric torsion and the bloat that followed.

Though life can be saved by immediate surgery to untwist the organ, the rate of fatality is high. Symptoms of gastric torsion are unusual restlessness, excessive salivation, attempts to vomit, rapid respiration, pain and the eventual bloating of the abdominal region.

The cause of gastric torsion can be attributed to overeating, excess gas formation in the stomach, poor function of the stomach or intestine, or general lack of exercise. As the food ferments in the stomach, gases form which may twist the stomach in a clockwise direction so that the gas is unable to escape. Surgery, where the stomach is untwisted counter-clockwise, is the safest and most successful way to correct the situation.

To avoid the threat of gastric torsion, it is wise to keep your dog well exercised to be sure the body is functioning normally. Make sure that food and water are available for the dog at all times, thereby reducing the tendency to overeat. With self-service dry feeding, where the dog is able to eat intermittently during the day, there is not the urge to "stuff" at one time.

If you notice any of the symptoms of gastric torsion, call your veterinarian immediately! Death can result within a matter of hours!

FEEDING THE RACING DOG

While the Samoyed is known to be capable of extreme drive over long distances, a relatively simple diet is required.

Owners who race their dogs—including the real professionals who have been in the racing game for a long time—will tell you that the basic diet is a good dog meal and that the average amount of food for a racing dog of average size is approximately a one-pound coffee can full. Most Northern breed dogs have voracious appetites and will overeat if permitted to do so, so try to establish the correct amount for keeping each of your racing dogs in proper flesh, and then stick to it.

Mother-daughter look-alikes. . . Ch. Pinehill's Pixie O'Whytekrest and Pinehill's Glory Be. Owners: Barbara and Mary Telychan and Lee and Sandy Wacenske of New Jersey.

The late General and Mrs. Allen, Samoyed fanciers and friends of Ruth Bates Young. While stationed at Fort Knox the Allens owned several Sammys. They are pictured here with one of the two puppies they purchased from Mrs. Young.

This ration of a good dog meal, plus drinking water, is all that is really required for a proper and balanced diet, even if your dog races. However, there are those who choose to supplement a racing dog's diet in the belief that the "extras" add to the all-around good health of the animal.

Alaskans, for instance, might add moose meat or other wild game meat to the diet. But in the Alaskan region mainly fish is used as an added ingredient. And when we mention fish, we mean to say the *entire* fish—inside and out, head and tail included!

Some owners of racing teams will supplement with liver, or keep their dogs on vitamins mixed in with the meal or feed. They might even use the vitamin tablets as treats or as a reward. Still others just feed the added vitamins a few days before a racing schedule begins. On the day of the race some drivers feed lumps of sugar or add Karo syrup to the ration. But those "in the know" will tell you that while it will not harm the dog, sugar and Karo syrup are instant energy and are burned up so quickly it will in no way sustain a dog throughout the entire distance of the race. Therefore, the proper basic diet is still the best way to condition a dog fully for racing

Photographer Harold McLaughlin of Morrison, Colorado has captured in this adorable puppy picture the essence of what endears the breed to all of us!

At home by the fireside: Ch. Yorza and friend. Owner, Mrs. John May of Trenton, New Jersey.

This same principle applies to the vitamin B shots which some owners of racing dogs believe to be of help. A dog that has been properly and substantially fed will not need any additional vitamin or energy supplements. There is always the risk of diarrhea when a diet is suddenly supplemented to any marked degree. Those that do add meat—or anything else for that matter—to the diet before racing their dogs do so for several days ahead of time so that the dog has time to adjust to it.

It is possible to buy huge frozen blocks of beef for the team and add it to the ration on a regular basis so it will not shock the dog's system. It is an unpleasant experience to have a racing dog with diarrhea, and diarrhea can certainly throw a dog off his performance and thereby hold back an entire team.

The correct procedure is to feed the dog his customary diet, to have him in the peak of condition, and use a suppository about an hour before the race if the dog has not emptied himself entirely without prompting.

DRINKING WATER

Just as it is not wise to feed before a race, it is not wise to let a racing dog drink too much water before a race. Watch the water intake carefully. If the dog is still thirsty as race time approaches, he usually will lick snow, but it is not wise to offer any water immediately before or immediately after a heat.

15. GENERAL CARE AND MANAGEMENT OF YOUR SAMOYED

TATTOOING

Ninety per cent success has been reported on the return of stolen or lost dogs that have been tattooed. More and more this simple, painless, inexpensive method of positive identification for dogs is being reported all over the United States. Long popular in Canada, along with nose prints, the idea gained interest in this country when dognapping started to soar as unscrupulous people began stealing dogs for resale to research laboratories. Pet dogs that wander off and lost hunting dogs have always been a problem. The success of tattooing has been significant.

Tattooing can be done by the veterinarian for a minor fee. There are several dog "registries" that will record your dog's number and help you locate it should it be lost or stolen. The number of the dog's American Kennel Club registration is most often used on thoroughbred dogs, or the owner's Social Security number in the case of mixed breeds. The best place for the tattoo is the groin. Some prefer the inside of an ear, and the American Kennel Club has rules that the judges officiating at the AKC dog shows not penalize the dog for the tattoo mark.

The tattoo mark serves not only to identify your dog should it be lost or stolen, but offers positive identification in large kennels where several litters of the same approximate age are on the premises. It is a safety measure against unscrupulous breeders "switching" puppies. Any age is a proper age to tattoo, but for safety's sake, the sooner the better.

The buzz of the needle might cause your dog to be apprehensive, but the pricking of the needle is virtually painless. The risk of infection is negligible when done properly, and the return of your beloved pet may be the reward for taking the time to insure positive identification for your dog. Your local kennel club will know of a dog registry in your area.

The Samoyed at his happiest. . . outdoors in the snow and master of all he surveys. One of Joyce Cain's Sammys atop his snow house in Ripon, Wisconsin.

OUTDOOR HOUSEBREAKING

If you are particular about your dog's behavior in the house, where you expect him to be clean and respectful of the carpets and furniture, you should also want him to have proper manners outdoors. Just because the property belongs to you doesn't necessarily mean he should be allowed to empty himself any place he chooses. Before long the entire yard will be fouled and odorous and the dog will be completely irresponsible on other people's property as well. Dogs seldom recognize property lines.

If your dog does not have his own yard fenced in, he should be walked on leash before being allowed to run free and before being penned up in his own yard. He will appreciate his own run being kept clean. You will find that if he has learned his manners outside, his manners inside will be better. Good manners in "toilet training" are especially important with big dogs!

OTHER IMPORTANT OUTDOOR MANNERS

Excessive barking is perhaps the most objectionable habit a dog indulges in out of doors. It annoys neighbors and makes for a noisy dog in the house as well. A sharp jerk on the leash will stop a dog from excessive barking while walking; trees and shrubs around a dog run will cut down on barking if a dog is in his own run. However, it is unfair to block off his view entirely. Give him some view—preferably of his own home—to keep his interest. Needless to say, do not leave a dog that barks excessively out all night.

You will want your dog to bark at strangers, so allow him this privilege. Then after a few "alerting" barks tell the dog to be quiet (with the same word command each time). If he doesn't get the idea, put him on leash and let him greet callers with you at the door until he does get the idea.

Do not let your dog jump on visitors either. Leash training may be necessary to break this habit as well. As the dog jumps in the air, pull back on the lead so that the dog is returned to the floor abruptly. If he attempts to jump up on you , carefully raise your knee and push him away by leaning against his chest.

Ch. Jan Mayen.

Do not let your dog roam free in the neighborhood no matter how well he knows his way home. Especially do not let your dog roam free to empty himself on the neighbors' property or gardens!

A positive invitation to danger is to allow your dog to chase cars or bicycles. Throwing tin cans or chains out of car windows at them has been suggested as a cure, but can also be dangerous if they hit the dog instead of the street. Streams of water from a garden hose or water pistol are the least dangerous, but leash control is still the most scientific and most effective.

If neighbors report that your dog barks or howls or runs from window to window while you are away, crate training or room training for short periods of time may be indicated. If you expect to be away for longer periods of time, put the dog in the basement or a single room where he can do the least damage. The best solution of all is to buy him another dog or cat for companionship. Let them enjoy each other while you are away and have them both welcome you home!

GERIATRICS

If you originally purchased good healthy stock and cared for your dog throughout his life, there is no reason why you cannot expect your dog to live to a ripe old age. With research and the remarkable foods produced for dogs, especially this past decade or so, his chances of longevity have increased considerably. If you have cared for him well, your dog will be a sheer delight in his old age, just as he was while in his prime.

We can assume you have fed him properly if he is not too fat. Have you ever noticed how fat people usually have fat dogs because

American and Canadian Ch. Saroma's Polar Prince pictured in all his beauty at eleven years of age. The famous Samoyed, one of the outstanding dogs in the history of the breed, is owned by Richard T. and Martha B. Beal of Mercer Island, Washington.

they indulge their dogs' appetite as they do their own? If there has been no great illness, then you will find that very little additional care and attention are needed to keep him well. Exercise is still essential, as is proper food, booster shots, and tender loving care.

Even if a heart condition develops, there is still no reason to believe your dog cannot live to an old age. A diet may be necessary, along with medication and limited exercise, to keep the condition under control. In the case of deafness, or partial blindness, additional care must be taken to protect the dog, but neither infirmity will in any way shorten his life. Prolonged exposure to temperature variances, overeating, excessive exercise, lack of sleep, or being housed with younger, more active dogs may take an unnecessary toll on the dog's energies and introduce serious trouble. Good judgment, periodic veterinary checkups and individual attention will keep your dog with you for many added years.

When discussing geriatrics, the question of when a dog becomes old or aged usually is asked. We have all heard the old saying that one year of a dog's life is equal to seven years in a human. This theory is strictly a matter of opinion, and must remain so, since so many outside factors enter into how quickly each individual dog "ages." Recently, a new chart was devised which is more realistically equivalent:

DOG	MAN
6 months	10 years
1 year	15 years
2 years	24 years
3 years	28 years
4 years	32 years
5 years	36 years
6 years	40 years*
7 years	44 years
8 years	48 years
9 years	52 years
10 years	56 years
15 years	76 years
21 years	100 years

It must be remembered that such things as serious illnesses, poor food and housing, general neglect and poor beginnings as puppies will take their toll on a dog's general health and age him more quickly than a dog that has led a normal, healthy life. Let your veterinarian help you determine an age bracket for your dog in his later years.

While good care should prolong your dog's life, there are several "old age" disorders to be on the lookout for no matter how well he may be doing. The tendency toward obesity is the most common, but constipation is another. Aging teeth and a slowing down of the digestive processes may hinder digestion and cause constipation, just as any major change in diet can bring on diarrhea. There is also the possibility of loss or impairment of hearing or eyesight which will also tend to make the dog wary and distrustful. Other behavioral changes may result as well, such as crankiness, loss of patience and lack of interest; these are the most obvious changes. Other ailments may manifest themselves in the form of rheumatism, arthritis, tumors and warts, heart disease, kidney infections, male prostatism and female disorders. Of course, all of these require a veterinarian's checking the degree of seriousness and proper treatment.

Take care to avoid infectious diseases. When these hit the older dog, they can debilitate him to an alarming degree, leaving him open to more serious complications and a shorter life.

DOG INSURANCE

Much has been said for and against canine insurance, and much more will be said before this kind of protection for a dog becomes universal and/or practical. There has been talk of establishing a Blue Cross-type plan similar to that now existing for humans. However, the best insurance for your dog is *you*! Nothing compensates for tender, loving care. Like the insurance policies for humans, there will be a lot of fine print in the contracts revealing that the dog is not covered after all. These limited conditions usually make the acquisition of dog insurance expensive and virtually worthless.

Great expectations. . . two Samoyeds wait patiently to see what Santa has brought. Photograph by Harold McLaughlin, Morrison, Colorado.

Ch. North Star Mist of Yate Sea, whelped in 1970. "Fluffy" is pictured here taking a win at a show on the way to her championship. The sire was Ch. Yate Sea Arctic King *ex* Yate Sea Blue Bell D'or. Owners are Walter Yates and Marie M. Gemeinhardt of Cedar Grove, New Jersey.

Blanket coverage policies for kennels or establishments which board or groom dogs can be an advantage, especially in transporting dogs to and from their premises. For the one-dog owner, however, whose dog is a constant companion, the cost for limited coverage is not necessary.

THE HIGH COST OF BURIAL

Pet cemeteries are mushrooming across the nation. Here, as with humans, the sky can be the limit for those who wish to bury their pets ceremoniously. The costs of satin-lined caskets, grave stones, flowers, etc. run the gamut of prices to match the emotions and means of the owner. This is strictly a matter of what the bereaved owner wishes to do.

IN THE EVENT OF YOUR DEATH. . .

This is a morbid thought perhaps, but ask yourself the question, "If death were to strike at this moment, what would become of my beloved dogs?"

Perhaps you are fortunate enough to have a relative, friend or spouse who could take over immediately, if only on a temporary basis. Perhaps you have already left instructions in your last will and testament for your pet's dispensation, as well as a stipend for their perpetual care.

Provide definite instructions before a disaster occurs and your dogs are carted off to the pound, or stolen by commercially minded neighbors with "resale" in mind. It is a simple thing to instruct your lawyer about your wishes in the event of sickness or death. Leave instructions as to feeding, etc., posted on your kennel room or kitchen bulletin board, or wherever your kennel records are kept. Also, tell several people what you are doing and why. If you prefer to keep such instructions private, merely place them in sealed envelopes in a known place with directions that they are to be opened only in the event of your demise. Eliminate the danger of your animals suffering in the event of an emergency that prevents your personal care of them.

KEEPING RECORDS

Whether or not you have one dog, or a kennel full of them, it is wise to keep written records. It takes only a few moments to record dates of inoculations, trips to the vet, tests for worms, etc. It can avoid confusion or mistakes, or having your dog not covered with immunization if too much time elapses between shots because you have to guess at the last shot.

Make the effort to keep all dates in writing rather than trying to commit them to memory. A rabies injection date can be a problem if you have to recall that "Fido had the shot the day Aunt Mary got back from her trip abroad, and, let's see, I guess that was around the end of June."

In an emergency, these records may prove their value if your veterinarian cannot be reached and you have to use another, or if you move and have no case history on your dog for the new veterinarian. In emergencies, you do not always think clearly or accurately, and if dates and types of serums used, etc., are a matter of record, the veterinarian can act more quickly and with more confidence.

16. YOUR DOG, YOUR VETERINARIAN, AND YOU!

The purpose of this chapter is to explain why you should never attempt to be your own veterinarian. Quite the contrary, we urge emphatically that you establish good liaison with a reputable veterinarian who will help you maintain happy, healthy dogs. Our purpose is to bring you up to date on the discoveries made in modern canine medicine and to help you work with your veterinarian by applying these new developments to your own animals.

A lovely head-study of Raquel, one of Joyce Cain's lovely Samoyeds.

Christmas of 1949 finds Ch. Yorza II and Kadra II posed in front of the Christmas tree. Owned by Katherine May of New Jersey.

We have provided here "thumbnail" histories of many of the most common types of diseases your dog is apt to come in contact with during his lifetime. We feel that if you know a little something about the diseases and how to recognize their symptoms, your chances of catching them in the preliminary stages will help you and your veterinarian effect a cure before a serious condition develops.

Today's dog owner is a realistic, intelligent person who learns more and more about his dog—inside and out—so that he can care for and enjoy the animal to the fullest. He uses technical terms for parts of the anatomy, has a fleeting knowledge of the miracles of surgery and is fully prepared to administer clinical care for his animals at home. This chapter is designed for study and/or reference and we hope you will use it to full advantage.

We repeat, we do *not* advocate your playing "doctor." This includes administering medication without veterinary supervision, or even doing your own inoculations. General knowledge of diseases, their symptoms and side effects will assist you in diagnosing diseases for your veterinarian. He does not expect you to be an expert, but will appreciate your efforts in getting a sick dog to him before it is too late and he cannot save its life.

ASPIRIN: A DANGER

There is a common joke about doctors telling their patients, when they telephone with a complaint, to take an aspirin, go to bed and let him know how things are in the morning! Unfortunately, that is exactly the way it turns out with a lot of dog owners who think aspirins are curealls and give them to their dogs indiscriminately. Then they call the veterinarian when the dog has an unfavorable reaction.

Aspirins are not panaceas for everything—certainly not for every dog. In an experiment, fatalities in cats treated with aspirin in one laboratory alone numbered ten out of 13 within a two-week period. Dogs' tolerance was somewhat better, as far as actual fatalities, but there was considerable evidence of ulceration in varying degrees on the stomach linings when necropsy was performed.

Aspirin has been held in the past to be almost as effective for dogs as for people when given for many of the everyday aches and pains. The fact remains, however, that medication of any kind should be administered only after veterinary consultation and a specific dosage suitable to the condition is recommended.

While aspirin is chiefly effective in reducing fever, relieving minor pains and cutting down on inflammation, the acid has been proven harmful to the stomach when given in strong doses. Only your veterinarian is qualified to determine what the dosage is, or whether it should be administered to your particular dog at all.

WHAT THE THERMOMETER CAN TELL YOU

You will notice in reading this chapter dealing with the diseases of dogs that practically everything a dog might contract in the way of sickness has basically the same set of symptoms. Loss of appetite, diarrhea, dull eyes, dull coat, warm and/or runny nose, and FEVER!

Therefore, it is most advisable to have a thermometer on hand for checking temperature. There are several inexpensive metal rectal-type thermometers that are accurate and safer than the glass variety which can be broken. This may happen either by dropping, or perhaps even breaking off in the dog because of improper insertion or an aggravated condition with the dog that makes him violently resist the injection of the thermometer. Either kind should be lubricated with Vaseline to make the insertion as easy as possible, after it has been sterilized with alcohol.

Ch. Winterland's Kim, Best In Show-winning Samoyed owned and shown by Mrs. Robert Heagy in the early 1960's. Carey Lindsay is the judge at this Sioux City, Iowa show.

The normal temperature for a dog is 101.5° Fahrenheit, as compared to the human 98.6°. Excitement as well as illness can cause this to vary a degree or two, but any sudden or extensive rise in body temperature must be considered as cause for alarm. Your first indication will be that your dog feels unduly "warm" and this is the time to take the temperature, not when the dog becomes very ill or manifests additional serious symptoms. With a thermometer on hand, you can check temperatures quickly and perhaps prevent some illness from becoming serious.

COPROPHAGY

Perhaps the most unpleasant of all phases of dog breeding is to come up with a dog that takes to eating stool. This practice, which is referred to politely as coprophagy, is one of the unsolved mysteries in the dog world. There simply is no explanation to why some dogs do it.

However, there are several logical theories, all or any of which may be the cause. Some say nutritional deficiencies; another says that dogs inclined to gulp their food (which passes through them not entirely digested) find it still partially palatable. There is another

One of our favorite all-time photographs: Samuel Silverstein's children Zona (3½ years old) and Grant (one year) showing their beautiful Samoyed Tanya exactly how they feel about her! Photo was taken in 1955.

theory that the preservatives used in some meat are responsible for an appealing odor that remains through the digestive process. Then again poor quality meat can be so tough and unchewable that dogs swallow it whole and it passes through them in large undigested chunks.

There are others who believe the habit is strictly psychological, the result of a nervous condition or insecurity. Others believe the dog cleans up after itself because it is afraid of being punished as it was when it made a mistake on the carpet as a puppy. Others claim boredom is the reason, or even spite. Others will tell you a dog does not want its personal odor on the premises for fear of attracting other hostile animals to itself or its home.

The most logical of all explanations and the one most veterinarians are inclined to accept is that it is a deficiency of dietary enzymes. Too much dry food can be bad and many veterinarians suggest trying meat tenderizers, monosodium glutamate, or garlic powder which gives the stool a bad odor and discourages the dog. Yeast or certain vitamins or a complete change of diet are even more often suggested. By the time you try each of the above you will probably discover that the dog has outgrown the habit anyway. However, the condition cannot be ignored if you are to enjoy your dog to the fullest.

There is no set length of time that the problem persists, and the only real cure is to walk the dog on leash, morning and night and after every meal. In other words, set up a definite eating and exercising schedule before coprophagy is an established pattern.

MASTURBATION

A source of embarrassment to many dog owners, masturbation can be eliminated with a minimum of training.

The dog which is constantly breeding anything and everything, including the leg of the piano or perhaps the leg of your favorite guest, can be broken of the habit by stopping its cause.

The over-sexed dog—if truly that is what he is—which will never be used for breeding can be castrated. The kennel stud dog can be broken of the habit by removing any furniture from his quarters or keeping him on leash and on verbal command when he is around people, or in the house where he might be tempted to breed pillows, people, etc.

Hormone imbalance may be another cause and your veterinarian may advise injections. Exercise can be of tremendous help. Keeping the dog's mind occupied by physical play when he is around people will also help relieve the situation.

Females might indulge in sexual abnormalities like masturbation during their heat cycle, or again, because of a hormone imbalance. But if they behave this way because of a more serious problem, a hysterectomy may be indicated.

Ch. Beta Sigma's Mufti, fraternity mascot for the Alpha Sigma Phi fraternity in Cincinnati, Ohio. Mufti led the college parades to the games on campus and was also a show dog known for his exceptionally good movement.

Ch. Moonlighter Moonshine O'Berl, pictured winning at ten months of age at a Winnebagoland Samoyed Fancier Show. Moonlighter finished at sixteen months with all majors (5, 4, 3, and 3) and a Best of Breed from the classes over Specials, two of them Group Winners. Handled by owner Jeanne Nonhof of Waldo, Wisconsin. Sire: Ch. Moonlighter's Hallmark *ex* Talosam's Mystic Star.

Wings Over Sea of Icefloe, nine months old (sitting in the chair), and Babyface Crystal in front of the trophy case. Both Samoyeds owned by Laura and Leo Povier of Detroit, Michigan.

A sharp "no!" command when you can anticipate the act, or a sharp "no!" when caught in the act will deter most dogs if you are consistent in your correction. Hitting or other physical abuse will only confuse a dog.

RABIES

The greatest fear in the dog fancy today is still the great fear it has always been—rabies!

What has always held true about this dreadful disease still holds true today. The only way rabies can be contracted is through the saliva of a rabid dog entering the bloodstream of another animal or person. There is, of course, the Pasteur treatment for rabies which is very effective. There was of late the incident of a little boy bitten by a rabid bat having survived the disease. However, the Pasteur treatment is administered immediately if there is any question of exposure. Even more than dogs being found to be rabid, we now know that the biggest carriers are bats, skunks, foxes, rabbits and other warm-blooded animals, which pass it from one to another, since they do not have the benefit of inoculation. Dogs that run free should be inoculated for protection against these animals. For city or house dogs that never leave their owner's side, it may not be as necessary.

Driftwayes Oni-Agra Rex, eleven-month-old male which won Best Senior Samoyed Puppy and Group 4 at a Hunterdon Hills Kennel Club all-breed match show. Owned by the Richard Peskins of Clinton, New Jersey.

For many years, Great Britain, because it is an island and because of the country's strictly enforced six-month quarantine, was entirely free of rabies. But in 1969, a British officer brought back his dog from foreign duty and the dog was found to have the disease soon after being released from quarantine. There was a great uproar about it, with Britain killing off wild and domestic animals in a great scare campaign, but the quarantine is once again down to six months and things seem to have returned to a normal, sensible attitude.

Health departments in rural towns usually provide rabies inoculations free of charge. If your dog is outdoors a great deal, or exposed to other animals that are, you might wish to call the town hall and get information on the program in your area. One cannot be too cautious about this dread disease. While the number of cases diminishes each year, there are still thousands being reported and there is still the constant threat of an outbreak where animals roam free. And never forget, there is no cure.

Ch. Winterway's Yukiko, owned by Mrs. Margaret Ochi of Rockville, Maryland. The sire was Ch. Kondako's Dancing Bear *ex* Ch. Kim's Lady Bug. Photo by Josephine Seelig.

Rabies is caused by a neurotropic virus which can be found in the saliva, brain and sometimes the blood of the warm-blooded animal afflicted. The incubation period is usually two weeks or as long as six months, which means you can be exposed to it without any visible symptoms. As we have said, while there is still no known cure, it can be controlled. It is up to every individual to help effect this control by reporting animal bites, educating the public to the dangers and symptoms and prevention of it, so that we may reduce the fatalities.

There are two kinds of rabies; one form is called "furious," and the other is referred to as "dumb." The mad dog goes through several stages of the disease. His disposition and behavior change radically and suddenly; he becomes irritable and vicious; the eating habits alter, and he rejects food for things like stones and sticks; he be-

Ruth Young's Ch. Cotton Fluff of Top Acres with some of her trophies.

comes exhausted and drools saliva out of his mouth almost constantly. He may hide in corners, look glassy eyed and suspicious, bite at the air as he races around snarling and attacking with his tongue hanging out. At this point paralysis sets in, starting at the throat so that he can no longer drink water though he desires it desperately; hence, the term hydrophobia is given. He begins to stagger and eventually convulse and death is imminent.

In "dumb" rabies paralysis is swift; the dog seeks dark, sheltered places and is abnormally quiet. Paralysis starts with the jaws, spreads down the body and death is quick. Contact by humans or other animals with the drool from either of these types of rabies on open skin can produce the fatal disease, so extreme haste and proper diagnosis is essential. In other words, you do not have to be bitten by a rabid dog to have the virus enter your system. An open wound or cut that comes in touch with the saliva is all that is needed.

The incubation and degree of infection can vary. You usually contract the disease faster if the wound is near the head, since the virus travels to the brain through the spinal cord. The deeper the wound, the more saliva is injected into the body, the more serious the infection. So, if bitten by a dog under any circumstances—or any warm-blooded animal for that matter—immediately wash out the wound with soap and water, bleed it profusely, and see your doctor as soon as possible.

Also, be sure to keep track of the animal that bit, if at all possible. When rabies is suspected the public health officer will need to send the animal's head away to be analyzed. If it is found to be rabies free, you will not need to undergo treatment. Otherwise, your doctor may advise that you have the Pasteur treatment, which is extremely painful. It is rather simple, however, to have the veterinarian examine a dog for rabies without having the dog sent away for positive diagnosis of the disease. A ten-day quarantine is usually all that is necessary for everyone's peace of mind.

Rabies is no respecter of age, sex or geographical location. It is found all over the world from North Pole to South Pole, and has nothing to do with the old wives' tale of dogs going mad in the hot summer months. True, there is an increase in reported cases during summer, but only because that is the time of the year for animals to roam free in good weather and during the mating season when the battle of the sexes is taking place. Inoculation and a keen eye for symptoms and bites on our dogs and other pets will help control the disease until the cure is found.

VACCINATIONS

If you are to raise a puppy, or a litter of puppies, successfully, you must adhere to a realistic and strict schedule of vaccination. Many puppyhood diseases can be fatal—all of them are debilitating.

Janet and John J. Horn's "Timo," otherwise known as Ite of Kalevalo. Timo (*Timo* is Finnish for Timothy) lives in Brick Township, New Jersey and was photographed by Robert Kirsch.

Yate Sea Bidushka, Ch. North Star Mist of Yate Sea, Ch. Cinnamon Snow of Yate Sea and Snow Hullabaloo, owned by Marie Gemeinhardt of Cedar Grove, New Jersey.

The English-bred Ch. Destiny of Top Acres, large in size but beautiful-ly put together and bearing a magnificent head. Imported by Ruth Bates Young, Medway, Ohio.

According to the latest statistics, 98 per cent of all puppies are being inoculated after 12 weeks of age against the dread distemper, hepati-tis and leptospirosis and manage to escape these horrible infections. Orphaned puppies should be vaccinated every two weeks until the age of 12 weeks. Distemper and hepatitis live-virus vaccine should be used, since they are not protected with the colostrum normally sup-plied to them through the mother's milk. Puppies weaned at six to seven weeks should also be inoculated repeatedly because they will no longer be receiving mother's milk. While not all will receive pro-tection from the serum at this early age, it should be given and they should be vaccinated once again at both nine and 12 weeks of age.

Leptospirosis vaccination should be given at four months of age with thought given to booster shots if the disease is known in the area, or in the case of show dogs which are exposed on a regular basis to many dogs from far and wide. While annual boosters are in order for distemper and hepatitis, every two or three years is sufficient for lep-tospirosis, unless there is an outbreak in your immediate area. The one exception should be the pregnant bitch since there is reason to believe that inoculation might cause damage to the fetus.

Strict observance of such a vaccination schedule will not only keep your dog free of these debilitating diseases, but will prevent an epidemic in your kennel, or in your locality, or to the dogs which are competing at the shows.

SNAKEBITE

As field trials and hunts and the like become more and more popular with dog enthusiasts, the incident of snakebite becomes more of a likelihood. Dogs that are kept outdoors in runs or dogs that work the fields and roam on large estates are also likely victims.

Most veterinarians carry snakebite serum, and snakebite kits are sold to dog owners for just such purpose. To catch a snakebite in time might mean the difference between life and death, and whether your area is populated with snakes or not, it behooves you to know what to do in case it happens to you or your dog.

Your primary concern should be to get to a doctor or veterinarian immediately. The victim should be kept as quiet as possible (excitement or activity spreads the venom through the body more quickly) and if possible the wound should be bled enough to clean it out before applying a tourniquet, if the bite is severe.

First of all, it must be determined if the bite is from a poisonous or non-poisonous snake. If the bite carries two horseshoe shaped pinpoints of a double row of teeth, the bite can be assumed to be non-poisonous. If the bite leaves two punctures or holes—the result of the two fangs carrying venom—the bite is very definitely poisonous and time is of the essence.

Recently, physicians have come up with an added help in the case of snakebite. A first aid treatment referred to as hypothermia, which is the application of ice to the wound to lower body temperature to a point where the venom spreads less quickly, minimizes swelling, helps prevent infection and has some influence on numbing the pain. If ice is not readily available, the bite may be soaked in ice-cold water. But even more urgent is the need to get the victim to a hospital or a veterinarian for additional treatment.

EMERGENCIES

No matter how well you run your kennel or keep an eye on an individual dog, there will almost invariably be some emergency at some time that will require quick treatment until you get the animal to the veterinarian. The first and most important thing to remember is to keep calm! You will think more clearly and your animal will need to know he can depend on you to take care of him. However, he will be frightened and you must beware of fear biting. Therefore, do not shower him with kisses and endearments at this time, no matter how

An impressive study of Ch. Yorza II of Arbee, dam of Mrs. Ruth Young's famous Ch. Sparkle Plenty of Top Acres. Yorza was owned by Mrs. John May of Trenton, New Jersey.

sympathetic you feel. Comfort him reassuringly, but keep your wits about you. Before getting him to the veterinarian try to alleviate the pain and shock.

If you can take even a minor step in this direction it will be a help toward the final cure. Listed here are a few of the emergencies which might occur and what you can do AFTER you have called the vet and told him you are coming.

BURNS

If you have been so foolish as not to turn your pot handles toward the back of the stove—for your children's sake as well as your dog's— and the dog is burned, apply ice or ice cold water and treat for shock. Electrical or chemical burns are treated the same; but with an acid or alkali burn, use, respectively, a bicarbonate of soda or vinegar solution. Check the advisability of covering the burn when you call the veterinarian.

DROWNING

Most animals love the water, but sometimes get in "over their heads." Should your dog take in too much water, hold him upside down and open his mouth so that water can empty from the lungs, then apply artificial respiration, or mouth-to-mouth resuscitation. Then treat for shock by covering him with a blanket, administering a stimulant such as coffee with sugar, and soothing him with voice and hand.

FITS AND CONVULSIONS

Prevent the dog from thrashing about and injuring himself, cover with a blanket and hold down until you can get him to the veterinarian.

FROSTBITE

There is no excuse for an animal getting frostbite if you are on your toes and care for the animal. However, should frostbite set in, thaw out the affected area slowly with a circulatory motion and stimulation. Use vaseline to help keep the skin from peeling off and/or drying out.

HEART ATTACK

Be sure the animal keeps breathing by applying artificial respiration. A mild stimulant may be used and give him plenty of air. Treat for shock as well, and get to the veterinarian quickly.

Snowy and Roy Anderson in Australia.

SUFFOCATION

Artificial respiration and treat for shock with plenty of air.

SUN STROKE

Cooling the dog off immediately is essential. Ice packs, submersion in ice water, and plenty of cool air are needed.

WOUNDS

Open wounds or cuts which produce bleeding must be treated with hydrogen peroxide and tourniquets should be used if bleeding is excessive. Also, shock treatment must be given, and the animal must be kept warm.

Ch. Silver Spray of Wychwood, bred and owned by Bernice Ashdown of Long Island, pictured winning several years ago under judge Charles Schwartz. Photo by Evelyn M. Shafer.

THE FIRST AID KIT

It would be sheer folly to try to operate a kennel or to keep a dog without providing for certain emergencies that are bound to crop up when there are active dogs around. Just as you would provide a first aid kit for people you should also provide a first aid kit for the animals on the premises.

The first aid kit should contains the following items:

> BFI or other medicated powder
> jar of Vaseline
> Q-tips
> bandage—1 inch gauze
> adhesive tape
> Band-Aids
> cotton
> boric acid powder

The Dingledines' Christmas card one year featured this lovely photograph signed by their dog Sniejok. The Dingledines live in New England.

A trip to your veterinarian is always safest, but there are certain preliminaries for cuts and bruises of a minor nature that you can care for yourself.

Cuts, for instance, should be washed out and medicated powder or Vaseline applied with a bandage. The lighter the bandage the better so that the most air possible can reach the wound. Q-tips can be used for removing debris from the eyes after which a mild solution of boric acid wash can be applied. As for sores, use dry powder on wet sores, and Vaseline on dry sores. Use cotton for washing out wounds and drying them.

A particular caution must be given here on bandaging. Make sure that the bandage is not too tight to hamper the dog's circulation. Also, make sure the bandage is made correctly so that the dog does not bite at it trying to get it off. A great deal of damage can be done to a wound by a dog tearing at a bandage to get it off. If you notice the dog is starting to bite at it, do it over or put something on the bandage that smells and tastes bad to him. Make sure, however, that the solution does not soak through the bandage and enter the wound. Sometimes, if it is a leg wound, a sock or stocking slipped on the dog's leg will cover the bandage edges and will also keep it clean.

HOW NOT TO POISON YOUR DOG

Ever since the appearance of Rachel Carson's book *Silent Spring,* people have been asking, "Just how dangerous are chemicals?" In the animal world where disinfectants, room deodorants, parasitic sprays, solutions and aerosols are so widely used, the question has taken on even more meaning. Veterinarians are beginning to ask, "What kind of disinfectant do you use?" or "Have you any fruit trees that have been sprayed recently?" When animals are brought in to their offices in a toxic condition, or for unexplained death, or when entire litters of puppies die mysteriously, there is good reason to ask such questions.

The popular practice of protecting animals against parasites has given way to their being exposed to an alarming number of commercial products, some of which are dangerous to their very lives. Even flea collars can be dangerous, especially if they get wet or somehow touch the genital regions or eyes. While some products are a great deal more poisonous than others, great care must be taken that they be applied in proportion to the size of the dog and the area to be covered. Many a dog has been taken to the vet with an unusual skin problem that was a direct result of having been bathed with a detergent rather than a proper shampoo. Certain products that are safe for dogs can be fatal for cats. Extreme care must be taken to read all ingredients and instructions carefully before use on any animal.

The same caution must be given to outdoor chemicals. Dog owners must question the use of fertilizers on their lawns. Lime, for in-

The lovely Ch. Silver Scion of Wychwood taking Best of Breed at a Morris and Essex Kennel Club Show several years ago.

stance, can be harmful to a dog's feet. The unleashed dog that covers the neighborhood on his daily rounds is open to all sorts of tree and lawn sprays and insecticides that may prove harmful to him, if not as a poison, as a producer of an allergy. Many puppy fatalities are reported when they consume mothballs.

There are various products found around the house which can be lethal, such as rat poison, boric acid, hand soap, detergents, and insecticides. The garage too may provide dangers: antifreeze for the car, lawn, garden and tree sprays, paints, etc., are all available for tipping over and consuming. All poisons should be placed on high shelves for the sake of your children as well as your animals.

Perhaps the most readily available of all household poisons are plants. Household plants are almost all poisonous, even if taken in small quantities. Some of the most dangerous are the elephant ear, the narcissus bulb, any kind of ivy leaves, burning bush leaves, the jimson weed, the dumb cane weed, mock orange fruit, castor beans, Scotch broom seeds, the root or seed of the plant called four o'clock, cyclamen, pimpernel, lily of the valley, the stem of the sweet pea, rhododendrons of any kind, spider lily bulbs, bayonet root, foxglove leaves, tulip bulbs, monkshood roots, azalea, wisteria, poinsettia leaves, mistletoe, hemlock, locoweed and arrowglove. In all, there are over 500 poisonous plants in the United States. Peach, elderberry and cherry trees can cause cyanide poisoning if the bark is consumed. Rhubarb leaves either raw or cooked can cause death or violent convulsions. Check out your closets, fields and grounds around your home to see what might be of danger to your pets.

Mrs. Walter (Judy) Schirber of Freehold, New Jersey poses at the gate with Kiska IX and Kira, whose registered name is Windom's Cameo of Silversea. This is the photograph Judy chose to use to accompany the column she writes for *Popular Dogs* magazine.

The exquisite Nanci—pictured in 1929 with a litter of Sammy puppies and two family friends which were ever so camera shy! Nanci was owned by the late Catherine L. Quereaux, a New York City lawyer.

Mr. Forbes, Maintenance Manager of O'Hare International Airport in Chicago and owner of Pratika of Top Acres, one of five litter sisters named by the Shah of Iran during a visit to Samoyed fancier General Allen at Fort Knox, Kentucky. The Shah gave them all names of white flowers (*Pratika* means white rose). Pratika is pictured here with Mr. Forbes' daughter and some of Pratika's many trophies and ribbons.

SYMPTOMS OF POISONING

Be on the lookout for vomiting, hard or labored breathing, whimpering, stomach cramps, and trembling as a prelude to the convulsions. Any delay in a visit to your veterinarian can mean death. Take along the bottle or package or a sample of the plant you suspect to be the cause to help the veterinarian determine the correct antidote.

The most common type of poisoning, which accounts for nearly one-fourth of all animal victims, is staphylococcic-infected food. Salmonella ranks third. These can be avoided by serving fresh food and not letting it lie around in hot weather.

There are also many insect poisonings caused by animals eating cockroaches, spiders, flies, butterflies, etc. Toads and some frogs give off a fluid which can make a dog foam at the mouth—and even kill him—if he bites just a little too hard!

Some misguided dog owners think it is "cute" to let their dogs enjoy a cocktail with them before dinner. There can be serious effects resulting from encouraging a dog to drink—sneezing fits, injuries as a result of intoxication, and heart stoppage are just a few. Whiskey for medicinal purposes or beer for brood bitches should be administered only on the advice of your veterinarian.

There have been cases of severe damage and death when dogs emptied ash trays and consumed cigarettes, resulting in nicotine poisoning. Leaving a dog alone all day in a house where there are cigarettes available on a coffee table is asking for trouble. Needless to say, the same applies to marijuana. The narcotic addict who takes his dog along with him on "a trip" does not deserve to have a dog. All the ghastly side effects are as possible for the dog as for the addict, and for a person to submit an animal to this indignity is indeed despicable. Don't think it doesn't happen. Ask the veterinarians that practice near some of your major hippie havens! Unfortunately, in all our major cities the practice is becoming more and more a problem for the veterinarian.

Be on the alert and remember that in the case of any type of poisoning, the best treatment is prevention.

Ch. Pratikas Pilot, magnificent male Samoyed who piled up an impressive array of Bests of Breed during his campaigning in 1957. Photo by Norton of Kent.

THE CURSE OF ALLERGY

The heartbreak of a child being forced to give up a beloved pet because he is suddenly found to be allergic to it is a sad but true story. Many families claim to be unable to have dogs at all; others seem to be able only to enjoy them on a restricted basis. Many children know animals only through occasional visits to a friend's house or the zoo.

While modern veterinary science has produced some brilliant allergists, such as Dr. Edward Baker of New Jersey, the field is still working on a solution for those who suffer from exposure to their pets. There is no permanent cure as yet.

Over the last quarter of a century there have been many attempts at a permanent cure, but none has proven successful, because the treatment was needed too frequently, or was too expensive to maintain over extended periods of time.

Marie Stukey, daughter of Bill Stukey, American Kennel Club representative for many years, and her Tazson's Snow King pictured when he was thirteen months of age. Marie Stukey is a grown woman now and lives in California.

However, we find that most people who are allergic to their animals are also allergic to a variety of other things as well. By eliminating the other irritants, and by taking medication given for the control of allergies in general, many are able to keep pets on a restricted basis. This may necessitate the dog's living outside the house, being groomed at a professional grooming parlor instead of by the owner, or merely being kept out of the bedroom at night. A discussion of this "balance" factor with your medical and veterinary doctors may give new hope to those willing to try.

A paper presented by Mathilde M. Gould, M.D., a New York allergist, before the American Academy of Allergists in the 1960's, and reported in the September-October 1964 issue of the *National Humane Review* magazine, offered new hope to those who are allergic by a method referred to as hyposensitization. You may wish to write to the magazine and request the article for discussion with your medical and veterinary doctors on your individual problem.

272

Ch. Silveracres Ivan wins Best of Breed at the Chicago International Kennel Club Show in April, 1970. "John" is handled by Leslie Lueck and owned by Joan Lueck of Oxford, Michigan. Mr. Lueck is the present American Kennel Club delegate for the Samoyed Club of America. Photo by William P. Gilbert.

Part of the teething process. . . puppies chew on everything and anything! For their own safety and your own peace of mind, make sure that any teething playthings you provide are veterinary-approved. This little fellow busily working on a rug is owned by Dick and Joan Peskin of Clinton, New Jersey.

DO ALL DOGS CHEW?

All young dogs chew! Chewing is the best possible method of cutting teeth and exercising gums. Every puppy goes through this teething process. True, it can be destructive if not watched carefully, and it is really the responsibility of every owner to prevent the damage before it occurs.

When you see a puppy pick up an object to chew, immediately remove it from his mouth with a sharp "No!" and replace the object with a Nylon or rawhide bone which should be provided for him to do his serious chewing. Puppies take anything and everything into their mouths so they should be provided with proper toys which they cannot chew up and swallow.

BONES

There are many opinions on the kind of bones a dog should have. Anyone who has lost a puppy or dog because of a bone chip puncturing the stomach or intestinal wall will say "no bones" except for the

Nylon or rawhide kind you buy in pet shops. There are those who say shank or knuckle bones are permissible. Use your own judgment, but when there are adequate processed bones which you know to be safe, why risk a valuable animal? Cooked bones, soft enough to be pulverized and put in the food can be fed if they are reduced almost to a powder. If you have the patience for this sort of thing, okay. Otherwise, stick to the commercial products.

As for dogs and puppies chewing furniture, shoes, etc., replace the object with something allowable and safe and put yourself on record as remembering to close closet doors. Keep the puppy in the same room with you so you can stand guard over the furniture.

Electrical cords and sockets, or wires of any kind, present a dangerous threat to chewers. Glass dishes which can be broken are hazardous if not picked up right after feeding.

Chewing can also be a form of frustration or nervousness. Dogs sometimes chew for spite, if owners leave them alone too long or too often. Bitches will sometimes chew if their puppies are taken away from them too soon; insecure puppies often chew thinking they're nursing. Puppies which chew wool or blankets or carpet corners or certain types of materials may have a nutritional deficiency or something lacking in their diet, such as craving the starch that might be left in material after washing. Perhaps the articles have been near something that tastes good and they retain the odor.

The act of chewing has no connection with particular breeds or ages, any more than there is a logical reason for dogs to dig holes outdoors or dig on wooden floors indoors.

So we repeat, it is up to you to be on guard at all times until the need—or habit—passes.

HIP DYSPLASIA

Hip dysplasia, or HD, is one of the most widely discussed of all animal afflictions, since it has appeared in varying degrees in just about every breed of dog. True, the larger breeds seem most susceptible, but it has hit the small breeds and is beginning to be recognized in cats as well.

While HD in man has been recorded as far back as 370 B.C., HD in dogs was more than likely referred to as rheumatism until veterinary research came into the picture. In 1935, Dr. Otto Schales, at Angell Memorial Hospital in Boston, wrote a paper on hip dysplasia and classified the four degrees of dysplasia of the hip joint as follows:

Grade 1—slight (poor fit between ball and socket)

Grade 2—moderate (moderate but obvious shallowness of the socket)

Grade 3—severe (socket quite flat)

Grade 4—very severe (complete displacement of head of femur at early age)

HD is an incurable, hereditary, though not congenital disease of the hip sockets. It is transmitted as a dominant trait with irregular manifestations. Puppies appear normal at birth but the constant wearing away of the socket means the animal moves more and more on muscle, thereby presenting a lameness, a difficulty in getting up and severe pain in advanced cases.

The degree of severity can be determined around six months of age, but its presence can be noticed from two months of age. The problem is determined by X-ray, and if pain is present it can be relieved temporarily by medication. Exercise should be avoided since motion encourages the wearing away of the bone surfaces.

Dogs with HD should not be shown or bred, if quality in the breed is to be maintained. It is essential to check a pedigree for dogs known to be dysplastic before breeding, since this disease can be dormant for many generations.

ELBOW DYSPLASIA

The same condition can also affect the elbow joints and is known as elbow dysplasia. This also causes lameness, and dogs so affected should not be used for breeding.

PATELLAR DYSPLASIA

Some of the smaller breeds of dogs also suffer from patella dysplasia, or dislocation of the knee. This can be treated surgically, but the surgery by no means abolishes the hereditary factor. Therefore, these dogs should not be used for breeding.

All dogs—in any breed—should be X-rayed before being used for breeding. The X-ray should be read by a competent veterinarian, and the dog declared free and clear.

HD PROGRAM IN GREAT BRITAIN

The British Veterinary Association (BVA) has made an attempt to control the spread of HD by appointing a panel of members of their profession who have made a special study of the disease to read X-rays. Dogs over one year of age may be X-rayed and certified as free. Forms are completed in triplicate to verify the tests. One copy remains with the panel, one copy is for the owner's veterinarian, and one for the owner. A record is also sent to the British Kennel Club for those wishing to check on a particular dog for breeding purposes.

THE UNITED STATES REGISTRY

In the United States we have a central Hip Dysplasia Foundation, known as the OFA (Orthopedic Foundation for Animals). This HD control registry was formed in 1966. X-rays are sent for expert evaluation by qualified radiologists.

Champion Alta of the Deep Powder, owned by Ann C. Hamlin of California and photographed by the noted dog photographer Joan Ludwig.

All you need do for complete information on getting an X-ray for your dog is to write to the Orthopedic Foundation for Animals at 817 Virginia Ave., Columbia, Mo., 65201, and request their dysplasia packet. There is no charge for this kit. It contains an envelope large enough to hold your X-ray film (which you will have taken by your own veterinarian), and a drawing showing how to position the dog properly for X-ray. There is also an application card for proper identification of the dog. Then, hopefully, your dog will be certified "normal." You will be given a registry number which you can put on his pedigree, use in your advertising, and rest assured your breeding program is in good order.

All X-rays should be sent to the address above. Any other information you might wish to have may be requested from Mrs. Robert Bower, OFA, Route 1, Constantine, Mo., 49042.

We cannot urge strongly enough the importance of doing this. While it involves time and effort, the reward in the long run will more than pay for your trouble. To see the heartbreak of parents and children when their beloved dog has to be put to sleep because of severe hip dysplasia as the result of bad breeding is a sad experience. Don't let this happen to you or to those who will purchase your puppies!

Additionally, we should mention that there is a method of palpation to determine the extent of affliction. This can be painful if the animal is not properly prepared for the examination. There have also been attempts to replace the animal's femur and socket. This is not only expensive, but the percentage of success is small.

For those who refuse to put their dog down, there is a new surgical technique which can relieve pain, but in no way constitutes a cure. This technique involves the severing of the pectinius muscle which for some unknown reason brings relief from pain over a period of many months—even up to two years. Two veterinary colleges in the United States are performing this operation at the present time. However, the owner must also give permission to "de-sex" the dogs at the time of the muscle severance. This is a safety measure to help stamp out hip dysplasia, since obviously the condition itself remains and can be passed on.

17. THE BLIGHT OF PARASITES

Anyone who has ever spent countless hours peering down intently at his dog's warm, pink stomach waiting for a flea to appear will readily understand why we call this chapter the "blight of parasites." For it is that dreaded onslaught of the pesky flea that heralds the subsequent arrival of worms.

If you have seen even one flea scoot across that vulnerable expanse of skin you can be sure there are more fleas lurking on other favorite areas of your dog. They seldom travel alone. So it is now an established fact that *la puce*, as the French would say when referring to the flea, has set up housekeeping on your dog and it is going to demand a great deal of your time before you manage to evict them completely, and probably just temporarily, no matter which species your dog is harboring.

Fleas are not always choosy about their host, but chances are your dog has what is commonly known as *Ctenocephalides canis*, the dog flea. If you are a lover of cats also, your dog might even be playing host to a few *Ctenocephalides felis*, the cat flea, or vice versa! The only thing you can be really sure of is that your dog is supporting an entire community of them, all hungry and all sexually oriented, and you are going to have to be persistent in your campaign to get rid of them.

One of the chief reasons they are so difficult to catch is that what they lack in beauty and eyesight (they are blind at birth, throughout infancy and see very poorly or are blind during adulthood,) they make up for in their fantastic ability to jump and scurry about.

While this remarkable ability to jump—some say 150 times the length of their bodies—stands them in good stead with circus entrepeneurs and has given them claim to fame as chariot pullers and acrobats in side show attractions, the dog owner can be reduced to tears at the very thought of the onset of fleas.

Modern research has provided a remedy in the form of flea sprays, dips, collars and tags which can be successful in varying degrees. But there are those who swear by the good old-fashioned methods of removing them by hand, which can be a challenge to your sanity as well as your dexterity.

Ch. Barney Boy won points toward his championship at the Chicago International show in 1952. Barney was from the Snowland bloodlines owned by Mrs. Harris of Philadelphia.

A uniform litter of Samoyed puppies sired by Canadian and American Ch. Noatak of Silver Moon *ex* Ch. Orions Capella of Tsar-Khan. Bred and owned by Patricia Morehouse, Kubla Khan Kennels in Los Angeles. Photo by Joan Ludwig.

Since the fleas' conformation (they are built like envelopes, long and flat) with their spiny skeletal system on the outside of their bodies is specifically provided for slithering through hair forests, they are given a distinct advantage to start with. Two antennae on the head select the best spot for digging and then two mandibles penetrate the skin and hit a blood vessel. It is also at this moment that the flea brings into play his spiny contours to prop himself against a few surrounding hairs which prevent him from being scratched off as he puts the bite on your dog. A small tubular tongue is then lowered into the hole to draw out blood and another tube is injected into the hole to pump the saliva of the flea into the wound which prevents the blood from clotting. This allows the flea to drink freely. Simultaneously your dog jumps into the air and gets one of those back legs into action scratching endlessly and in vain.

Now while you may catch an itinerant flea as he mistakenly shortcuts across your dog's stomach, the best hunting grounds are usually in the deep fur down along the dog's back from neck to the base of the tail. However, the flea like every other creature on earth must have water, so several times during its residency it will make its way to the moister areas of your dog, such as the corners of the mouth, the eyes or the genital areas. This is when the flea collars and tags are useful. The fumes from them prevent the fleas from passing the neck to get to the head of your dog.

Your dog can usually support several generations of fleas if he doesn't scratch himself to death or go out of his mind with the itching in the interim. The population of the flea is insured by the strong mating instinct and the wise personal decision of the female flea as to the best time to deposit her eggs. She has the useful capacity to store semen until the time is right to lay the eggs after some previous brief encounter with a passing member of the opposite sex.

When that time comes for her to lay the eggs, she does so without so much as a backward glance and moves on. The dog, during a normal day's wandering, shakes the eggs off along his way, and there the eggs remain until hatched and the baby fleas are ready to jump back on a dog. If any of the eggs remain on the dog, chances are your dog will help them emerge from their shells with his scratching when some adult flea passes in the vicinity.

Larval fleas look like very small and slender maggots; they begin their lives feasting off their own egg shells until your dog comes along and offers the return to the world of adult fleas, whose excrement provides the predigested blood pellets they must have to thrive. They cannot survive on fresh blood, nor are they capable at this tender age of digging for it themselves. We are certain that the expression "two can eat as cheaply as one" originated after some curious scientist made a detailed study of the life cycle of the flea.

After a couple of weeks of this free loading, the baby flea makes his own cocoon and becomes a pupa. This stage lasts long enough for the larval flea to grow legs, mandibles, and sharp spines and to flatten out and in general get to be identifiable as the commonly known and obnoxious *Ctenocephalides canis*. The process can take several weeks or several months, depending on weather conditions, heat, moisture, etc., but generally three weeks is all that is required to enable it to start chomping on your dog in its own right.

And so the life of the flea is renewed and begun again, and if you don't have plans to stem the tide, you will certainly see a population explosion that will make the human one resemble an endangered species. Getting rid of fleas can be accomplished by the aforementioned spraying of the dog, or the flea collars and tags, but air, sunshine and a good shaking out of beds, bedding, carpets, cushions, etc., certainly must be undertaken to get rid of the eggs or larvae lying around the premises.

However, if you love the thrill of the chase, and have the stomach for it, you can still try to catch them on safari across your dog's stomach. Your dog will love the attention, that is, if you don't keep pinching a bit of skin instead of that little blackish critter. Chances are

Pictured at eight weeks of age is Ch. Tempest of Misty Way with two litter mates and proud owner. Tempest was Top Brood Bitch in the breed in 1968. Photo by Joe Matheson.

"Hey, want to watch TV with me?" Three-month-old Oakwood Farm's Diko Kafana invites company. The sire was American and Canadian Ch. Oakwood Farm's Kari J'Go Diko and the breeder Joan Lueck of Oxford, Michigan.

great you will come up with skin rather than the flea and your dog will lose interest and patience.

Should you be lucky enough to get hold of one, you must either squeeze it to death (which isn't likely) or break it in two with a sharp, strong fingernail (which also isn't likely) or you must release it *underwater* in the toilet bowl and flush immediately. This prospect is only slightly more likely. We strongly suggest that you shape up, clean up, shake out and spray—on a regular basis.

There are those people, however, who are much more philosophical about the flea, since, like the cockroach, it has been around since the beginning of the world. For instance, that old-time philosopher, David Harum, who has been much quoted with his remark, "A reasonable amount of fleas is good for a dog. They keep him from broodin' on bein' a dog." We would rather agree with John Donne who in his *Devotions* reveals that, "The flea, though he kill none, he does all the harm he can." This is especially true if your dog is a show dog! If the scratching doesn't ruin the coat, the inevitable infestations of the parasites the fleas will leave with your dog will!

So we readily see that dogs can be afflicted by both internal and external parasites. The external parasites are known as the aforementioned fleas, plus ticks and lice; while all of these are bothersome, they can be treated. However, the internal parasites, or worms of various kinds, are usually well-infested before discovery and require more substantial means of ridding the dog of them completely.

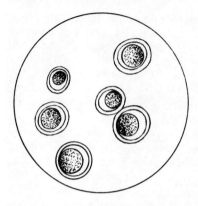

**Round Worm
(Ascarid)**

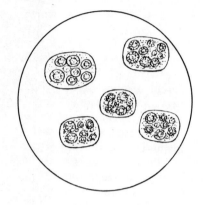

Tapeworm

Hookworm

Whipworm

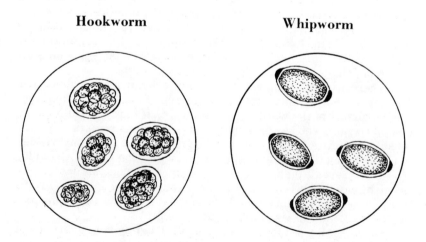

Eggs of certain parasites commonly seen in dogs.

INTERNAL PARASITES

The most common worms are the round worms. These, like many other worms, are carried and spread by the flea and go through a cycle within the dog host. They are excreted in egg or larval form and passed on to other dogs in this manner.

Worm medicine should be prescribed by a veterinarian, and dogs should be checked for worms at least twice a year, or every three months if there is a known epidemic in your area, and during the summer months when fleas are plentiful.

Major types of worms are hookworms, whipworms, tapeworms (the only non-round worm in this list), ascarids (the "typical" round worms), heartworms, kidney and lung worms. Each can be peculiar to a part of the country or may be carried by a dog from one area to another. Kidney and lung worms are quite rare, fortunately. The others are not. Symptoms for worms might be vomiting intermittently, eating grass, lack of pep, bloated stomach, rubbing their tail along the ground, loss of weight, dull coat, anemia and pale gums, eye discharge, or unexplained nervousness and irritability. A dog with worms will usually eat twice as much as he normally would also.

Never worm a sick dog, or a pregnant bitch after the first two weeks she has been bred, and never worm a constipated dog. . . it will retain the strong medicine within the body for too long a time. The best, safest way to determine the presence of worms is to test for them before they do excessive damage.

HOW TO TEST FOR WORMS

Worms can kill your dog if the infestation is severe enough. Even light infestations of worms can debilitate a dog to the point where he is more susceptible to other serious diseases that can kill, if the worms do not.

Today's medication for worming is relatively safe and mild, and worming is no longer the traumatic experience for either dog or owner that it used to be. Great care must be given, however, to the proper administration of the drugs. Correct dosage is a "must" and clean quarters are essential to rid your kennel of these parasites. It is almost impossible to find an animal that is completely free of parasites, so we must consider worming as a necessary evil.

However mild today's medicines may be, it is inadvisable to worm a dog unnecessarily. There are simple tests to determine the presence of worms and this chapter is designed to help you learn how to make these tests yourself. Veterinarians charge a nominal fee for this service, if it is not part of their regular office visit examination. It is a simple matter to prepare fecal slides that you can read yourself on a periodic basis. Over the years it will save you much time and money, especially if you have more than one dog or a large kennel.

All that is needed by way of equipment is a microscope with 100x power. These can be purchased in the toy department in a department or regular toy store for a few dollars, depending on what else you want to get with it, but the basic, least expensive sets come with the necessary glass slides and attachments.

After the dog has defecated, take an applicator stick, or a toothpick with a flat end, or even an old-fashioned wooden matchstick, and gouge off a piece of the stool about the size of a small pea. Have one of the glass slides ready with a large drop of water on it. Mix the two together until you have a cloudy film over a large area of the slide. This smear should be covered with another slide, or a cover slip—though it is possible to obtain readings with just the one open slide. Place your slide under the microscope and prepare to focus in on it. To read the slide you will find that your eye should follow a certain pattern. Start at the top and read from left to right, then right back to the left side and then left over to the right side once again until you have looked at every portion of the slide from the top left to the bottom right side, as illustrated here:

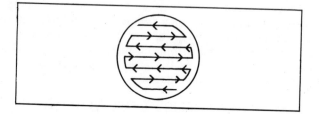

Make sure that your smear is not too thick or watery or the reading will be too dark and confused to make proper identification. Included in this chapter are drawings which will show you what to look for when reading the slides to identify the four most common varieties of worms. If you decide you would rather not make your own fecal examinations, but would prefer to have the veterinarian do it, the proper way to present a segment of the stool for him to examine is as follows:

After the dog has defecated, a portion of the stool, say a square inch from different sections of it, should be placed in a glass jar or plastic container, and labeled with the dog's name and address of the owner. If the sample cannot be examined within three to four hours after passage, it should be refrigerated. Your opinion as to what variety of worms you suspect is sometimes helpful to the veterinarian and may be noted on the label of the jar you submit to him for the examination.

Checking for worms on a regular basis is advisable not only for the welfare of the dog but for the protection of your family, since most worms are transmissible, under certain circumstances, to humans.

18. DICTIONARY OF DOG DISEASES

AN AID TO DIAGNOSIS
—A—

ABORTION—The premature expulsion of embryos from the uterus. If part of a fetus is left in the uterus, serious infection may occur. The first indication of this will be high fever, dry nose and lethargy. The immediate services of a veterinarian are necessary.

ABSCESS—A skin eruption characterized by a localized collection of pus formed as a result of disintegrating tissues of the body. Abscesses may be acute or chronic. An acute abscess forms rapidly and will more than likely burst within a week. It is accompanied by pain, redness, heat and swelling, and may cause a rise in temperature. An abscess is usually the result of infection of a bacterial nature. Treatment consists of medication in the form of antibiotics and salves, ointments, powders or a poultice designed to bring it to a head. A chronic abscess is a slow-developing headless lump surrounded by gathering tissue. This infection is usually of internal origin, and painless unless found in a sensitive area of the body. The same antibiotics and medications are used. Because abscesses of this nature are slow in developing, they are generally slow in dissolving.

ACARUS—One of the parasitic mites which cause mange.

ACHONDROPLASIA—A disease which results in the stunting of growth, or dwarfing of the limbs before birth.

ADENOMA—A non-inflammatory growth or benign tumor found in a prominent gland; most commonly found in the mammary gland of the bitch.

AGALACTIA—A contagious, viral disease resulting in lowered or no production of milk by a nursing bitch. It usually appears in warm weather, and is accompanied by fever and loss of appetite. Abscesses may also form. In chronic cases the mammary gland itself may atrophy.

ALARIASIS—An infection caused by flukes (*Alaria arisaemoides*), which are ingested by the dog. They pass on to the bronchial tract and into the small intestine where they grow to maturity and feed on intestinal contents.

Snow King's Bear Wolf, one-year-old Samoyed owned by the Snow King Samoyed Kennels of Stuart J. Rein, Bowie, Maryland.

Ch. Beau Geste of Misty Way pictured winning first in American-bred Class and Reserve Winners Dog at the September, 1972 Los Angeles Specialty Show under judge Charles Hamilton. Handler is J. Masley. Sire was Ch. Star's Boloff of Altai *ex* Ch. Silver Trinkets of Misty Way. Owned by the Misty Way Kennels. Photo by Joan Ludwig.

Saint Barbello of Top Acres shown with Wayne Gillette at a March, 1957 dog show in Indianapolis, where he was Winners Dog on that day.

ALLERGY—Dogs can be allergic as well as people to outdoor or indoor surroundings, such as carpet fuzz, pillow stuffings, food, pollen, etc. Recent experiments in hyposensitization have proved effective in many cases when injections are given with follow-up "boosters." Sneezing, coughing, nasal discharges, runny, watery eyes, etc., are all symptomatic.

ALOPECIA—A bare spot, or lack of full growth of hair on a portion of the body; another name for baldness and can be the end result of a skin condition.

AMAUROSIS—Sometimes called "glass eye." A condition that may occur during a case of distemper if the nervous system has been affected, or head injuries sustained. It is characterized by the animal bumping into things or by a lack of coordination. The condition is incurable and sooner or later the optic nerve becomes completely paralyzed.

ANALGESIA—Loss of ability to feel pain with the loss of consciousness or the power to move a part of the body. The condition may be induced by drugs which act on the brain or central nervous system.

ANAL SAC OBSTRUCTION—The sacs on either side of the rectum, just inside the anus, at times may become clogged. If the condition persists, it is necessary for the animal to be assisted in their opening, so that they do not become infected and/or abscess. Pressure is applied by the veterinarian and the glands release a thick, horrible-smelling excretion. Antibiotics or a "flushing" of the glands if infected is the usual treatment, but at the first sign of discomfort in the dog's eliminating, or a "sliding along" the floor, it is wise to check for clogged anal glands.

ANASARCA—Dropsy of the connective tissues of the skin. It is occasionally encountered in fetuses and makes whelping difficult.

ANEMIA—A decrease of red blood cells which are the cells that carry oxygen to the body tissues. Causes are usually severe infestation of parasites, bad diet, or blood disease. Transfusions and medications can be given to replace red blood cells, but the disease is sometimes fatal.

ANEURYSM—A rupture or dilation of a major blood vessel, causing a bulge or swelling of the affected part. Blood gathers in the tissues forming a swelling. It may be caused by strain, injury, or when arteries are weakened by debilitating disease or old age. Surgery is needed to remove the clot.

ANESTROUS—When a female does not come into heat.

ANTIPERISTALSIS—A term given to the reverse action of the normal procedures of the stomach or intestine, which brings their contents closer to the mouth.

ANTIPYRETICS—Drugs or methods used to reduce temperature during fevers. These may take the form of cold baths, purgatives, etc.

ANTISPASMODICS—Medications which reduce spasms of the muscular tissues and soothe the nerves and muscles involved.

ANTISIALICS—Term applied to substances used to reduce excessive salivation.

ARSENIC POISONING—Dogs are particularly susceptible to this type of poisoning. There is nausea, vomiting, stomach pains and convulsions, even death in severe cases. An emetic may save the animal in some cases. Salt or dry mustard (1 tablespoon mixed with 1 teaspoonful of water) can be effective in causing vomiting until the veterinarian is reached.

A lovely candid picture of the Schirbers' Kiska IX at a Fourth of July barbecue in 1970, when she was two years and ten months old. The Schirbers own the Warlord Samoyeds in Freehold, New Jersey.

Ch. Suffolk Prince Taiga, bred by George Price and owned by Dr. Charles Wright, is pictured following his Winners Dog win at the Westchester Kennel Club show in 1970 on the way to championship. The sire was Suffolk Nik *ex* Suffolk Snowflake.

Ch. Sam O'Khan's Kubla Khan, owned by Patricia Morehouse of Los Angeles, California and photographed by Joan Ludwig. Khan was top Samoyed sire in 1971 according to *Kennel Review* magazine and has sired eleven American and one Canadian champion to date. He was first in Stud Dog Class at the 1972 National Specialty and first in Stud Dog Class at the Samoyed Specialty in San Diego in 1973. His sire was American and Canadian Ch. Noatak of Silver Moon; bred by Francis FitzPatrick.

Two of the Sterling Hills' children with part of a litter of Sammys sired by Ruth Young's Silver Flare of Wychwood.

ARTHRITIS—A painful condition of the joints which results in irritation and inflammation. A disease that pretty much confines itself to older dogs, especially in the larger breeds. Limping, irritability and pain are symptomatic. Anti-inflammatory drugs are effective after X-ray determines the severity. Heat and rest are helpful.

ASCITES—A collection of serous fluid in the abdominal cavity, causing swelling. It may be a result of heavy parasitic infestation or a symptom of liver, kidney, tuberculosis or heart diseases.

ASPERGILLOSIS—A disease contracted from poultry and often mistaken for tuberculosis since symptoms are quite similar. It attacks the nervous system and sometimes has disastrous effects on the respiratory system. This fungus growth in the body tissue spreads quickly and is accompanied by convulsions. The dog rubs his nose and there is a bloody discharge.

ASTHMA—Acute distress in breathing. Attacks may occur suddenly at irregular intervals and last as long as half an hour. The condition may be hereditary or due to allergy or heart condition. Antihistamines are effective in minor attacks.

ATAXIA—Muscular incoordination or lack of movement causing an inhibited gait, although the necessary organs and muscle power are coherent. The dog may have a tendency to stagger.

ATOPY—Manifestations of atopy in the dog are a persistent scratching of the eyes and nose. Onsets are usually seasonal—the dog allergic to, say, ragweed will develop the condition when ragweed is in season, or say, house dust all year round. Most dogs afflicted with atopy are multi-sensitive and are affected by something several months out of the year. Treatment is by antihistamines or systemic corticosteroids, or both.

Off and running for a frolic in the backyard! Photographer Harold Mc-
Laughlin of Morrison, Colorado, captures his Sammy on film as he
takes off for some exercise.

—B—

BABESIA GIBSONI (or Babesiosis)—A parasitic disease of the
tropics, reasonably rare in the U.S.A. to date. Blood tests can re-
veal its presence and like other parasitic infections the symptoms
are loss of appetite, no pep, anemia and elevations in temperature
as the disease advances, and enlarged spleen and liver are sometimes evident.

BALANITIS—The medical term for a constant discharge of pus from the penis which causes spotting of clothing or quarters or causes the dog to clean himself constantly. When bacteria gather at the end of the sheath, it causes irritations in the tissue and pus. If the condition becomes serious, the dog may be cauterized or ointment applied.

BLASTOMYCOSIS—A rare infectious disease involving the kidneys and liver. The animal loses its appetite and vomits. Laboratory examination is necessary to determine presence.

BRADYCARDIA—Abnormal slowness of the heartbeat and pulse.

BRONCHITIS—Inflammation of the mucus lining in the respiratory tract, the windpipe or trachea, and lungs. Dampness and cold are usually responsible and the symptoms usually follow a chill, or may be present with cases of pneumonia or distemper. Symptoms are a nagging dry cough, fever, quickened pulse rate, runny nose, perhaps vomiting, and congested nasal passages which must be kept open. Old dogs are particularly affected. It is a highly transmissible disease and isolation from other animals is important. Antibiotics are given.

BRUCELLA CANIS—An infectious disease associated with abortion in bitches in the last quarter of gestation, sterility or stillbirths. A comparable is testicle trouble in male dogs. It is highly contagious and can be diagnosed through blood tests and animals having the infection should be isolated.

—C—

CANCER (tumors, neoplasia, etc.)—A growth of cells which serve no purpose is referred to as a cancer. The growth may be malignant or benign. Malignancy is the spreading type growth and may invade the entire body. Treatment, if the condition is diagnosed and caught in time, may be successful by surgical methods, drugs, or radioactive therapy. Haste in consulting your veterinarian cannot be urged too strongly.

CANKER (Otitis)—A bacterial infection of the ear where the ear may drain, have a dreadful odor, and ooze a dark brown substance all the way out to the ear flap. Cause of canker can be from mites, dirt, excessive hair growth in the ear canal, wax, etc. A daily cleaning and administering of antifungal ointment or powder are in order until the condition is cured. Symptoms are the dog shaking his head, scratching his ear and holding the head to the side.

CARIES—A pathologic change causing destruction of the enamel on teeth and subsequent invasion of the dentine; in other words, a cavity in a tooth. This may result in bad breath, toothache, digestive disorders, etc., depending upon the severity. Cavities in dogs are rare, though we hear more and more of false teeth being made for dogs and occasionally even root canal work for show dogs.

CASTRATION—Surgical removal of the male gonads or sex organs. An anesthesia is necessary and the animal must be watched for at least a week to see that hemorrhage does not occur. It is best performed at an early age—anywhere from three to nine months. Older dogs suffering from a hormonal imbalance or cancer of the gonads are castrated.

CATARACT—An opaque growth covering the lens of the eye. Surgical removal is the only treatment. Cataract may be a result of an injury to the eye or in some cases may be an inherited trait.

CELLULITIS—Inflammation of the loose subcutaneous tissue of the body. A condition which can be symptomatic of several other diseases.

CHEILITIS—Inflammation of the lips.

CHOLECYSTITIS—A condition affecting the gall bladder. The onset is usually during the time an animal is suffering from infectious canine hepatitis. Removal of the gall bladder, which thickens and becomes highly vascular, can effect a complete cure.

CHOREA—Brain damage as a result of distemper which has been severe is characterized by convulsive movements of the legs. It is progressive and if it affects the facial muscles, salivating or difficulty in eating or moving the jaws may be evident. Sedatives may bring relief, but the disease is incurable.

CHOROIDITIS—Inflammation of the choroid coat of the eye which is to be regarded as serious. Immediate veterinary inspection is required.

COCCIDIOSIS—An intestinal disease of parasitic nature and origin. Microscopic organisms reproduce on the walls of the intestinal tract and destroy tissue. Bloody diarrhea, loss of weight and appetite and general lethargy result. Presence of parasites is determined by fecal examination. Sulfur drugs are administered and a complete clean up of the premises is in order since the parasite is passed from one to to another through floor surfaces or eating utensils.

COLOSTRUM—A secretion of the mammary glands for the first day or so after the bitch gives birth. It acts as a purgative for the young, and contains antibodies against distemper, hepatitis and other bacteria.

CONJUNCTIVITIS—Inflammation of the conjunctiva of the eye.

CONVULSIONS—A fit, or violent involuntary contractions of groups of muscles, accompanied by unconsciousness. They are in themselves a symptom of another disease, especially traceable to one affecting the brain; i.e., rabies, or an attack of encephalitis or distemper. It may also be the result of a heavy infestation of parasites or toxic poisonings. Care must be taken that the animal does not injure itself and a veterinarian must be consulted to determine and eliminate the cause.

Oni-Agra's Chiefson, bred by Beverly Ward and owned by the Richard Peskins, Driftwaye Samoyeds Clinton, New Jersey. The sire of this lovely six-year-old is Kobe's Oni-Agra Chief of Encino, and the dam is Mac's Snow Queen.

CRYPTORCHID—A male animal in which neither testicle is present or descended. This condition automatically bars a dog from the show ring.

CYANOSIS—A definite blueness seen in and around the mucous membranes of the face; i.e. tongue, lips and eyes. It is usually synonymous with a circulatory obstruction or heart condition.

CYSTITIS—A disease of the urinary tract which is characterized by inflammation and/or infection in the bladder. Symptoms are straining, frequent urination with little results or with traces of blood, and perhaps a fever. Antibiotics, usually in the sulfur category, as well as antiseptics are administered. This is a condition which is of great discomfort to the animal and is of lengthy duration. Relief must be given by a veterinarian, who will empty bladder by means of catheter or medication to relax the bladder so that the urine may be passed.

DEMODECTIC MANGE—A skin condition caused by a parasitic mite, *Demodex*, living in hair follicles. This is a difficult condition to get rid of and is treated internally as well as externally. It requires diligent care to free the animal of it entirely.

DERMATITIS—There are many forms of skin irritations and eruptions but perhaps the most common is "contact dermatitis." Redness and itching are present. The irritation is due to something the animal has been exposed to and to which it is allergic. The irritant must be identified and removed. Antihistamines and anti-inflammatory drugs are administered, and in severe cases sedatives or tranquilizers are prescribed to lessen the dog's scratching.

DIABETES (Insipidus)—A deficiency of antidiuretic hormone produced by the posterior pituitary gland. It occurs in older animals and is characterized by the animal's drinking excessive amounts of water and voiding frequently. Treatment is by periodic injection of an antidiuretic drug for the rest of the animal's life.

DIABETES (Mellitus)—Sometimes referred to as sugar diabetes, this is a disorder of the metabolism of carbohydrates caused by lack of insulin production by the cells of the pancreas. Symptoms are the same as in the insipidus type, and in severe cases loss of weight, vomiting or coma may occur. Blood and urine analysis confirm its presence. It is treated by low carbohydrate diet, oral medication and/or insulin injections.

Silver Rocket of Wychwood, owned by Juliette Chessor. Sire: Silver Heritage of Wychwood; dam: Zamerina of Kobe. She was bred by Bernice Ashdown. This picture shows the typical "Samoyed smile."

DIGITOXIN—A medication given to a dog with congestive heart failure. Dosage is, of course, adjusted to severeness of condition and size of the individual animal.

DISC ABNORMALITIES (Intervertebral)—Between each bone in the spine is a connecting structure called an intervertebral disc. When the disc between two vertebrae becomes irritated and protrudes into the spinal canal it forms lesions and is painful. (This is a disease which particularly affects the Dachshund because of its long back in comparison to length of legs.) Paralysis of the legs, reluctance to move, and loss of control of body functions may be symptoms. X-ray and physical examination will determine extent of the condition. Massage helps circulation and pain relievers may be prescribed. Surgery is sometimes successful and portable two-wheel carts which support the hindquarters help.

DISTEMPER—Highly transmissible disease of viral origin which spreads through secretions of nose, eyes or direct oral contact. May be fatal in puppies under 12 weeks. Symptoms of this disease are alternately high and low fevers, runny eyes and nose, loss of appetite and general lassitude, diarrhea and loss of weight. This disease sometimes goes into pneumonia or convulsions if the virus reaches the brain. Chorea may remain if infection has been severe or neglected. Antibiotics are administered and fluids and sedation may be advised by your veterinarian. If the dog has been inoculated, the disease may remain a light case, BUT it is not to be treated lightly. Warmth and rest are also indicated.

DROPSY—Abnormal accumulation of fluid in the tissues or body cavities. Also referred to as edema when accumulations manifest themselves below the skin. In the stomach region it is called ascites. Lack of exercise or poor circulation, particularly in older dogs, may be the cause. While the swellings are painless, excess accumulations in the stomach can cause digestive distress or heart disturbances, and may be associated with diabetes. Occasional diarrhea, lack of appetite, loss of weight, exhaustion, emaciation and death may occur if the condition is not treated.

DYSGERMINOMA—A malignant ovarian tumor. Symptoms are fever, vaginal discharge, vomiting and diarrhea. Tumors vary in size, though more commonly are of the large size and from reports to date, the right ovary is more commonly affected. Radiotherapy may be successful; if not, surgery is required.

—E—

EAR MANGE—Otodectic mange, or parasitic otitis externa. Ear mites suck lymph fluids through the walls of the ear canal. Infections are high when mites are present and a brownish, horrible smelling ooze is present deep down in the canal all the way out to the flap where the secretion has a granular texture. The dog shakes his head, rubs and scrapes. In extreme cases convulsions

Ch. Frost Star, C.D., owned by Ruth Young of Medway, Ohio.

or brain damage may result. The ear must be cleaned daily and drugs of an antibiotic and anti-inflammatory nature must be given.

ECLAMPSIA—A toxemia of pregnancy. Shortly before the time a bitch whelps her puppies, her milk may go bad. She will pant as a result of high fever, and go into convulsions. The puppies must be taken away from the mother immediately. This is usually the result of an extreme lack of calcium during pregnancy. Also known as milk fever.

ECTROPION—All breeders of dogs with drooping eyelids or exaggerated haws will be familiar with this condition, where the lower eyelid turns out. It can be a result of an injury, as well as hereditary in some breeds, but can be corrected surgically.

ECZEMA—Eczema is another form of skin irritation which may confine itself to redness and itching, or go all the way to a scaly skin surface or open wet sores. This is sometimes referred to as "hot spots." A hormone imbalance or actual diet deficiency may prevail. Find the cause and remove it. Medicinal baths and ointments usually provide a cure, but cure is a lengthy process and the condition frequently recurs.

EDEMA—Abnormal collections of fluids in the tissues of the body.

ELBOW DYSPLASIA—Term applies to a developmental abnormality of the elbow joints. It is hereditary.

EMPHYSEMA—Labored breathing caused by distended or ruptured lungs. May be acute or chronic and is not uncommon.

EMPYEMA—Accumulation of pus or purulent fluid, in a body cavity resembling an abscess. Another term for pleurisy.

ENCEPHALITIS—Brain fever associated with meningitis. An inflammation of the brain caused by a virus, rabies or perhaps tuberculosis. It may also be caused by poisonous plants, bad food or lead poisoning. Dogs go "wild," running in circles, falling over, etc. Paralysis and death frequently result. Cure depends on extent of infection and speed with which it is diagnosed and treated.

ENDOCARDITIS—Inflammation and bacterial infection of the smooth membrane that lines the inside of the heart.

ENTERITIS—Intestinal inflammation of serious import. It can be massive or confine itself to one spot. Symptoms are diarrhea, bloody at times, vomiting, and general discomfort. Antibiotics are prescribed and fluids, if the diarrhea and vomiting have been excessive. Causes are varied; may follow distemper or other infections or bacterial infection through intestinal worms.

A magnificent trio of Samoyeds representing three generations of champions for Joyce E. Cain of Ripon, Wisconsin.

ENTROPION—A turning in of the margin of the eyelids. As a result, the eyelashes rub on the eyeball and cause irritation resulting in a discharge from the eye. Here again it is a condition peculiar to certain breeds—particularly Chow Chows—or may be the result of an injury which failed to heal properly. Infection may result as the dog will rub his eyes and cause a swelling. It is painful, but can be cured surgically.

ENTEROTOXEMIA—A result of toxins and gases in the intestine. As bacteria increase in the intestine, intermittent diarrhea and/or constipation results from maldigestion. If the infection reaches the kidney through the circulatory system, nephritis results. The digestive system must be cleaned out by use of castor oil or colonic irrigation, and outwardly by antibiotics.

Ch. Silver Moon with a puppy in front of the fireplace with the Charles Tucker Brood Bitch Trophy which she won in 1963, 1964 and 1965. At left is the A.E. Mason Trophy won by her son, American and Canadian Ch. Noatak of Silver Moon. Owned by Robert and Bonita Bowles of Renton, Washington. Silver Moon is also the dam of Best In Show winner Ch. Star Nika Altai of Silver Moon.

Ch. Cinnamon Snow of Yate Sea, whelped in January, 1970. The sire was Ch. Yate Sea Arctic King *ex* Yate Sea White Krystal. Owners are John and Marie Gemeinhardt of Cedar Grove, New Jersey.

EOSINOPHILIC MYOSITIS—Inflammation of the muscles dogs use for chewing. Persistent attacks usually lasting one or more weeks. They come and go over long periods of time, coming closer and closer together. Difficulty in swallowing, swelling of the face, or even the dog holding his mouth open will indicate the onset of an attack. Anti-inflammatory drugs are the only known treatment. Cause unknown, outlook grave.

EPILEPSY—The brain is the area affected and fits and/or convulsions may occur early or late in life. It cannot be cured; however, it can be controlled with medication. Said to be hereditary. Convulsions may be of short duration or the dog may just appear to be dazed. It is rarely fatal. Care must be taken to see that the dog does not injure itself during an attack.

EPIPHORA—A constant tearing which stains the face and fur of dogs. It is a bothersome condition which is not easily remedied either with outside medication or by surgical tear duct removal. There has been some success in certain cases reported from a liquid medication given with the food and prescribed by veterinarians. This condition may be caused by any one or more of a number of corneal irritations, such as nasal malfunction or the presence of foreign matter in the superficial gland of the third eyelid. After complete examination as to the specific cause, a veterinarian can decide whether surgery is indicated.

ESOPHAGEAL DIVERTICULUM—Inflammation or sac-like protrusions on the walls of the esophagus resembling small hernias. It is uncommon in dogs, but operable, and characterized by gagging, listlessness, temperature and vomiting in some cases.

—F—

FALSE PREGNANCY (or pseudopregnancy)—All the signs of the real thing are present in this heart-breaking and frustrating condition. The bitch may even go into false labor near the end of the 63-day cycle and build a nest for her hoped-for puppies. It may be confirmed by X-ray or a gentle feeling for them through the stomach area. Hormones can be injected to relieve the symptoms.

FROSTBITE—Dead tissue as a result of extreme cold. The tissues become red, swollen and painful, and may peel away later, causing open lesions. Ointments and protective coverings should be administered until irritation is alleviated.

FUSOSPIROCHETAL DISEASE—Bad breath is the first and most formidable symptom of this disease of the mouth affecting the gums. Bloody saliva and gingivitis or ulcers in the mouth may also be present, and the dog may be listless due to lack of desire to eat. Cleaning the teeth and gums daily with hydrogen peroxide in prescribed dosage by the veterinarian is required. Further diagnosis of the disease can be confirmed by microscopic examination of smears, though these fusiform bacteria might be present in the mouth of a dog which never becomes infected. Attempts to culture these anaerobes have been unsuccessful.

—G—

GASTRIC DILATION—This is an abnormal swelling of the abdomen due to gas or overeating. Consumption of large amounts of food especially if dry foods are eaten, and then large quantities of water make the dog "swell." The stomach twists so that both ends are locked off. Vomiting is impossible, breathing is hampered and the dog suffers pain until the food is expelled. Dogs that gulp their food and swallow air with it are most susceptible. Immediate surgery may be required to prevent the stomach from bursting. Commonly known as bloat.

GASTRITIS—Inflammation of the stomach caused by many things— spoiled food which tends to turn to gas, overeating, eating foreign bodies, chemicals or even worms. Vomiting is usually the first symptom though the animal will usually drink great quantities of water which more often than not it throws back up. A 24-hour fast which eliminates the cause is the first step toward cure. If vomiting persists chunks of ice cubes put down the throat may help. Hopefully the dog will lick them himself. Keep the dog on a liquid diet for another 24 hours before resuming his regular meals.

GASTRO-ENTERITIS—Inflammation of the stomach and intestines. There is bleeding and ulceration in the stomach and this serious condition calls for immediate veterinary help..

GASTRODUODENITIS—Inflammation of the stomach and duodenum.

GINGIVITIS or gum infection—Badly tartared teeth are usually the cause of this gum infection characterized by swelling, redness at the gum line, bleeding and bloody saliva. Bad breath also. Improper diet may be a cause of it. Feeding of only soft foods as a steady diet allows the tartar to form and to irritate the gums. To effect a cure, clean the teeth and perhaps the veterinarian will also recommend antibiotics.

Eleven little snowballs all getting ready to settle down for a nap. All are owned by the Beckmans of Clayton, Illinois.

GLAUCOMA—Pressure inside the eyeball builds up, the eyeball becomes hard and bulgy and a cloudiness of the entire corneal area occurs. The pupil is dilated and the eye is extremely sensitive. Blindness is inevitable unless treatment is prompt at the onset of the disease. Cold applications as well as medical prescriptions are required with also the possibility of surgery, though with no guarantee of success.

GLOSSITIS—Inflammation of the tongue.

GOITER—Enlargement of the thyroid gland, sometimes requiring surgery. In minor cases, medication—usually containing iodine—is administered.

HARELIP—A malformation of the upper lip characterized by a cleft palate. Difficulty in nursing in exaggerated cases can result in starvation or puny development. Operations can be performed late in life.

HEART DISEASE—Heart failure is rare in young dogs, but older dogs which show an unusual heavy breathing after exercise or are easily tired may be victims of heart trouble, and an examination is in order. As it grows worse, wheezing, coughing or gasping may be noticed. Other symptoms indicating faulty circulation may manifest themselves as the animal retains more body fluids as the circulation slows down. Rest, less exercise, and non-fattening diets are advised and medication to remove excess fluids from the body are prescribed. In many cases, doses of digitalis may be recommended.

HEARTWORM (*Dirofilaria immitis*)—This condition does not necessarily debilitate a working dog or a dog that is extremely active. It is diagnosed by a blood test and a microscopic examination to determine the extent of the microfilariae. If positive, further differentials are made for comparison with other microfilariae. Treatment consists of considerable attention to the state of nutrition, and liver and kidney functions are watched closely in older dogs. Medication is usually treatment other than surgery and consists of dithiazine iodine therapy over a period of two weeks. Anorexia and/or fever may occur and supplemental vitamins and minerals may be indicated. Dogs with heavy infestations are observed for possible foreign protein reaction from dying and decomposing worms, and are watched for at least three months.

HEATSTROKE—Rapid breathing, dazed condition, vomiting, temperature, and collapse in hot weather indicate heatstroke. It seems to strike older dogs especially if they are overweight or have indulged in excessive activity. Reduce body temperature immediately by submerging dog in cold water, apply ice packs, cold enemas, etc. Keep dog cool and quiet for at least 24 hours.

HEMATOMA—A pocket of blood that may collect in the ear as a result of an injury or the dog's scratching. Surgery is required to remove the fluid and return skin to cartilage by stitching.

HEMOPHILIA—Excessive bleeding on the slightest provocation. Only male subjects are susceptible and it is a hereditary disease passed on by females. Blood coagulants are now successfully used in certain cases.

HEPATITIS, Infectious canine—This disease of viral nature enters the body through the mouth and attacks primarily the liver. Puppies are the most susceptible to this disease and run a fever and drink excessive amounts of water. Runny eyes, nose, vomiting, and general discomfort are symptoms. In some cases blood build-

Ch. Hadessi of Ta, photographed several years ago.

Narguess "on guard" under the livingroom window at General Allen's home in Japan. General Allen purchased "Narci" from Ruth Bates Young of Medway, Ohio.

Celestial's Orion the Hunter, pictured winning at a Winnebagoland Samoyed Fanciers show at nine months of age with his owner-handler Anne Copeland of Palatine, Illinois. Sired by Celestial's Taurus the Bull *ex* Celestial's Blonde Bombshell, this young male is linebred to the great American and Canadian Ch. Tod Acres Fang seven times in six generations.

ers or even blood transfusions are administered since the virus has a tendency to thin the blood. This depletion of the blood often leaves the dog open to other types of infection and complete recovery is a lengthy process. Antibiotics are usually given and supplemental diet and blood builders are a help. Vaccination for young puppies is essential.

HERNIA (diaphragmatic)—An injury is usually responsible for this separation or break in the wall of the diaphragm. Symptoms depend on severity; breathing may become difficult, there is some general discomfort or vomiting. X-rays can determine the extent of damage and the only cure is surgery.

HERNIA (umbilical)—Caused by a portion of the abdominal viscera protruding through a weak spot near the navel. Tendency toward hernia is said to be largely hereditary.

Victor of Top Acres and Ch. Cotton Fluff of Top Acres, owned by Ruth Bates Young.

HIP DYSPLASIA—or HD is a wearing away of the ball and socket of the hip joint. It is a hereditary disease. The symptoms of this bone abnormality are a limp and an awkwardness in raising or lowering the body. X-ray will establish severity and it is wise in buying or selling a dog of any breed to insist on a radiograph to prove the animal is HD clear. The condition can be detected as early as three months and if proven the dog should have as little exercise as possible. There is no cure for this condition. Only pain relievers can be given for the more severe cases. No animal with HD should be used for breeding.

HOOKWORM—Hookworms lodge in the small intestines and suck blood from the intestinal wall. Anemia results from loss of blood. Loss of weight, pale gums, and general weakness are symptoms. Microscopic examination of the feces will determine presence.

Emphasis on diet improvement and supplements to build up the blood is necessary and, of course, medication for the eradication of the hookwórms. This can be either oral or by veterinary injection.

HYDROCEPHALUS—A condition also known as "water head" since a large amount of fluid collects in the brain cavity, usually before birth. This may result in a difficult birth and the young are usually born dead or die shortly thereafter. Euthanasia is recommended on those that do survive since intelligence is absent and violence to themselves or to others is liable to occur.

HYDRONEPHROSIS—Due to a cystic obstruction the kidney collects urine which cannot be passed through the ureter into the bladder, causing the kidney to swell (sometimes to five times its normal size) and giving pain in the lumbar region. The kidney may atrophy, if the condition goes untreated.

—I—

ICHTHYOSIS—A skin condition over elbows and hocks. Scaliness and cracked skin cover the area particularly that which comes in contact with hard surfaces. Lubricating oils well rubbed into the skin and keeping the animal on soft surfaces are solutions.

IMPETIGO—Skin disease seen in puppies infested by worms, distemper, or teething problems. Little soft pimples cover the surface of the skin. Sulfur ointments and ridding the puppy of the worms are usually sufficient cure as well.

INTERDIGITAL CYSTS—Growths usually found in the legs. They are painful and cause the dog to favor the paw or not walk on it at all. Surgery is the only cure and antibiotic ointments to keep dirt and infection out are necessary.

INTESTINAL OBSTRUCTIONS—When a foreign object becomes lodged in the intestines and prevents passage of stool constipation results from the blockage. Hernia is another cause of obstruction or stoppage. Pain, vomiting, loss of appetite are symptoms. Fluids, laxatives or enemas should be given to remove blockage. Surgery may be necessary after X-ray determines cause. Action must be taken since death may result from long delay or stoppage.

IRITIS—Inflammation of the iris or colored part of the eye. May be caused by the invasion of foreign bodies or other irritants.

—J—

JAUNDICE—A yellow discoloration of the skin. Liver malfunction causes damage by bile seeping into the circulatory system and being dispensed into the body tissue, causing discoloration of the skin. It may be caused by round worms, liver flukes or gall stones. It may be either acute or chronic and the animal loses ambition, convulses or vomits, sometimes to excess. It may be cured once the cause has been eliminated. Neglect can lead to death.

American and Canadian Ch. Scherezade of Kubla Khan, bred by Patricia Morehouse and owned by Sandy Adams of Portland, Oregon, pictured here after a Best of Breed win over Specials from the classes. The sire was Ch. Sam O'Khan's Kubla Khan *ex* Ch. Icelandic Princess Zoe.

—K—

KERATITIS—Infection of the cornea of the eye. Distemper or hepatitis may be a cause. Sensitivity to light, watery discharge and pain are symptomatic. Treatment depends on whether the lesion is surface irritation or a puncture of the cornea. Warm compresses may help until the veterinarian prescribes the final treatment. Sedatives or tranquilizers may be prescribed to aid in preventing the dog from rubbing the eye.

KIDNEY WORM—The giant worm that attacks the kidney and kidney tissue. It can reach a yard in length. The eggs of this rare species of worm are passed in the dog's urine rather than the feces. These worms are found in raw fish. It is almost impossible to detect them until at least one of the kidneys is completely destroyed or an autopsy reveals its presence. There is no known cure at this point and, therefore, the only alternative is not to feed raw fish.

—L—

LEAD POISONING—Ingestion of lead-based paints or products such as linoleum containing lead is serious. Symptoms are vomiting, behavior changes and/or hysteria or even convulsions in severe cases. It can be cured by medication if caught early enough. Serious damage can be done to the central nervous system. Blood samples are usually taken to determine amount in the blood. Emetics may be required if heavy intake is determined.

LEPTOSPIROSIS—This viral infection is dangerous and bothersome because it affects many organs of the body before lodging itself in the kidneys. Incubation is about two weeks after exposure to the urine of another affected dog. Temperature, or subtemperature, pain and stiffness in the hindquarters are not uncommon, nor is vomiting. Booster shots after proper vaccination at a young age are usually preventative, but once afflicted, antibiotics are essential to cure.

LOCKJAW (tetanus)—Death rate is very high in this bacterial disease. Puncture wounds may frequently develop into lockjaw. Symptoms are severe. As the disease progresses high fever and stiffness in the limbs becomes serious though the dog does not lose consciousness. Sedatives must be given to help relax the muscles and dispel the spasms. When the stiffness affects the muscles of the face, intravenous feeding must be provided. If a cure is effected, it is a long drawn out affair. Lockjaw bacteria are found in soil and in the feces of animals and humans.

LYMPHOMA (Hodgkins disease)—Malignant lymphoma most frequently is found in dogs under four years of age, affects the lymph glands, liver and spleen. Anorexia and noticeable loss of weight are apparent as well as diarrhea. Depending on area and organ, discharge may be present. The actual neoplasm or tumorous growth may be surrounded by nodules or neoplastic tissue which should be surgically removed under anesthesia.

—M—

MAMMARY NEOPLASMS—25 per cent of all canine tumors are of mammary origin. About half of all reported cases are benign. They are highly recurrent and, when cancerous, fatalities are high. Age or number of litters has nothing to do with the condition itself or the seriousness.

MANGE—The loss of a patch of hair usually signals the onset of mange, which is caused by any number of types of microscopic mites. The veterinarian will usually take scrapings to determine which of the types it is. Medicated baths and dips plus internal and external medication is essential as it spreads rapidly and with care can be confined to one part of the body. Antibiotics are prescribed.

312

Ch. Karasam of Misty Way, Top Samoyed in the West and #3 in the nation in 1968 and 1969. Handler is Ray Brinlee for owners Peggy and Mike McCarthy of Eugene, Oregon. Karasam, pictured here taking Best of Breed, went on to win the Group at this Richland Kennel Club Show. Judge pictured is Noah Bloomer.

MASTITIS (mammary gland infection)—After the birth of her young, a bitch may be beset by an infection causing inflammation of the mammary glands which produce milk for the puppies. Soreness and swelling make it painful for her when the puppies nurse. Abscess may form and she will usually run a fever. Hot compresses and antibiotics are necessary and in some instances hormone therapy.

MENINGITIS—Inflammation affecting the membranes covering the brain and/or spinal cord. It is a serious complication which may result from a serious case of distemper, tuberculosis, hardpad, head injury, etc. Symptoms are delirium, restlessness, high temperature, and dilated pupils in the eyes. Paralysis and death are almost certain.

METRITIS—This infection, or inflammation of the uterus, causes the dog to exude a bloody discharge. Vomiting and a general lassitude are symptoms. Metritis can occur during the time the bitch is in season or right after giving birth. Antibiotics are used, or in severe cases hysterectomy.

MONORCHIDISM—Having only one testicle.

MOTION SICKNESS—On land, on sea, or in the air, your dog may be susceptible to motion sickness. Yawning, or excessive salivation, may signal the onset, and there is eventual vomiting. One or all of the symptoms may be present and recovery is miraculously fast once the motion ceases. Antinauseant drugs are available for animals which do not outgrow this condition.

MYELOMA—Tumor of the bone marrow. Lameness and evidence of pain are symptoms as well as weight loss, depression and palpable tumor masses. Anemia or unnatural tendency to bleed in severe cases may be observed. The tumors may be detected radiographically, but no treatment has yet been reported for the condition.

—N—

NEONATAL K-9 HERPESVIRUS INFECTION—Though K-9 herpesvirus infection, or CHV, has been thought to be a disease of the respiratory system in adult dogs, the acute necrotizing and hemorrhagic disease occurs only in infant puppies. The virus multiplies in the respiratory system and female genital tracts of older dogs. Puppies may be affected in the vaginal canal. Unfortunately the symptoms resemble other neonatal infections, even hepatitis, and only after autopsy can it be detected.

NEPHROTIC SYNDROME—Symptoms may be moist or suppurative dermatitis, edema or hypercholesteremia. It is a disease of the liver and may be the result of another disease. Laboratory data and biopsies may be necessary to determine the actual cause if it is other than renal disease. This is a relatively uncommon thing in dogs, and liver and urinal function tests are made to determine its presence.

Chipper and Mr. Eugene Thommassen on his mountain property in Tennessee.

Ch. Suffolk Princess Bukhara with her litter of puppies sired by Ch. Suffolk Czar Nicholas. Bred and owned by Jack Price of Oakdale, New York.

NEURITIS—Painful inflammation of a nerve.

NOSEBLEED (epistaxis)—A blow or other injury which causes injury to the nasal tissues is usually the cause. Tumors, parasites, foreign bodies, such as thorns or burs or quills, may also be responsible. Ice packs will help stem the tide of blood, though coagulants may also be necessary. Transfusions in severe cases may be indicated.

—O—

ORCHITIS—Inflammation of the testes.

OSTEOGENESIS IMPERFECTA—Or "brittle bones" is a condition that can be said to be both hereditary and dietary. It may be due to lack of calcium or phosphorus or both. Radiographs show "thin" bones with deformities throughout the skeleton. Treatment depends on cause.

OSTEOMYELITIS (enostosis)—Bone infection may develop after a bacterial contamination of the bone, such as from a compound fracture. Pain and swelling denote the infection and wet sores may accompany it. Lack of appetite, fever and general inactivity can be expected. Antibiotics are advised after X-ray determines severity. Surgery eliminates dead tissue or bone splinters to hasten healing.

OTITIS—Inflammation of the ear.

—P—

PANCREATITIS—It is difficult to palpate for the pancreas unless it is enlarged, which it usually is if this disease is present. Symptoms

Ch. Yorza II of Arbee poses with her replica in snow. Yorza is owned by Mrs. John May of Trenton, New Jersey.

Suffolk Woly Buly of Oakwood photographed winning at his first show at eight months of age, handled by Jack Price. This 1973 Specialty Show held by the Potomac Valley Samoyed Club was judged by Arnold Wolfe. Owner is Amelia Price of Oakdale, New York. Shafer photo.

to note are as in other gastronomic complaints such as vomiting, loss of appetite, anorexia, stomach pains and general listlessness. This is a disease of older dogs though it has been diagnosed in young dogs as well. Blood, urine and stool examination and observation of the endocrine functions of the dog are in order. Clinical diseases that may result from a serious case of pancreatitis are acute pancreatitis which involves a complete degeneration of the pancreas, atrophy, fibrous and/or neoplasia, cholecystitis. Diabetes mellitus is also a possibility.

PATELLAR LUXATION—"Trick knees" are frequent in breeds that have been "bred down" from Standard to Toy size, and is a condition where the knee bone slips out of position. It is an off again, on again condition that can happen as a result of a jump or excessive exercise. It if is persistent, anti-inflammatory drugs may be given or in some cases surgery can correct it.

PERITONITIS—Severe pain accompanies this infection or inflammation of the lining of the abdominal cavity. Extreme sensitivity to touch, loss of appetite and vomiting occur. Dehydration and weight loss is rapid and anemia is a possibility. Antibiotics should

A most impressive lineup of the Snowland Kennels Sammys; this photo became the back cover on the October, 1970 issue of *Popular Dogs* magazine.

kill the infection and a liquid diet for several days is advised. Pain-killers may be necessary or drainage tubes in severe cases.

PHLEBITIS—Inflammation of a vein.

PLACENTA—The afterbirth which accompanies and has been used to nourish the fetus. It is composed of three parts; the chorion, amnion, and allantois.

POLYCYTHEMIA VERA—A disease of the blood causing an elevation of hemoglobin concentration. Blood-letting has been effective. The convulsions that typify the presence can be likened to epileptic fits and last for several minutes. The limbs are stiff and the body feels hot. Mucous membranes are congested, the dog may shiver, and the skin has a ruddy discoloration. Blood samples must be taken and analyzed periodically. If medication to reduce the production of red blood cells is given, it usually means the dog will survive.

PROCTITIS—Inflammation of the rectum.

PROSTATITIS—Inflammation of the prostate gland.

PSITTACOSIS—This disease which affects birds and people has been diagnosed in rare instances in dogs. A soft, persistent cough indicates the dog has been exposed, and a radiograph will show a cloudy portion on the affected areas of the lung. Antibiotics such as aureomycin have been successful in the known cases and cure has been effected in two to three weeks' time. This is a highly contagious disease, to the point where it can be contracted during a post mortem.

PYOMETRA—This uterine infection presents a discharge of pus from the uterus. High fever may turn to below normal as the infection persists. Lack of appetite with a desire for fluids and frequent urination are evidenced. Antibiotics and hormones are known cures. In severe cases, hysterectomy is performed.

—R—

RABIES (hydrophobia)—The most deadly of all dog diseases. The Pasteur treatment is the only known cure for humans. One of the viral diseases that affects the nervous system and damages the brain. It is contracted by the intake, through a bite or cut, of saliva from an infected animal. It takes days or even months for the symptoms to appear, so it is sometimes difficult to locate, or isolate, the source. There are two reactions in a dog to this disease. In the paralytic type of rabies the dog can't swallow and salivates from a drooping jaw, and progressive paralysis eventually overcomes the entire body. The animal goes into coma and eventually dies. In the furious type of rabies the dog turns vicious, eats strange objects, in spite of a difficulty in swallowing, foams at the mouth, and searches out animals or people to attack—hence the expression "mad dog." Vaccination is available for dogs that run loose.

Examination of the brain is necessary to determine actual diagnosis.

RECTAL PROLAPSE—Diarrhea, straining from constipation or heavy infestations of parasites are the most common cause of prolapse which is the expulsion of a part of the rectum through the anal opening. It is cylindrical in shape, and must be replaced within the body as soon as possible to prevent damage. Change in diet, medication to eliminate the cause, etc. will effect a cure.

RETINAL ATROPHY—A disease of the eye that is highly hereditary and may be revealed under ophthalmoscopic examination. Eventual blindness inevitably results. Dogs with retinal atrophy should not be used for breeding. Particularly prominent in certain breeds where current breeding trends have tended to change the shape of the head.

RHINITIS—Acute or chronic inflammation of the mucous membranes of the nasal passages. It is quite common in both dogs and cats. It is seldom fatal, but requires endless "nursing" on the part of the owner for survival, since the nose passages must be kept open so the animal will eat. Dry leather on the nose though there is excessive discharge, high fever, sneezing, etc., are symptoms. Nose discharge may be bloody and the animal will refuse to eat, making it listless. The attacks may be recurrent and medication must be administered.

RICKETS—The technical name for rickets is osteomalacia and is due to not enough calcium in the body. The bones soften and the legs become bowed or deformed. Rickets can be cured if caught in early stages by improvement in diet.

RINGWORM—The dread of the dog and cat world! This is a fungus disease where the hair falls out in circular patches. It spreads rapidly and is most difficult to get rid of entirely. Drugs must be administered "inside and out!" The cure takes many weeks and much patience. Ultraviolet lights will show hairs green in color so it is wise to have your animal, or new puppy, checked out by the veterinarian for this disease before introducing him to the household. It is contracted by humans.

ROOT CANAL THERAPY—Injury to a tooth may be treated by prompt dental root canal therapy which involves removal of damaged or necrotic pulp and placing of opaque filling material in the root canal and pulp chamber.

—S—

SALIVARY CYST—Surgery is necessary when the salivary gland becomes clogged or non-functional, causing constant salivation. A swelling becomes evident under the ear or tongue. Surgery will release the accumulation of saliva in the duct of the salivary gland, though it is at times necessary to remove the salivary gland in its

Laura and Leo Povier's Ch. Crystal with one of the memorial trophies offered in memory of Samoyeds at some of the shows.

A magnificent
headstudy of
Ch. Martingale
Snowland Taz,
taken in 1952.

entirety. Zygomatic salivary cysts are usually a result of obstructions in the four main pairs of salivary glands in the mouth. Infection is more prevalent in the parotid of the zygomatic glands located at the rear of the mouth, lateral to the last upper molars. Visual symptoms may be protruding eyeballs, pain when moving the jaw, or a swelling in the roof of the mouth. If surgery is necessary, it is done under general anesthesia and the obstruction removed by dissection. Occasionally, the zygomatic salivary gland is removed as well. Stitches or drainage tubes may be necessary or dilation of the affected salivary gland. Oral or internal antibiotics may be administered.

SCABIES—Infection from a skin disease caused by a sarcoptic mange mite.

SCURF (dandruff)—A scaly condition of the body in areas covered with hair. Dead cells combined with dried sweat and sebaceous oil gland materials.

SEBORRHEA—A skin condition also referred to as "stud tail," though studding has nothing to do with the condition. The sebaceous or oil-forming glands are responsible. Accumulation of dry skin, or scurf, is formed by excessive oily deposits while the hair becomes dry or falls out altogether.

SEPTICEMIA—When septic organisms invade the bloodstream, it is called septicemia. Severe cases are fatal as the organisms in the

A figure of a beautiful white Samoyed and an enchanting if incongruous grouping with baby seal and two curious penguins. Artist Carol Moorland Marshall captures this ancient breed in these two pieces from her collection of her original dog figurines.

Prayer time at the Phil Baird household includes everyone, including their Samoyed, Regal Frosty.

Two-week-old puppy owned by Marjorie Van Ornum peeks out from under the bed.

blood infiltrate the tissues of the body and all the body organs are affected. Septicemia is the result of serious wounds, especially joints and bones. Abscess may form. High temperature and/or shivering may herald the onset, and death occurs shortly thereafter since the organisms reproduce and spread rapidly. Close watch on all wounds, antibiotics and sulfur drugs are usually prescribed.

SHOCK (circulatory collapse)—The symptoms and severity of shock vary with the cause and nervous system of the individual dog. Severe accident, loss of blood, and heart failure are the most common cause. Keep the dog warm, quiet and get him to a veterinarian right away. Symptoms are vomiting, rapid pulse, thirst, diarrhea, "cold, clammy feeling" and then eventually physical collapse. The veterinarian might prescribe plasma transfusion, fluids, perhaps oxygen, if pulse continues to be too rapid. Tranquilizers and sedatives are sometimes used as well as antibiotics and steroids. Relapse is not uncommon, so the animal must be observed carefully for several days after initial shock.

SINUSITIS—Inflammation of a sinus gland that inhibits breathing.

SNAKEBITE—The fact must be established as to whether the bite was poisonous or non-poisonous. A horse-shoe shaped double row of toothmarks is a non-poisonous bite. A double, or two-hole puncture, is a poisonous snake bite. Many veterinarians now carry anti-venom serum and this must be injected intramuscularly almost immediately. The veterinarian will probably inject a tranquilizer and other antibiotics as well. It is usually a four-day wait before the dog is normal once again, and the swelling completely gone. During this time the dog should be kept on medication.

SPIROCHETOSIS—Diarrhea which cannot be checked through normal anti-diarrhea medication within a few days may indicate spirochetosis; while spirochetes are believed by some authorities to be present and normal to gastrointestinal tracts, unexplainable diarrhea may indicate its presence in great numbers. Large quantities could precipitate diarrhea by upsetting the normal balance of the organ, though it is possible for some dogs which are infected to have no diarrhea at all.

SPONDYLITIS—Inflammation and loosening of the vertebrae.

STOMATITIS—Mouth infection. Bleeding or swollen gums or excessive salivation may indicate this infection. Dirty teeth are usually the cause. Antibiotics and vitamin therapy are indicated; and, of course, scraping the teeth to eliminate the original cause. See also GINGIVITIS.

STRONGYLIDOSIS—Disease caused by strongyle worms that enter the body through the skin and lodge in the wall of the small intestine. Bloody diarrhea, stunted growth, and thinness are general symptoms, as well as shallow breathing. Heavy infestation or neglect leads to death. Isolation of an affected animal and medication will help eliminate the problem, but the premises must also be cleaned thoroughly since the eggs are passed through the feces.

SUPPOSITORY—A capsule comprised of fat or glycerine introduced into the rectum to encourage defecation. A paper match with the ignitible sulfur end torn off may also be used. Medicated suppositories are also used to treat inflammation of the intestine.

—T—

TACHYCARDIA—An abnormal acceleration of the heartbeat. A rapid pulse signaling a disruption in the heart action. Contact a veterinarian at once.

TAPEWORM—There are many types of tapeworms, the most common being the variety passed along by the flea. It is a white, segmented worm which lives off the wall of the dog's intestine and keeps growing by segments. Some of these are passed and can be

A beautiful headstudy of Marie Gillette's Ch. Jomay of Singing Trees, photographed by Jennette Gifford.

seen in the stool or adhering to the hairs on the rear areas of the dog or even in his bedding. It is a difficult worm to get rid of since, even if medication eliminates segments, the head may remain in the intestinal wall to grow again. Symptoms are virtually the same as for other worms: debilitation, loss of weight, occasional diarrhea, and general listlessness. Medication and treatment should be under the supervision of a veterinarian.

TETANUS (lockjaw)—A telarius bacillus enters the body through an open wound and spreads where the air does not touch the wound. A toxin is produced and affects the nervous system, particularly the brain or spine. The animal exhibits a stiffness, slows down considerably and the legs may be extended out beyond the body even when the animal is in a standing position. The lips have a twisted appearance. Recovery is rare. Tetanus is not common in dogs, but it can result from a bad job of tail docking or ear cropping, as well as from wounds received by stepping on rusty nails.

THALLOTOXICOSIS or thallium poisoning—Thallium sulfate is a cellular-toxic metal used as a pesticide or rodenticide and a ready cause of poisoning in dogs. Thallium can be detected in the urine by a thallium spot test or by spectrographic analysis by the veterinarian. Gastrointestinal disturbances signal the onset with vomiting, diarrhea, anorexia and stomach cramps. Sometimes a cough or difficulty in breathing occurs. Other intestinal disorders may also manifest themselves as well as convulsions. In mild cases the disease may be simply a skin eruption, depending upon the damage to the kidneys. Enlarged spleens, edema or nephrosis can develop. Antibiotics and a medication called dimercaprol are helpful, but the mortality rate is over 50 per cent.

THROMBUS—A clot in the blood vessel or the heart.

TICK PARALYSIS— Seasonal tick attacks or heavy infestations of ticks can result in a dangerous paralysis. Death is a distinct reality at this point and immediate steps must be taken to prevent total paralysis. The onset is observed usually in the hindquarters. Lack of coordination, a reluctance to walk, and difficulty in getting up can be observed. Complete paralysis kills when infection reaches the respiratory system. The paralysis is the result of the saliva of the tick excreted as it feeds.

TOAD POISONING—Some species of toads secrete a potent toxin. If while chasing a toad your dog takes it in his mouth, more than likely the toad will release the toxin from its parotid glands which will coat the mucous membranes of the dog's throat. The dog will salivate excessively, suffer prostration, cardiac arrhythmia. Some tropical and highly toxic species cause convulsions that result in death. Caught in time, there are certain drugs that can be used to counteract the dire effects. Try washing the dog's mouth with large amounts of water and get him to a veterinarian quickly.

A touching moment captured at the Pennsylvania S.P.C.A. during the blessing of the animals ceremony held to commemorate the birthday of the patron saint of animals, St. Francis of Assisi.

TONSILLECTOMY—Removal of the tonsils. A solution called epinephrine, injected at the time of surgery, makes excessive bleeding almost a thing of the past in this otherwise routine operation.

TOXEMIA—The presence of toxins in the bloodstream, which normally should be eliminated by the excretory organs.

TRICHIASIS—A disease condition of the eyelids, the result of neglect of earlier infection or inflammation.

—U—

UREMIA—When poisonous materials remain in the body, because they are not eliminated through the kidneys, and are recirculated in the bloodstream. A nearly always fatal disease—sometimes within hours—preceded by convulsions and unconsciousness. Veterinary care and treatment are urgent and imperative.

Taymyra Eenya, a five-year-old granddaughter of Kobe's North Star of Encino, owned by Richard Peskin of Clinton, New Jersey.

URINARY BLADDER RUPTURE—Injury or pelvic fractures are the most common causes of a rupture in this area. Anuria usually occurs in a few days when urine backs up into the stomach area. Stomach pains are characteristic and a radiograph will determine the seriousness. Bladder is flushed with saline solution and surgery is usually required. Quiet and little exercise is recommended during recovery.

—V—

VENTRICULOCORDECTOMY—Devocalization of dogs, also known as aphonia. In diseases of the larynx this operation may be used. Portions of the vocal cords are removed by manual means or by electrocautery. Food is withheld for a day prior to surgery and premedication is administered. Food is again provided 24 hours after the operation. At the end of three or four months, scar tissue develops and the dog is able to bark in a subdued manner. Complications from surgery are few, but the psychological effects on the animal are to be reckoned with. Suppression of the barking varies from complete to merely muted, depending on the veterinarian's ability and each individual dog's anatomy.

—W—

WHIPWORMS—Parasites that inhabit the large intestine and the cecum. Two to three inches in length, they appear "whip-like" and symptoms are diarrhea, loss of weight, anemia, restlessness or even pain, if the infestation is heavy enough. Medication is best prescribed by a veterinarian. Cleaning of the kennel is essential, since infestation takes place through the mouth. Whipworms reach maturity within thirty days after intake.

19. PURSUING A CAREER IN DOGS

One of the biggest joys for those of us who love dogs is to see someone we know or someone in our family grow up in the fancy and go on to enjoy the sport of dogs in later life. Many dog lovers, in addition to leaving codicils in their wills, are providing in other ways for veterinary scholarships for deserving youngsters who wish to make their association with dogs their profession.

Unfortunately, many children who have this earnest desire are not always able to afford the expense of an education that will take them through veterinary school, and they are not eligible for scholarships. In recent years, however, we have had a great innovation in this field—a college course for those interested in earning an Animal Science degree, which costs less than half of what it costs to complete veterinary courses. These students have been a boon to the veterinarians, and a number of colleges are now offering the program.

With each passing year, the waiting rooms of veterinarians have become more crowded, and the demands on the doctors' time for research, consultation, surgery and treatment have consumed more and more of the working hours over and above his regular office hours. The tremendous increase in the number of dogs and cats and other domestic animals, both in cities and in the suburbs, has resulted in an almost overwhelming consumption of veterinarians' time.

Until recently most veterinary help consisted of kennel men or women who were restricted to services more properly classified as office maintenance rather than actual veterinary assistance. Needless to say, their part in the operation of a veterinary office is both essential and appreciated, as are the endless details and volumes of paperwork capably handled by office secretaries and receptionists. However, still more of a veterinarian's duties could be handled by properly trained semiprofessionals.

With exactly this additional service in mind, many colleges are now conducting two-year courses in animal science for the training of such semiprofessionals, thereby opening a new field for animal technologists. The time saved by the assistance of these trained semiprofessionals will relieve veterinarians of the more mechanical chores

Kubla Khan Teddy Bear, first in Puppy Dog Class at six months at a San Diego Specialty Show. Sired by Ch. Sam O'Khan's Kubla Khan *ex* Ch. Orions Capella of Tsar-Khan. Bred and owned by Patricia Morehouse, Los Angeles.

and will allow them more time for diagnosing and general servicing of their clients.

"Delhi Tech," the State University Agricultural and Technical College at Delhi, New York, has recently graduated several classes of these technologists, and many other institutions of learning are offering comparable two-year courses at the college level. Entry requirements are usually that each applicant must be a graduate of an approved high school or have taken the State University admissions examination. In addition, each applicant for the Animal Science Technology program must have some previous credits in mathematics and science, with chemistry an important part of the science background.

The program at Delhi was a new educational venture dedicated to the training of competent technicians for employment in the biochemical field and has been generously supported by a five-year grant, designated as a "Pilot Development Program in Animal Science." This grant provided both personal and scientific equipment with such obvious good results when it was done originally pursuant to a contract with the United States Department of Health, Education, and Welfare. Delhi is a unit of the State University of New York and is accredited by the Middle States Association of Colleges and Secondary Schools. The campus provides offices, laboratories and animal quarters and is equipped with modern instruments to train technicians in laboratory animal care, physiology, pathology, microbiology, anesthesia, X-ray and germ-free techniques. Sizable animal colonies are maintained in air-conditioned quarters: animals housed include mice, rats, hamsters, guinea-pigs, gerbils and rabbits, as well as dogs and cats.

First-year students are given such courses as livestock production, dairy food science, general, organic and biological chemistry, mammalian anatomy, histology and physiology, pathogenic microbiology and quantitative and instrumental analysis, to name a few. Second year students matriculate in general pathology, animal parasitology, animal care and anesthesia, introductory psychology, animal breeding, animal nutrition, hematology and urinalysis, radiology, genetics, food sanitation and meat inspection, histological techniques, animal laboratory practices and axenic techniques. These, of course, may be supplemented by electives that prepare the student for contact with the public in the administration of these duties. Such recommended electives include public speaking, botany, animal reproduction and other related subjects.

In addition to Delhi and the colleges which got in early on the presentation of these courses, more and more universities are offering training for animal technologists. Students at the State University of Maine, for instance, receive part of their practical training at the Animal Medical Center in New York City, and after this actual experience can perform professionally immediately upon entering a veterinarian's employ.

Frosty Dawn of Sonlaski and Top Acres Silver Storm of Sunlaski pose in Florida with their owner's husband.

Taken in 1954, the lovely Crystal with her friend Polar, at home in an easy chair.

A six-week-old puppy waits for the Christmas celebrating to begin! Misty Way's Goody Two Shoes, photographed in 1973, was sired by Bo Jingles of Misty Way *ex* Whitecliff's Kerry of Misty Way. Owner is Peggy McCarthy of Eugene, Oregon.

Under direct veterinary supervision they are able to perform all of the following procedures as a semi-professional:

*Recording of vital information relative to a case. This would include such information as the client's name, address, telephone number and other facts pertinent to the visit. The case history would include the breed, age of the animal, its sex, temperature, etc.

*Preparation of the animal for surgery

*Preparation of equipment and medicaments to be used in surgery.

*Preparation of medicaments for dispensing to clients on prescription of the attending veterinarian.

*Administration and application of certain medicines.

*Administration of colonic irrigations.

*Application or changing of wound dressings.

*Cleaning of kennels, exercise runs and kitchen utensils.

*Preparation of food and the feeding of patients.

*Explanation to clients on the handling and restraint of their pets, including needs for exercise, house training and elementary obedience training.

*First-aid treatment for hemorrhage, including the proper use of tourniquets

*Preservation of blood, urine and pathologic material for the purpose of laboratory examination

*General care and supervision of the hospital or clinic patients to insure their comfort.

*Nail trimming and grooming of patients.

High school graduates with a sincere affection and regard for animals and a desire to work with veterinarians and perform such clinical duties as mentioned above will find they fit in especially well. Women particularly will be useful since, over and beyond the strong maternal instinct that goes so far in the care and the recovery phase when dealing with animals, women will find the majority of the positions will be in the small animal field, their dexterity will also fit in well. Students having financial restrictions that preclude their education and licensing as full-fledged veterinarians can in this way pursue careers in an area close to their actual desire. Their assistance in the pharmaceutical field, where drug concerns deal with laboratory animals, covers another wide area for trained assistance. The career

A boy and his dog. . . this charming photo submitted by Ruth Young.

opportunities are varied and reach into job opportunities in medical centers, research institutions and government health agencies; at present, the demand for graduates far exceeds the current supply of trained personnel.

As far as the financial remunerations, yearly salaries are estimated at an average of $5,000.00 for a starting point. As for the estimate of basic college education expenses, they range from $1800.00 to $2200.00 per year for out-of-state residents, and include tuition, room and board, college fees, essential textbooks and limited personal expenses. These personal expenses, of course, will vary with individual students, as well as the other expenses, but we present an average. It is obvious that the costs are about half of the costs involved in becoming a full-fledged veterinarian, however.

Champion Silver Surf of Wildcliffe, pictured at a dog show, is owner-handled by Roy Wallace and Eileen M. Woodworth of Cleveland, Ohio.

PART TIME KENNEL WORK

Youngsters who do not wish to go on to become veterinarians or animal technicians can get valuable experience and extra money by working part-time after school and weekends, or full-time during summer vacations, in a veterinarian's office. The exposure to animals and office procedure will be time well spent.

Another great help to veterinarians has been the housewife who loves animals and wishes to put in some time at a job away from the house, especially if her children are grown or away at college. If she can clean up in her own kennel she can certainly clean up in a veterinarian's office, and she will learn much about handling and caring for her own animals while she is making money.

Kennel help is also an area that is wide open for retired men. They are able to help out in many areas where they can learn and stay active, and most of the work allows them to set their own pace.

The gentility that age and experience bring is also beneficial to the animals they will deal with; for their part, the men find great reward in their contribution to animals and will be keeping their hand in the business world as well.

PROFESSIONAL HANDLERS

For those who wish to participate in the sport of dogs and whose interests or abilities do not center around the clinical aspects of the fancy, there is yet another avenue of involvement.

For those who excel in the show ring, who enjoy being in the limelight and putting their dogs through their paces, a career in professional handling may be the answer. Handling may include a weekend of showing a few dogs for special clients, or it may be a full-time career which can also include boarding, training, conditioning, breeding and showing of dogs for several clients.

Depending on how deeply your interest runs, the issue can be solved by a lot of preliminary consideration before it becomes necessary to make a decision. The first move would to to have a long, serious talk with a successful professional handler to learn the pros and cons of such a profession. Watching handlers in action from ringside as they perform their duties can be revealing. A visit to their kennels for

Pinehill's Pride O'Whytekrest, whelped in 1973 and pictured here at eleven weeks of age. Pride's sire was Ch. Pinehill's Country Boy ex Pinehill's In The Ribbons. Pride is the grandson of Best In Show winner American and Canadian Ch. Shaloon of Drayalene and the Group winner Ch. Chu-San's Silver Folly. Owners are Barbara and Mary Telychan of Edison, New Jersey.

Snow Hullabaloo pictured winning at the 1969 Ramapo Kennel Club show. Whelped in March, 1967, Snow is owned by Linda and Marie Gemeinhardt of Cedar Grove, New Jersey.

an on-the-spot revelation of the behind-the-scenes responsibilities is essential! And working for them full or part time would be the best way of all to resolve any doubt you might have!

Professional handling is not all glamour in the show ring. There is plenty of "dirty work" behind the scenes 24 hours of every day. You must have the necessary ability and patience for this work, as well as the ability and patience to deal with CLIENTS—the dog owners who value their animals above almost anything else and would expect a great deal from you in the way of care and handling. The big question you must ask yourself first of all is: do you *really* love dogs enough to handle it. . .

DOG TRAINING

Like the professional handler, the professional dog trainer has a most responsible job! You not only need to be thoroughly familiar with the correct and successful methods of training a dog but also

Rinda of Singing Trees photographed at Lake Yellowstone by Jennette Gifford of Carmel, Indiana, waiting for her master to return from fishing.

American and Canadian Ch. Snow Cloud of Cedarwood photographed with her handler and some of her many ribbons. Patricia Morehouse, Los Angeles, California.

must have the ability to communicate with dogs. True, it is very rewarding work, but training for the show ring, obedience, or guard dog work must be done exactly right for successful results to maintain a business reputation.

Training schools are quite the vogue nowadays, with all of them claiming success. But careful investigation should be made before enrolling a dog. . . and even more careful investigation should be made of their methods and of their actual successes before becoming associated with them.

GROOMING PARLORS

If you do not wish the 24-hour a day job which is required by a professional handler or professional trainer, but still love working with and caring for dogs, there is always the very profitable grooming business. Poodles started the ball rolling for the swanky, plush grooming establishments which sprang up like mushrooms all over the major cities, many of which seem to be doing very well. Here again, handling dogs and the public is necessary for a successful operation, as well as skill in the actual grooming of the dogs, and of all breeds.

While shops flourish in the cities, some of the suburban areas are now featuring mobile units which by appointment will visit your home with a completely equipped shop on wheels and will groom your dog right in your own driveway!

THE PET SHOP

Part-time or full-time work in a pet shop can help you make up your mind rather quickly as to whether or not you would like to have a shop of your own. For those who love animals and are concerned with their care and feeding, the pet shop can be a profitable and satisfying association. Supplies which are available for sale in these shops are almost limitless, and a nice living can be garnered from pet supplies if the location and population of the city you choose warrant it.

Mrs. George Brown and "Kukie" at home in Greenville, Pennsylvania. Note charming ceramic Samoyed ashtray on the coffee table. This photo was taken about 1964.

Luchow's Pride of Top Acres, once owned by Jan Mitchell and named after his famous restaurant in downtown New York City. While in New York, Pride sired two litters, one by Countess Tolstoy's dam Belka. He is now at Ruth Bates Young's Top Acres Kennels in Medway, Ohio, where he is siring additional litters. Pride was also owned by Kurt Unkelbach.

"Yes, chewing carpet can be delicious. . .

. . . once you get a piece of it!" Samoyed puppies are known for their tendency to chew and should be provided with safe chew toys. This puppy belongs to Bob and Wanda Krauss of Madison, Wisconsin.

DOG JUDGING

There are also those whose professions or age or health prevent them from owning or breeding or showing dogs, and who turn to judging at dog shows after their active years in the show ring are no longer possible. Breeder-judges make a valuable contribution to the fancy by judging in accordance with their years of experience in the fancy, and the assignments are enjoyable. Judging requires experience, a good eye for dogs and an appreciation of a good animal.

MISCELLANEOUS

If you find all of the aforementioned too demanding or not within your abilities, there are still other aspects of the sport for you to enjoy and participate in at will. Writing for the various dog magazines, books or club newsletters, dog photography, portrait painting, club activities, making dog coats, or needlework featuring dogs, typing pedigrees or perhaps dog walking. All, in their own way, contribute to the sport of dogs and give great satisfaction. Perhaps, where Samoyeds are concerned, you may wish to learn to train for racing, or sled hauling, or you might even wish to learn the making of the sleds!

The magnificent Ch. Kazan of Kentwood, Best In Show winner at the Ventura County Dog Show in 1962.

This adorable Samoyed puppy embodies all the charm and beauty which endears the breed to dog lovers all over the world. Owned and photographed by Harold McLaughlin, professional photographer and owner of the Silveracres Samoyed Kennels in Morrison, Colorado.

20. SAMOYED STORIES

Perhaps the most significant story about this beautiful breed goes back to the days when Mrs. Clara Kilburn-Scott, who, along with her husband, has done so much to establish the breed in England and here, brought back to Britain the world-famous Samoyed named Antarctic Buck.

Buck was first seen by Mrs. Scott sitting dejectedly in a cage in a zoo in Sydney, Australia. Buck had been with the Southern Cross (Borchgrevinks) expedition to the South Pole and had ended up as an attraction at the zoo, where he was expected to live out the rest of his life. Mrs. Scott felt sorry for the dog and after two attempts managed to obtain Buck and return with him to her native England. There Buck distinguished himself as a stud force with just two litters to his credit and appears in many pedigrees of Samoyeds which have become famous in the breed and in the show ring in England. Buck unfortunately died of distemper before he could be used as a sire to meet the demand.

LAIKA IN SPACE

These great white dogs have a way of attracting attention and getting into the limelight, and not just because they are so lovely to look at or because they are such excellent working dogs. A true story to bear witness to this fact is a recent happening which made newspaper headlines in the Midwest.

We all remember that it was a dog looking very much like a Sammy which the Russians chose to send off on a space trip several years ago. Laika was its name, and Laika's adventure in space led to a strange and amusing. . . and as yet unsolved. . . tale of events in Gresham, Illinois.

An untagged dog looking very much like Laika—and thought by many townspeople to be Laika—appeared on the main street of town, looking confused and obviously disturbed by the unfamiliar surroundings. The local police were called out, and they assumed that it was one of the three Samoyeds belonging to Charles and Edla Lawrence, which had escaped from their yard and were running free. They picked up the dog and brought it to the Lawrence house and put it in the run in the back yard. Imagine the Lawrences' surprise when they returned home and found four Samoyeds in the yard instead of three!

Ch. Kondako's Fryers' Snow White, owned by Clifton and Mary Fryer of Paradise, Pennsylvania. The four-week-old puppy in the picture was sired by Ch. Gentle Giant of Snow Country.

In December, 1957 this litter of California-bred Whitecliff Sammy puppies was getting ready to greet new owners and their show ring careers.

Dog lovers that they are, the Lawrences offered to keep the dog until the owner could be found. So far no one has claimed the dog. But one thing is certain. . . the unknown visitor has expressed no desire to return to either Russia or to space!

SAMOYEDS IN EDUCATION

As further proof of the versatility of the Samoyed, I repeat here the story I heard recently of yet another avenue of success to which this dog can claim fame. We are all aware of their work as herders, haulers, show dogs and obedience dogs, but there is now a famous Samoyed who is very active in the fields of education and public relations. His name is Nikkolad of Top Acres. In his work he is also known as Sergeant Safety, since he and his owner, Sgt. Jerry Howard of the Indiana State Police, are the mainstays of the Indiana Safety Education program. Sgt. Howard gives talks on safety four or five times a week at schools, churches and other public affairs and takes Nikkolad along as the symbol of safety. Nikkolad adores the attention, and his picture appears on all of the safety posters and billboards. He is booked for appearances on television programs in connection with the campaign.

What makes Nikkolad's appearances so important is that he not only helps impress the importance of safety on the public but also is a

The magnificent Snow Chief, sired by the imported Ch. Sport of the Arctic ex Olga Pazie of Oh, bred by Ruth Young at her Top Acres Kennels in Medway, Ohio.

Ch. Karasam's Cowboy of Misty Way is pictured winning Best of Breed at the 1973 Portland Kennel Club show under judge Dr. Frank Booth. Sired by Ch. Karasam of Misty Way *ex* Silver Tassle of Misty Way. Handled by Ray Brinlee for owner Peggy McCarthy of Eugene, Oregon.

The late Mrs. Mason of San Francisco, California, with three of her Samoyeds, Queenie (10 months), Sissy and Snowcap. Sissy flushed rabbits after parachuting 1400 feet out of an airplane! Mrs. Mason, a top breeder on the West Coast in earlier years, is wearing a coat made from Samoyed hair that has been corded and woven.

good specimen of the breed to put before the public, so we Samoyed lovers can all be proud to have him as the center of attention, endearing our breed to the public and helping to spread the word for pure-bred dogs.

THE NAME'S THE SAME

One of my favorite Sammy stories is the tale about the attempt to change the name of the breed. *Samoyed* is the Russian word for cannibal, and the tribes which owned and bred the dogs originally were supposed to have been cannibals, which is how they got their name. However, because Mr. Kilburn-Scott had given the Bjelkiers the name of Samoyed, or cannibal, some of the few remaining Samoyed people went to Joseph Stalin with a petition expressing their wish to change the name! Needless to say, they petitioned unsuccessfully!

Hauling the United States mail in Idaho in 1947. Lloyd Van Sickle is shown driving Agnes Mason's Samoyed team. Rex, the lead dog, was well known for facing blizzards during cross-country travel at the head of his team.

Ruth Bates Young of Medway, Ohio with her imported Ch. Sport of the Arctic.

SAMOYEDS IN PUBLIC RELATIONS

Because of their spectacular appearance, Samoyeds have always been "naturals" for public attention. In addition to their success in the show ring, and as racers, haulers, herders, guard dogs and obedience dogs, they keep active in related fields, individually and in teams.

One team which comes to mind is the famous one owned by Mrs. Agnes Mason and bred at her Whiteway Kennels in Sacramento, Calif. This team has distinguished itself by carrying the U.S. mail in the high Sierras. It has rescued snowbound people and has actually parachuted out of planes to help rescue air crash victims. In 1954, Rex of Whiteway, lead dog on the team, broke the world's record by pulling 1,870 pounds of weight all by himself.

A San Diego team with a load of food, medicine, clothing and toys crossed the United States border to deliver its cargo to Tijuana, Mexico, to an orphanage. Others, proudly trained by their owners, are frequent attractions at county fairs, hospital shows, on entertainment tours, and at public service events. We should all be proud of them.

FOOD FOR THOUGHT

Ruth Bates Young of Medway, Ohio sent me the following story, which was sent to her by Mrs. Agnes Mason and had been copied from the late Mrs. Quereaux' scrapbook. It was taken from the Letters to the Editor column of the August 14, 1946 issue of the *Illustrated Sporting and Dramatic News*. I feel it bears repeating.

"Sir: A short time ago you published a photo I sent you of "Gyp," a 23-year-old dog discovered by Mr. Bob Martin, living in Essex and believed to be the oldest dog in Britain. Your publication of this photo made a stir and within a few days Mr. Martin was told of an even old-

Victor of Top Acres, sire of five champions and a stud force at the Top Acres Kennels of Ruth Young in Ohio several years ago.

er dog living in Bristol. This rival claimant to the title of "oldest dog" is so remarkable that I am sending you his photograph herewith, together with a few brief particulars.

Breed: White Samoyed, aged 24 years, condemned in 1914 by original owner as unmanageable and sent to Bristol Dogs Home where present owner, Mr. Herbert of Bristol, saw and bought him. Docile, affectionate, and well-mannered, but a demon where other dogs are concerned. He has frequently jumped from an upper story window into the street to drive off strange dogs. Ten years ago, he was run over by a motorcycle and had two ribs broken but is still hale and hearty. At 24 he is deaf and has only 2 teeth but is still game for a 3 mile walk or scamper in the garden. Yours faithfully, B.D. Wratten."

Yate Sea King Cossack with litter sister Yate Sea Ahdoolo Misty Pearl, photographed at three months of age. The sire was Fyodor of Kobe *ex* Ch. North Star Mist of Yate Sea. Cossack is owned by Philip Sellar of Upper Montclair, New Jersey; Pearl is owned by the Gemeinhardts of Cedar Grove, New Jersey.

Ch. Winterland's Kim, owned by Robert and Bernice Heagy. Sire: Starik of Wimundstrev; dam: Nanook of Winterland. Photo by Don Mosca.

LUCKY WINNER

At the June, 1947 Pasadena Kennel Club show in California, the Pacific Coast Division of the Samoyed Club of America hosted the parent club Specialty show. A twelve-year-old girl named Shirley Hill bought a raffle ticket for one dollar with great hopes for winning the Samoyed puppy which was offered as the prize.

Shirley Hill not only won the puppy, later to become Ch. Verla's Prince Comet, but got herself a Best in Show-winning dog! Her Prince would soon win Best of Breed over 110 Samoyeds at another parent club Specialty and went on to win fourth place in the Working Group at that 1950 event. A year later Prince won a Best in Show under judge Albert E. Van Court at the San Gabriel Kennel Club Show over an all-breed entry of 750 dogs. Lucky winner, to be sure!

Shirley Ann Hill with her Best In Show-winning Sammy won in a raffle, Ch. Verla's Prince Comet. Photographed by Joan Ludwig at one of the California shows.

Shirley Ann Hill of Arcadia, California and her Ch. Verla's Prince Comet win top honors as Best at the Samoyed Club of America National Specialty Show at San Mateo the year that John Cross, Jr. officiated as judge at this major event.

A Samoyed fun match at Colonel Edward Wentworth's estate in Chesterton, Indiana, overlooking Lake Michigan. Colonel Wentworth was at one time head of the Union Stock Yards in Chicago. Photograph by Arthur E. Anderson.

SAMOYED LOYALTY

Colonel Edward Wentworth, a vice president of the Armour Meat Packing Company in Chicago, came into the breed by way of a family tragedy, tragedy which to me epitomizes the extent of loyalty accredited to this marvelous breed.

Colonel and Mrs. Wentworth's son owned a Samoyed, and the dog had chosen to die with the boy in a college fraternity house fire. Colonel Wentworth maintained several of the breed out of respect and reverence and served the dog fancy by serving as Chief Steward for the prestigious International Kennel Club of Chicago as well.

21. GLOSSARY OF DOG TERMS

ACHILLES HEEL—The major tendon attaching the muscle of the calf from the thigh to the hock

AKC—The American Kennel Club. Address: 51 Madison Avenue, N.Y., N.Y. 10010

ALBINO—Pigment deficiency, usually a congenital fault, which renders skin, hair and eyes pink

AMERICAN KENNEL CLUB—Registering body for canine world in the United States. Headquarters for the stud book, dog registrations, and federation of kennel clubs. They also create and enforce the rules and regulations governing dog shows in the U.S.A.

ALMOND EYE—The shape of the eye opening, rather than the eye itself, which slants upwards at the outer edge, hence giving it an almond shape

ANUS—Anterior opening found under the tail for purposes of alimentary canal elimination

ANGULATION—The angles formed by the meeting of the bones

APPLE-HEAD—An irregular roundedness of topskull. A domed skull

APRON—On long-coated dogs, the longer hair that frills outward from the neck and chest

BABBLER—Hunting dog that barks or howls while out on scent

BALANCED—A symmetrical, correctly proportioned animal; one with correct balance with one part in regard to another

BARREL—Rounded rib section; thorax; chest

BAT EAT—An erect ear, broad at base, rounded or semicircular at top, with opening directly in front

BAY—The howl or bark of the hunting dog

BEARD—Profuse whisker growth

BEAUTY SPOT—Usually roundish colored hair on a blaze of another color. Found mostly between the ears

BEEFY—Overdevelopment or overweight in a dog, particularly hindquarters

BELTON—A color designation particularly familiar to Setters. An intermingling of colored and white hairs

BITCH—The female dog

Proud as punch! This puppy knows just how to pose for the photographer, in this case his owner, Harold McLaughlin of Morrison, Colorado.

BLAZE—A type of marking. White strip running up the center of the face between the eyes

BLOCKY—Square head

BLOOM—Dogs in top condition are said to be "in full bloom"

BLUE MERLE—A color designation. Blue and gray mixed with black. Marbled-like appearance

BOSSY—Overdevelopment of the shoulder muscles

BRACE—Two dogs which move as a pair in unison

BREECHING—Tan-colored hair on inside of the thighs

BRINDLE—Even mixture of black hairs with brown, tan or gray

BRISKET—The forepart of the body below the chest

BROKEN COLOR—A color broken by white or another color

BROKEN-HAIRED—A wiry coat

BROKEN-UP FACE—Receding nose together with deep stop, wrinkle, and undershot jaw

BROOD BITCH—A female used for breeding

BRUSH—A bushy tail

BURR—Inside part of the ear which is visible to the eye

Ch. Elkenglo's Dash O'Silver, owned and handled by Elma L. Miller. The picture shows this fine Samoyed winning Best of Breed at the Samoyed Club of America under judge Clifford H. Chamberlain. Photo by William Brown.

BUTTERFLY NOSE—Parti-colored nose or entirely flesh color

BUTTON EAR—The edge of the ear which folds to cover the opening of the ear

CANINE—Animals of the family Canidae which includes not only dogs but foxes, wolves, and jackals

CANINES—The four large teeth in the front of the mouth often referred to as fangs

CASTRATE—The surgical removal of the testicles on the male dog

CAT-FOOT—Round, tight, high-arched feet said to resemble those of a cat

CHARACTER—The general appearance or expression said to be typical of the breed

CHEEKY—Fat cheeks or protruding cheeks

CHEST—Forepart of the body between the shoulder blades and above the brisket

CHINA EYE—A clear blue wall eye

CHISELED—A clean cut head, especially when chiseled out below the eye

CHOPS—Jowls or pendulous lips

CLIP—Method of trimming coats according to individual breed standards

CLODDY—Thick set or plodding dog

CLOSE-COUPLED—A dog short in loins; comparatively short from withers to hipbones

COBBY—Short-bodied; compact

COLLAR—Usually a white marking, resembling a collar, around the neck

CONDITION—General appearance of a dog showing good health, grooming and care

CONFORMATION—The form and structure of the bone or framework of the dog in comparison with requirements of the Standard for the breed

CORKY—Active and alert dog

COUPLE—Two dogs

COUPLING—Leash or collar-ring for a brace of dogs

COUPLINGS—Body between withers and the hipbones indicating either short or long coupling

COW HOCKED—when the hocks turn toward each other and sometimes touch

CRANK TAIL—Tail carried down

CREST—Arched portion of the back of the neck

CROPPING—Cutting or trimming of the ear leather to get ears to stand erect

CROSSBRED—A dog whose sire and dam are of two different breeds

CROUP—The back part of the back above the hind legs. Area from hips to tail

CROWN—The highest part of the head; the topskull

Ch. Hadesse of Ta, one of the five litter sisters named by the Shah of Iran after beautiful white flowers. Hadesse was bred by Ruth Young.

Ch. Beta Sigma's Mufti wins Best of Breed under judge James Trullinger at the Dayton Ohio Kennel Club Show in 1966; Chuck Herendeen handles for owner Ruth Bates Young of the Top Acres Kennels in Medway, Ohio.

Estalene Beckman with Ch. Kymric Taz of Top Acres, photographed at a dog show near St. Louis, Missouri.

CRYPTORCHID—Male dog with neither testicle visible

CULOTTE—The long hair on the back of the thighs

CUSHION—Fullness of upper lips

DAPPLED—Mottled marking of different colors with none predominating

DEADGRASS—Dull tan color

DENTITION—Arrangement of the teeth

DEWCLAWS—Extra claws, or functionless digits on the inside of the four legs; usually removed at about three days of age

DEWLAP—Loose, pendulous skin under the throat

DISH-FACED—When nasal bone is so formed that nose is higher at the end than in the middle or at the stop

DISQUALIFICATION—A dog which has a fault making it ineligible to compete in dog show competition

DISTEMPER TEETH—Discolored or pitted teeth as a result of having had distemper

DOCK—To shorten the tail by cutting

DOG—A male dog, though used freely to indicate either sex

Ch. Dmitri of Snowdrift, a son of Ch. Frost Star, C.D., at the age of four years, six months.

Ch. Sammy-Ed II of Shining Star, owned by Winford G. Messier. Sire: Ch. Bunky III of Lucky Dee; dam: Antique of Shining Star. Photo by Evelyn Shafer.

Tundra Princess Starya, owned by M. Estalene Beckman. Sire: Ch. Frolnick of Sammar; dam: Tundra Princess Vicki. Starya is the dam of many champion Samoyeds. Photo by Maxwell.

DOMED—Evenly rounded in topskull; not flat but curved upward

DOWN-FACED—When nasal bone inclines toward the tip of the nose

DOWN IN PASTERN—Weak or faulty pastern joints; a let-down foot

DROP EAR—The leather pendant which is longer than the leather of the button ear

DRY NECK—Taut skin

DUDLEY NOSE—Flesh-colored or light brown pigmentation in the nose

ELBOW—The joint between the upper arm and the forearm

ELBOWS OUT—Turning out or off the body and not held close to the sides

EWE NECK—Curvature of the top of neck

EXPRESSION—Color, size and placement of the eyes which give the dog the typical expression associated with his breed

FAKING—Changing the appearance of a dog by artificial means to make it more closely resemble the Standard. White chalk to whiten fur, etc.

FALL—Hair which hangs over the face

FEATHERING—Long hair fringe on ears, legs, tail, or body

FEET EAST AND WEST—Toes turned out

FEMUR—The large heavy bone of the thigh

FIDDLE FRONT—Forelegs out at elbows, pasterns close, and feet turned out

FLAG—A long-haired tail

FLANK—The side of the body between the last rib and the hip

FLARE—A blaze that widens as it approaches the topskull

FLAT BONE—When girth of the leg bones is correctly elliptical rather than round

FLAT-SIDED—Ribs insufficiently rounded as they meet the breastbone

FLEWS—Upper lips, particularly at inner corners

FOREARM—Bone of the foreleg between the elbow and the pastern

FOREFACE—Front part of the head, before the eyes; muzzle

FROGFACE—Usually overshot jaw where nose is extended by the receding jaw

FRINGES—Same as feathering

FRONT—Forepart of the body as viewed head-on

FURROW—Slight indentation or median line down center of the skull to the top

GAY TAIL—Tail carried above the top line

GESTATION—The period during which the bitch carries her young; 63 days in the dog

GOOSE RUMP—Too steep or sloping a croup

GRIZZLE—Bluish-gray color

GUN-SHY—When a dog fears gun shots

GUARD HAIRS—The longer stiffer hairs which protrude through the undercoat

HARD-MOUTHED—The dog that bites or leaves tooth marks on the game he retrieves

HARE-FOOT—A narrow foot

HARLEQUIN—A color pattern, patched or pied coloration, predominantly black and white

HAW—A third eyelid or membrane at the inside corner of the eye

HEEL—The same as the hock

HEIGHT—Vertical measurement from the withers to the ground, or shoulder to the ground

HOCK—The tarsus bones of the hind leg which form the joint between the second thigh and the metatarsals.

HOCKS WELL LET DOWN—When distance from hock to the ground is close to the ground

HOUND—Dog commonly used for hunting by scent

HOUND-MARKED—Three-color dogs; white, tan and black, predominating color mentioned first

HUCKLEBONES—The top of the hipbones

HUMERUS—The bone of the upper arm

Mrs. Thomassen and friends with "Chipper," her lovely Sammy from Top Acres Kennels. Chipper and Mrs. Thomassen live in Chattanooga, Tennessee.

INBREEDING—The mating of closely related dogs of the same standard, usually brother to sister

INCISORS—The cutting teeth found between the fangs in the front of the mouth

ISABELLA—Fawn or light bay color

KINK TAIL—A tail which is abruptly bent, appearing to be broken

KNUCKLING-OVER—An insecurely knit pastern joint often causes irregular motion while dog is standing still

LAYBACK—Well placed shoulders

LAYBACK—Receding nose accompanied by an undershot jaw

LEATHER—The flap of the ear

LEVEL BITE—The front or incisor teeth of the upper and lower jaws meet exactly

Ellbur's Rhonda of Drayalene, owned and handled by Helene L. Spathold and bred by E.L. Colburn. Sire: Ch. Barceia's Shondi of Drayalene; dam: Rocketa of Drayalene.

Kobe's Babbette of Encino, owned by Mrs. M.R. Tucker and handled by W.F. Hixson. She is shown completing her championship at the Harbor Cities Kennel Club under judge Alva Rosenberg. Photo by Joan Ludwig.

Ch. Barceia's Shondi of Drayalene, owned by E.L. Colburn and bred by Helene Spathold. Shondi was Best of Breed at Santa Barbara under Mrs. F.V. Crane. Photo by Bennett Associates.

Ch. Ilma of Blakewood, owned and handled by Elma L. Miller. Ilma is shown going Best of Opposite Sex to Best of Breed at the Samoyed Club of America under the late Charles A. Schwartz. Photo by Evelyn Shafer.

LINE BREEDING—The mating of related dogs of the same breed to a common ancestor. Controlled inbreeding. Usually grandmother to grandson, or grandfather to granddaughter.

LIPPY—Lips that do not meet perfectly

LOADED SHOULDERS—When shoulder blades are out of alignment due to overweight or overdevelopment on this particular part of the body

LOIN—The region of the body on either side of the vertebral column between the last ribs and the hindquarters

LOWER THIGH—Same as second thigh

LUMBER—Excess fat on a dog

LUMBERING—Awkward gait on a dog

MANE—Profuse hair on the upper portion of neck

MANTLE—Dark-shaded portion of the coat or shoulders, back and sides

MASK—Shading on the foreface

MEDIAN LINE—Same as furrow

MOLARS—Rear teeth used for actual chewing

MOLERA—Abnormal ossification of the skull

MONGREL—Puppy or dog whose parents are of two different breeds

MONORCHID—A male dog with only one testicle apparent

MUZZLE—The head in front of the eyes—this includes nose, nostrils and jaws as well as the foreface

MUZZLE-BAND—White markings on the muzzle

NICTITATING EYELID—The thin membrane at the inside corner of the eye which is drawn across the eyeball. Sometimes referred to as the third eyelid

NOSE—Scenting ability

OCCIPUT—The upper crest or point at the top of the skull

OCCIPITAL PROTUBERANCE—The raised occiput itself

OCCLUSION—The meeting or bringing together of the upper and lower teeth.

OLFACTORY—Pertaining to the sense of smell

OTTER TAIL—A tail that is thick at the base, with hair parted on under side

OUT AT SHOULDER—The shoulder blades are set in such a manner that the joints are too wide, hence jut out from the body

OUTCROSSING—The mating of unrelated individuals of the same breed

OVERHANG—A very pronounced eyebrow

OVERSHOT—The front incisor teeth on top overlap the front teeth of the lower jaw. Also called pig jaw.

PACK—Several hounds kept together in one kennel

PADDLING—Moving with the forefeet wide, to encourage a body roll motion

PADS—The underside, or soles, of the feet

Silver Frost's Crystal Holly, whelped April 22, 1973, and bred and owned by Nancy L. Brotherton of Short Hills, New Jersey. Holly is pictured here at three months of age. The sire was Deablo Siber Star and the dam Canadian Ch. Snowflake's Perdita.

Ch. Silver Crest's Sikandi, owned by Helene Spathold. Sire: White Frost's Tybo; dam: Ch. White Beauty of Lucky Dee. This bitch has enjoyed a fine show career and has proven her worth as a good producer.

PARTI-COLORED—Variegated in patches of two or more colors
PASTERN—The collection of bones forming the joint between the radius and ulna and the metacarpals
PEAK—Same as occiput
PENCILING—Black lines dividing the tan colored hair on the toes
PIED—Comparatively large patches of two or more colors. Also called parti-colored or piebald
PIGEON-BREAST—A protruding breastbone
PIG JAW—Jaw with overshot bite
PILE—The soft hair in the undercoat
PINCER BITE—A bite where the incisor teeth meet exactly
PLUME—A feathered tail which is carried over the back
POINTS—Color on face, ears, legs and tail in contrast to the rest of the body color
POMPON—Rounded tuft of hair left on the end of the tail after clipping
PRICK EAR—Carried erect and pointed at tip

Ch. Tod-Acres Fang, owned by John and Lila Weir. Sire: Ch. Stormy Weather; dam: Tod-Acres Starlet. This dog is the sire of a Best In Show winner.

PUPPY—Dog under one year of age

QUALITY—Refinement, fineness

QUARTERS—Hind legs as a pair

RACY—Tall, of comparatively slight build

RAT TAIL—The root thick and covered with soft curls—tip devoid of hair or having the appearance of having been clipped

RINGER—A substitute for close resemblance

RING TAIL—Carried up and around and almost in a circle

ROACH BACK—Convex curvature of back

ROAN—A mixture of colored hairs with white hairs. Blue roan, orange roan, etc.

ROMAN NOSE—A nose whose bridge has a convex line from forehead to nose tip. Ram's nose

ROSE EAR—Drop ear which folds over and back revealing the burr

ROUNDING—Cutting or trimming the ends of the ear leather

RUFF—The longer hair growth around the neck

SABLE—A lacing of black hair in or over a lighter ground color

SADDLE—A marking over the back, like a saddle

SCAPULA—The shoulder blade

SCREW TAIL—Naturally short tail twisted in spiral formation

SCISSORS BITE—A bite in which the upper teeth just barely overlap the lower teeth

SELF COLOR—One color with lighter shadings

SEMIPRICK EARS—Carried erect with just the tips folding forward

SEPTUM—The line extending vertically between the nostrils

SHELLY—A narrow body which lacks the necessary size required by the Breed Standard

SICKLE TAIL—Carried out and up in a semicircle

SLAB SIDES—Insufficient spring of ribs

SLOPING SHOULDER—The shoulder blade which is set obliquely or "laid back"

SNIPEY—A pointed nose

SNOWSHOE FOOT—Slightly webbed between the toes

SOUNDNESS—The general good health and appearance of a dog in its entirety

SPAYED—A female whose ovaries have been removed surgically

SPECIALTY CLUB—An organization to sponsor and promote an individual breed

SPECIALTY SHOW—A dog show devoted to the promotion of a single breed

Ishrar's Snow Belle, owned by Virginia Reilly and bred by Margaret and Nancy Dunagan. This handsome Samoyed is shown taking five points under judge Mrs. Robert Ward. Photo by Joan Ludwig.

SPECTACLES—Shading or dark markings around the eyes or from eyes to ears

SPLASHED—Irregularly patched color on white or vice versa

SPLAY FOOT—A flat or open-toed foot

SPREAD—The width between the front legs

SPRING OF RIBS—The degree of rib roundness

SQUIRREL TAIL—Carried up and curving slightly forward

STANCE—Manner of standing

STARING COAT—Dry harsh hair, sometimes curling at the tips

STATION—Comparative height of a dog from the ground—either high or low

STERN—Tail of a sporting dog or hound

STERNUM—Breastbone

STIFLE—Joint of hind leg between thigh and second thigh. Sometimes called the ham

STILTED—Choppy, up-and-down gait of straight-hocked dog

STOP—The step-up from nose to skull between the eyes

STRAIGHT-HOCKED—Without angulation; straight behind

SUBSTANCE—Good bone. Or in good weight, or well muscled dog

SUPERCILIARY ARCHES—The prominence of the frontal bone of the skull over the eye

Ch. Joli Knika, owned and handled by Cliff Cabe. Sire: Ch. Tod-Acres Fang; dam: Ch. Kobe's Nanuck of Encino. This Samoyed is a Best In Show winner. Photo by Danny Cox.

Ch. Rokandi of Drayalene, bred, owned, and handled by Helene K. Spathold. Sire: Ch. Yurok of Whitecliff; dam: Ch. Silver Crest's Sikandi. Rokandi is shown winning Best of Breed under judge O. Carley Harrisman at the Reno Kennel Club. Photo by Bennett Associates.

SWAYBACK—Concave curvature of the back between the withers and the hipbones

TEAM—Four dogs usually working in unison

THIGH—The hindquarter from hip joint to stifle

THROATINESS—Excessive loose skin under the throat

THUMB-MARKS—Black spots in the tan markings on the pasterns

TICKED—Small isolated areas of black or colored hairs on a white background

TIMBER—Bone, especially of the legs

TOPKNOT—Tuft of hair on the top of head

TRIANGULAR EYE—The eye set in surrounding tissue of triangular shape. A three-cornered eye

TRI-COLOR—Three colors on a dog, white, black and tan

TRUMPET—Depression or hollow on either side of the skull just behind the eye socket; comparable to the temple area in man

TUCK-UP—Body depth at the loin

TULIP EAR—Ear carried erect with slight forward curvature along the sides

TURN-UP—Uptilted jaw

TYPE—The distinguishing characteristics of a dog to measure its worth against the Standard for the breed

Just five weeks old and completely uninhibited by the camera! Joyce Cain's litter being trained for the show ring!

American and Canadian Ch. Scherezade of Kubla Khan pictured at nine weeks of age with the Tucker Memorial Brood Bitch trophy won by her paternal grandmother. Owned by Patricia Morehouse of Los Angeles, California.

Mrs. George Brown, sister of Ruth Bates Young of the Top Acres Kennel in Medway, Ohio, visits and enjoys the company of a litter of Sammy puppies.

UNDERSHOT—The front teeth of the lower jaw overlapping or projecting beyond the front teeth of the upper jaw

UPPER-ARM—The humerus bone of the foreleg between the shoulder blade and forearm

VENT—Tan-colored hair under the tail

WALLEYE—A blue eye also referred to as a fish or pearl eye

WEAVING—When the dog is in motion, the forefeet or hind feet cross

WEEDY—A dog too light of bone

WHEATEN—Pale yellow or fawn color

WHEEL-BACK—Back line arched over the loin; roach back

WHELPS—Unweaned puppies

WHIP TAIL—Carried out stiffly straight and pointed

WIRE-HAIRED—A hard wiry coat

WITHERS—The peak of the first dorsal vertebra; highest part of the body just behind the neck

WRINKLE—Loose, folding skin on forehead and/or foreface

Jennette Gifford took this charming photograph of one of her Samoyed puppies; it ranks among the author's favorites. Note drop of water on the chin.

INDEX

A

Abergavenny Championship, 34
Adams, Gertrude, 64
Alacbra, 30
All American Championship Sled
  Dog Races, 95, 96
Allergy, 272, 273
Alta, 49
American Dog Derby, 94
American Kennel Club, 36, 37, 64,
  122, 126, 152, 205
  Address, 111
  Registration, 58
Standard for the breed, 59
Ancestry of Samoyeds, 26, 27
Antarctic Bru, 28
Antarctic Buck, 26, 36, 37
Appearance, Standard for, 59
Arctic wolf, 22
Artificial Insemination, 152
Asian Wolves, 21
Attla, George, Jr., 101
Ayesha, 30, 33

B

Balto, 84
Bathing, 131, 132
Bitches, 18
Bjelkiers, 23, 351
Black Nordbrin, 30
Blank, Mrs. Jean, 43
Breeding, 145, 146, 147, 149
Births,
  Breech, 158, 159
  Dry, 159
Bones, 274, 275
Boothby, Lady May, 34
Borg, Mrs. Sidney, 37
Boris of Glacier, 34
Bowles, Robert, 55
Brechenridge, Richard, 35
Bristol Dogs Home, 353

Bristol, Lloyd, 55
Bryar, Jean, 101
Burial, 245
Burr, Charles, 64

C

Caesarian Section, 160
Cammack, Mrs. F.A., 33
Canis aureus, 13
Canis sibiricus, 24
Career, Pursuing a, in Dogs, 331,
  333, 335, 336, 337
Castrating, 170
Castren, M., 24
Chamberlain,
  Ardath, 49
  Clifford, 49, 55, 64
Championships, Qualifying for, 213
Chewing, 75, 77, 274
Chukchi dog, 19
Coat, Standard for, 59
Colman, Mrs. Gordon F., 30
Color, Standard for, 61
Commands, 190
Coprophagy, 251
Creveld, Miss I., 34
Cross, J.W., 35
Ctenocephalides canis, 279
Ctenocephalides felis, 279

D

Darwin Charles, 82, 83
Dawes, B.P., 64
Demidoff, Lorna, 101
de Witte of Argenteau, 36
Diet, All Meat, 229
Diseases, 287, 330
Disposition, 89
  Standard for, 64
Disqualifications, 64
Dodge, Mrs. Geraldine, 40

Dog degree,
  Companion Excellent, 196
  Tracking, 198
  Utility, 196
Dog Diseases, Dictionary of, 287, 330
Dog Insurance, 188
Dog Judging, 345
Dog Show,
  Types of, 215
Dog Sled Derby, 101
Dog Training, 340
Doyles, J.M., 44
Dondianes Siberian Ranook, 138
Dondianes Czaruke, 138
Donerna Kennels, 37
Donerna's Barin, 37
Drinking Water, 238
Drying, 132
Duffy,
  Lorna, 138
  Mrs. Vincent, 138
Dunlap, Bunty, 101
Dyer, Joe, 55
Dysplasia, 275, 276, 278
  Elbow, 276
  Hip, 275
  Patellar, 276

E

Ear Care, 139
Ears, Standard for, 62
Edelweiss, 34
Edwards, Mrs. D., 33, 34
Elkanglo's Dash O'Silver, 55
Elkhound, 13
Emergencies, 262, 263, 264
Episiotomy, 162
Esquimaux Dog, 20, 21
Etah, 27, 36
Eye Care, 139
Eyes, Standard for, 62
Expeditions, 19
  Abruzzi, 26
  Borchgrevinks, 26, 28
  Fram, 24, 26
  Jessup North Pacific, 19
  Nansen, 36
  Western Union Telegraph, 19
Explorers,
  Abruzzi, 26

Amundsen, 24, 27, 36
Borchgrevink, 24
Borgoras, 19
Byrd, 25
Fiala and Baldwin, 24
Jackson, 26
Jochelson, 19
Kenner, 19
Kerr, 24
Marco Polo, 19
Nansen, 36
Reed, 19
Shackleton, 24
Stefanson, 19
Swenson, 19
Vanderlip, 19

F

Farman, Mr. Edgar, 26
Feeding, 158, 223
  Adult Dog, 226
  Newborn Puppies, 223
  Racing Dog, 235, 236, 238
Feet, Standard for, 61
First Aid Kit, 266, 267, 268, 270
Fleas, 280, 281, 282
Frolnick of Sammar, 39
Front Legs, Standard for, 61

G

Gait, Standard for, 61
Gastric Torsion, 234
Gavin, Shirley, 102
Geldings, 82
General Care and Management, 239
Genetics, 141, 143, 144
Geriatrics, 242
Gestation Period, 152
Girvan, Thomas, 37
Gleason, Georgia, 64
Glossary of,
  Dog Terms, 359, 378
  Racing Terms, 106, 108, 109, 110
Godsol, Major B., 34
Goodrich Trust Fund Trophy, 44
Grand Duke Nicholas, 30, 36
Gray-Landsberg, Mr. E., 30
Great Serum Run, 83, 84
Greenacre Kennels, 57

Grooming, 13
  Parlors, 341
  Puppy, 134, 135
Gyp, 353

H

Handlers,
  Professional, 219, 222, 339
  Cost of, 220
Harnessing Methods, 78, 79, 80, 81
Harris, Helen, 64
Hasova, 30
Head, Standard for, 62
Height, Standard for, 59
Hill, Shirley, 45, 356
History, 13
Home Exercise, 70
Housebreaking, 123, 240
Howard, Sgt. Jerry, 349
Huckins, Darlene, 102
Hudson, Miss Elizabeth, 37
Humphries, Martha, 64, 138
Hunington, Jimmy, 100
Huslia Hustler, 101

I

Iceland Kennel, 34
Iditarod Trail Race, 98
Ingle, Mrs. L.D., 33
Internal Parasites, 285, 286
International Kennel Club, 358
Ivan of Taz, 34
Ivens, Dr., 40

J

Jacko, 26
Jackson, Major F., 26
Jaws and teeth, standard for, 62
Jingo, 44
Juliet Goodrich Trust Fund Trophy,
  44
Johannsen, Britt Inger, 96

K

Kasson, Gunnar, 84
Keeshunden, 13
Keyte-Perry, Miss, 35
Khatoonian, Irene Phillips, 43
Kieff, 31

Kilburn-Scott, 351
  Clara, 26, 28, 30
  Ernest, 64
  Mrs., 35
King Edward VII, 26
Kobe Kennels, 34
Kosko, 33
Knudsen, Chris, 45
Kvik and Flo, 26

L

Labor, 156, 157
Laika, 347
Landsberg, Mrs., 30
Lawrence,
  Charles, 347
  Ella, 347
  Vera, 64
Lead Dog, 82
Leader Dog, 22
Levorsen, Bella, 101
Litter, Evaluating the, 167
Lombard, Louise, 101
London, Jack, 28
Losonsky, Rosie, 104
Lulhaven's Snowmist Ensign, 56
Lundgren, Carol, 102, 104
Lurcock, Miss, 33

M

McBain, Anastasia, 40
Macinnes, Kit, 102, 104
Magnus of Kobe, 34
Malamute, 13
Manners, Outdoor, 240, 241
Marker, Miss, 30
Marshall, J.J., 39, 40
Martin, Bob, 353
Martingale Snowland Taz, 43
Martyska of Argenteau, 36
Mason, Agnes, 40, 64, 353
Mason Trophy, 44
Masturbation, 252, 255
Mating, 146, 150, 151
Mendel, Gregor, 141
Mesopotamian desert wolf, 21
Meyer, Marie, 40, 44
Michael, Mrs., 34
Miles, Vernon, 64

Miller,
  Lucille, 64
  Mrs. E.L., 55
Mitchell, Willoughby, J., 38
Morris and Essex Kennel Club, 40
Morrison, McLaren, 33, 34
Moustan, 30
Moustan of Argenteau, 36
Mustan of Farningham, 31
Musti, 28
Mutt, 95

N

Nansen, Mrs., 101
Nastja, 31
Nentsi, 23
Nichols, Miss Ruth, 37
Nikkolad of Top Acres, 349
Noel of Snowland, 40
Nootka dogs, 13
Nordly's Sammy, 44
Norka Kennels, 37, 39
Norka's Viking, 39
Norris, Natalie, 102, 104
North American Championship
  Race, 98
Nose, Standard for, 62
Nutrition, 223

O

Obedience, 179
  Lessons, 182
  Trials, 193, 213
  Samoyed in, 200
Obesity, 229
Obi Kennels, 31

P

Paddy, Mrs. F., 34
Parasites, 279, 282, 283, 285, 286
Parke-Cliffe Kennels, 37
Parker, Barbara, 102, 104
Pasadena Kennel Club, 356
Pearla of Kobe, 34
Pedigrees, Power of, 174, 178
Perry, Mrs. D.L., 34
Peter, 30
Pet shop, 343
Phillips System, 43
Planned Parenthood, 122

Point Show Classes, 208, 209, 210
Poisoning, 270
Polar Light, 30
Polka of Halfway, 30
Pregnancy, False, 160
Princess de Montyglyon, 27, 36
Prize Ribbons, 212
Puppies, 78, 154
  Feeding, 223
  Grooming, 134, 135
  Newborn, 232, 233
  Orphaned, 230
  Purchase Price, 129, 130
Puppy, 86, 87, 89
  Socializing Your, 162
Puxley, Miss, 30

Q

Quebec Race, 100
Quereaux, Mrs., 353
Queen Alexandra, 26
Quinlan, Miss, 34

R

Rabies, 255, 258, 259
Racing, 85, 86, 87, 88, 90, 92, 93, 94
  in Alaska, 97, 98, 99
  in Canada, 100
Racing Dog Feeding, 235, 236, 238
Real Arctic, 26
Rear End, Standard for, 61
Rearing, 163, 166
Records, Keeping, 246
Reid,
  Harry, 37
  Mr. and Mrs. H., 39
Reeves, Wh. H., 44
Rex of White Way, 45
Ricker, Mrs. E.P., 101
Ringer, Mrs. F., 30
Roberts, Percy, 37
Romer, Mrs. Frank, 37
Rosenbaum, M., 40
Rosenberg, Alva, 39
Ruick,
  Berta, 64
  S.K., 64
Russian Laikas, 13
Ruth,
  Alta, 49
  Roy, 49

S

Sam O'Khan's Chingis Khan, 44
Samoyed,
    Ancestry of, 26, 27
    History, 13
    In Education, 349
    In Obedience, 200
    In Public Relations, 353
    Maturity, 70
    People, 23, 24, 35
    Puppy, 68
    Stories, 347
    Temperament, 65, 66, 67, 68
    Top-winning, 56
    Tribe, 14
Samoyed Club of America, 37, 38,
    40, 49, 55, 356
San Gabriel Kennel Club, 356
Scott, Joe E., 64
Seager, Dr. Stephen W.J., 152
Seekins, Mrs. Robert, 64
Seeley,
    Alfred, 37
    Short, 101
Sewell, Mr. Frank, 26
Shedding, 137, 138
Sheet,
    James, 44
    Joan, 44
Shelley, Warren, 64
Sheppard, Carol, 102, 104
Sheridan, Miss Mildred, 37
Shondra of Drayalene, 55
Showing, 201
Showmanship Competition, Junior,
    213
Shows,
    Match, 201
    Point, 202, 205, 207
Siberian, 21
Siberian Keeno, 30, 35
Siberian Shaman, 34
Silver Spray of Wychwood, 43
Simon, Mrs., 30
Sled Dog, 78, 94, 95, 96
Sled Dog Derby, 97
Sled Dog Racing Events, 94, 95
Smirnow, Louis, 38, 64
Snakebite, 262
Snow Cloud, 31

Sora, 36
Spaying, 170
Spitz, 13
Standard for the Breed, 59
Standard, Story of the, 64
Sterilizing, 174
Stillman, Ruth, 49
Stillway, Lady, 28
Stonehenge, 19, 21
Stud fee, 150
Surf of the Arctic, 33
Swartz, Charles, 44
Sweet Missy of Sammar, 40

T

Tail, Standard for, 64
Taimir Kennels, 34
Tamera, 37
Tattooing, 239
Tawgy Samoyed, 24
Team dogs, 81, 82
Teeth, 140
    Standard for, 62
Temperament and Personality, 65,
    66, 67, 68
Temperature, 249, 251
Thomson-Glover, Miss J.V., 31
Thynne, Mrs. Stuart, 30, 31
Tibetan wolf, 21
Tiger Boy of Norka, 39
Tiki, 56, 57, 58
Timmins, Miss, 33
Tinsey, 26
Tobolsk, 37
Toledo Kennel Club, 40
Top of the World Kennels, 37
Torso, Standard for, 62
Toula of Tazov, 33
Training, 88, 179, 182, 186, 187
    Formal school, 191
    Advanced, 193
    Trials, 193

U

Urgo-Samoyeds, 23

V

Vaccination, 259, 261
Van Court, Albert, 55, 356

Van Heusen, Mrs. Ada, 37
Verla's Prince Comet, 35, 45, 356
Veterinarian, 247
Veterinary Inspection, 125
Viking, 31
Vinton, Mr. and Mrs. F.L., 37

W

Wainwright, Mrs. King, 37
Ward, Robert, 55, 64
Weaning, 225
Wells, Joyce, 102, 104
Wentworth, Col. Edward, 40
Westchester Kennel Club, 49
Westminster Kennel Club, 39
Weyer, Dr. Edward Moffat, Jr., 22
Whelping, 154, 155
  in the wilds, 17
Whirtay Petchora, 28
White Fang of Kobe, 34
White, Sonny, 56
Whiteway Kennels, 353

Wing, Anne, 102, 104
Winter, 33
Women Mushers, 101
Women's World Championships
  Race Winners, 104
Worms, 124, 284
  Test for, 285, 286
Wright,
  Shari, 102, 104
  Vera, 102, 104

Y

Young, Ruth Bates, 353
Yugarello, 30
Yugor of Halfway, 30
Yurak Kennels, 37
Yurak Samoyed, 24
Yurok of Whitecliff, 43

Z

Zahra, 33
Zor of Altai, 49